CHILD BEHAVIOR

*the text of this book is printed
on 100% recycled paper*

CHILD BEHAVIOR

by FRANCES L. ILG, M.D., *Director, Gesell Institute of Child Development*

and LOUISE BATES AMES, PH.D., *Director of Research*

Co-authors of INFANT AND CHILD IN THE CULTURE OF TODAY *and* THE CHILD FROM FIVE TO TEN

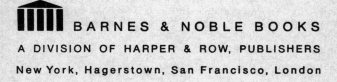

BARNES & NOBLE BOOKS

A DIVISION OF HARPER & ROW, PUBLISHERS

New York, Hagerstown, San Francisco, London

A hardcover edition of this book is also published by Harper & Row.

First BARNES & NOBLE BOOKS edition published 1972.

STANDARD BOOK NUMBER: 06-463344-6

78 79 80   12 11 10 9 8 7 6

Contents

PART THREE

Foreword

by

Arnold Gesell

This book bears the title of a syndicated newspaper column which has carried and still carries the by-line of Dr. Frances L. Ilg (M.D.) and Dr. Louise B. Ames (Ph.D.). The column first appeared in 1951. The spontaneous response of its readers has served to define the specific problems and anxieties which most commonly arise in the rearing of today's children. A sensitive awareness of these children, their parents, and also their teachers is amply reflected in the pages of the present volume. The topics are discussed concretely, but not too dogmatically. The approach is straightforward, the style direct. The writers have visualized their task as one of mutual, two-way communication.

The resultant book incorporates and adapts the column material. The opening paragraph of the opening chapter sets the theme— namely the theme of *growth*. To understand a child, we try to understand his ways of growth, for growth is the prime essence of life, and above all child life. The child grows as a unit in mind, body and personality. He is born into a culture, subject to the powerful influences of home, school and community. But he is also subject to deep-seated growth forces which shape his individuality. Each and every part of the child's nature has to grow—his sense of self, his fears, his affections and his curiosities; his feelings toward mother and father, brothers and sisters and playmates; his attitudes toward sex; his judgments of good and bad, of ugly and beautiful; his respect for truth and justice; his sense of humor; his ideas about life and death, violence, nature, deity. A book which deals concretely with the ages and stages of *child behavior* should sharpen our insight into that most intricate of all cycles—the cycle of child development.

Both authors have brought a rich fund of knowledge and experience to bear upon their intricate subject. Both have been active participants in a wider co-operative research now extending over a period of some twenty years. Under the auspices of the former Clinic of Child Development of the Medical School at Yale University, a research staff charted the behavior characteristics of thirty-four advancing age levels from birth to age ten. The results of these studies are reported in earlier publications. The Yale Clinic was terminated in 1948. In 1950 the present authors and Janet Learned, Ph.D., founded The Gesell Institute of Child Development, Inc., in order to continue the tradition of developmental research and service which began at Yale in 1911. The current studies of the Institute are concentrated on the years from ten to sixteen. The volume on *Child Behavior* is mainly limited to the first ten years of life. It does not in any sense attempt to summarize previous publications, but focuses on the analysis, interpretation and management of relatively normal manifestations and deviations of child development.

Dr. Ilg has had an extraordinary clinical contact with children of all ages from infancy through adolescence. Many of the children she has followed from age to age, with the intimate co-operation of their parents, who became collaborators in the investigation of the problems of normal and atypical behavior growth. Dr. Ilg has approached these problems from the standpoint of pediatrics, with an interest both in the somatic and functional expressions of development. As a form of supervisory medicine, *developmental pediatrics* must be based on a clinical science of normal child development. The concept of growth and development has comparable implications for a preventive child psychiatry and for the education of childhood and youth. Dr. Ilg in her extensive clinical work has demonstrated the functions of an inclusive *developmental examination* in the diagnosis and guidance of child behavior.

Dr. Louise B. Ames, since her postgraduate days, has been engaged in systematic and objective studies in the broad field of developmental psychology. She has contributed numerous papers on child

development, based on film analysis of research records, and also on
direct experimental and naturalistic observation. She is coauthor of
two recent volumes detailing the Rorschach responses of childhood
(from two to ten) and of old age (from seventy to a hundred).

During the past three years, Dr. Ames has conducted a weekly
half-hour TV program from Boston, sponsored jointly by Station
WBZ and the Boston *Globe,* as a public service. This is an unre-
hearsed program based on problems of child behavior as submitted
by four guests and also by letters from the audience clientele. These
letters are carefully considered in advance in consultation with Dr.
Ilg. Some of the questions raised and answered now reappear on the
printed pages of this book.

There is a slowly rising tide of intelligent interest in the methods
and principles of child care. There is a challenging quest for more
knowledge and also for a guiding philosophy which will safeguard
the worth and dignity of the individual child. In an age of violence
it seems that the conservation of individual growth is the surest
method of preserving a democratic culture. For this we need vastly
more knowledge and spiritual wisdom than we now possess. But it
is the goal of the life sciences to deepen our understanding of the
laws of human growth and to provide us with a more informed
philosophy of growth. Best of all, such a philosophy will foster a
greater enjoyment of our children and a genial appreciation of their
fine potentials.

Acknowledgments

This book, though not of a research nature, like all our publications stems directly from the systematic research carried on for many years by us and our colleagues, first at Yale and now at the Gesell Institute, under the direction of Dr. Arnold Gesell. Acknowledgment is therefore made first of all to Dr. Gesell for his guidance, leadership, and inspiration through many years.

Very grateful thanks are due to Mr. Robert M. Hall, President of the Post-Hall Syndicate, for making possible the publication of our syndicated daily column. Much of the material in the present volume has previously appeared in newspaper form, and Mr. Hall has generously allowed its republication.

We are extremely grateful to Mr. Richard N. Walker, Research Assistant at the Gesell Institute, for careful editorial help.

We must also, as in any publication, thank the many parents who, by sharing with us their experiences and problems, are continually adding to our knowledge of child behavior and how it grows.

Part One

1

How Behavior Grows

BEHAVIOR grows! Behavior has pattern and shape just as does physical structure. This is something that today's parents are beginning to recognize more and more—that just as your child's body grows in a reasonably patterned manner, so also does his behavior.

Gone are the days when psychologists likened the child's body to a lump of clay which you the parent could mold in any direction you chose. Nowadays most of us recognize the fact that though the child's behavior can be strongly influenced by the kind of home and other surroundings in which he grows up, many of the changes which will take place in his behavior are determined from within.

Does this mean, then, that all you as parents have to do is just sit back and watch your child grow? By no means. It is your responsibility, as well as your privilege, to provide him with the best possible environment. But the more you know about him, the better job you can do in providing him with the right kind of environment. The more you know about the normal changes which ordinarily take place in behavior as a child grows, the more successful you can be in guiding your child along the complicated path which leads to maturity.

Our observations of child behavior have led us to believe that almost any kind of behavior you can think of (eating, sleeping, talking, moving about, getting on with other people, even thinking about religion or understanding such complicated things as time and space) develops by means of remarkably patterned and largely predictable stages.

Knowledge of these growth stages can help you a good deal and in a great many ways. To begin with, it can give you an idea of what to expect. A good many things—approximately what your child's personality will be like, what abilities he will express, the speed with which he will progress through the expected stages—you can find out only by watching him develop. But what the stages in the development of any given behavior are likely to be, we can tell you in advance.

You may thus know not only what they are going to be but, roughly, when you may expect them to occur. You can be prevented from feeling too much surprise or discouragement when an unattractive (to you) stage of behavior occurs because you will know in advance that many behaviors, as they develop, do seem to have to go through phases which are not very attractive to the child's adult caretakers.

Also, knowledge of what to expect can help to keep you from being impatient or discouraged when a desired ability is slow in developing because you will have been forewarned that before the stage you are looking for can be expected to appear, several other, less effective stages have to be gone through. Thus if you know that five steps lead up to the behavior you are looking for, you won't expect your child to jump suddenly from one to five. You will be able to wait more or less patiently while he goes through steps two, three and four, and you will be able to take some of his backstepping more gracefully.

This book is going to tell you of the stages by which many of the commoner child behavior patterns develop in the first ten years of life. It is also going to tell you a little about the ages themselves— what 2-year-olds and 3-year-olds and 4-year-olds and the others are like, and what general changes you can expect from age to age.

It is going to tell you something about the different kinds of personalities and how they behave. The stages of behavior which more or less have to take place as a child develops are in many ways remarkably similar from child to child. To get to the top, the child has to climb all the steps. But, though the steps are pretty much the same for everybody, the way each child climbs these steps (or goes through the basic stages) is a little different for every child. The way in which he goes through the stages and the way he expresses the common patterns of behavior vary according to his own basic individuality.

Thus we can tell you about the common stages of development. You yourself, however, are the one who will need to discover and appreciate your own child's individuality. What we can tell you about different kinds of individuality is a beginning and will help you. But it is only a beginning. Recognizing and appreciating your child's basic personality is one of the most difficult but one of the most rewarding tasks of parenthood.

Ages and stages we can tell you about. These come first and are the easiest because they are most alike for all children. We can also help you with individuality or personality, though it is still up to you to recognize and appreciate your own particular child's individuality. A third equally important factor which you need to think about is the child's environment. What is the best environment for your particular child at his particular age? How can the environment act effectively to bring out the very best in your child's particular kind of personality? Here we can give you a few clues. In general, we can say, this or that is a good kind of environment to provide. In general, this or that works pretty well when you have this kind of problem. But here, even more than elsewhere, things are pretty much up to you. You will know best what kind of an environment your child needs. You are the one who has to provide it.

You have a challenging, but an exciting, task on your hands when you set out to bring up a child. We hope we can make that task a little easier for you by giving you this information about how children grow.

BETTER OR WORSE STAGES

As the child's body grows, it tends to get larger and larger. Physical growth may seem to stand still now and then, but at least it doesn't go backward. Your child is not likely suddenly one day to get smaller.

Behavior growth is more complicated. We can be pretty sure that as he grows older your child will get bigger, but unfortunately we cannot always guarantee that he will get better. In the long run he will become more self-sufficient. He will be able to use his body and his words and his thoughts more effectively. We can be assured that the 10-year-old is less exacting of his parents' time and patience than is the 18-monther. And in many ways the late-adolescent is more joy and less trouble to his parents than he was as a baby or preschooler.

But scientific studies of normal children have shown that this general trend toward "improvement" in behavior is not steady and uninterrupted. It does not go forward consistently and without setback. Each new age level tends to bring its own advantages and disadvantages.

The baby who used to be so docile about being fed may at a year demand his own feeding implements, with which he splashes in his food and generally disrupts the business of feeding. The added maturity of the 2½-year-old who at two years may have been so easy to manage through his daily routines may cause him to demand, "Me do it myself." Added maturity may bring a drive toward independence in the 6-year-old which expresses itself in, "No, I won't. Try and make me!"—though at five he took pleasure in obeying his mother. Added maturity may turn a helpful 10-year-old into a rebellious Eleven who shouts angrily, "I don't *want* to help with the dishes." It may change an enthusiastic, outgoing 14-year-old into a brooding, moody Fifteen.

Fortunately, all of these changes do not occur simply at random. Rather, as we have suggested, they take place in a lawful and patterned way.

Thus in general (and there are of course exceptions) ages when the child seems to be in better balance, both with himself and with the people and forces in his world, alternate with ages when he appears to be unhappy and confused within himself and also at cross-purposes with much of the outside world. We sometimes think of this as an alternation of stages of equilibrium and disequilibrium. It isn't really quite as simple as this, but it is helpful to think of the trend of growth as readjusting itself between better or worse stages.

So that if your child's behavior suddenly takes a turn for the worse, the reason for this turn may not necessarily be that something has gone wrong in his environment. Or that he is just naturally "bad." It may be that a stage of equilibrium has been succeeded, as it often will be, by a stage of disequilibrium. Thus 2-year-old equilibrium quite normally breaks up and behavior becomes worse at two and a half. The good 5-year-old becomes the explosive Six. Docile Ten becomes recalcitrant Eleven.

"Better" or "worse" behavior tends to alternate with the ages in a fairly lawful sequence of unfolding. There is a second, equally rhythmic alternation. Too concentrated or "focal" behavior, as we call it, at one time, is followed by too diffuse, widespread, or "peripheral" behavior at a succeeding time. A good example of focal behavior is seen in the average 5-year-old who tends to hug his mother's skirts, to shadow her wherever she goes. Six, in contrast, is in a peripheral stage. He may be all over the neighborhood, never at home, always ready for new places, people, experiences. It is the task of growth eventually to help the individual be neither one extreme nor the other, but to intermesh these extremes.

You may prefer your child's stages of equilibrium to those of disequilibrium. You may enjoy him most when he is conservative and close to home. Or you may prefer him when he is expansive and adventurous. But whichever you prefer, try to have patience with its opposite. Because the child seems to grow through these opposite extremes. One kind of behavior appears to be as necessary to growth as the other.

We can try to smooth over the child's "worse" stages, curb some of his expansiveness, or try to spread him out a little when he is in a too-close-to-home stage. But if we can accept all of these extremes, "for better or for worse," as necessary parts of growth, and not just blame them on somebody (teacher, other parent, neighbor, child himself), we will be looking at things realistically.

SUGGESTIONS

Each kind of behavior which will interest you (eating, sleeping, elimination, all the others) develops, as we have told you, through a series of patterned stages. In Part Two of this volume we are going to discuss these behaviors.

But it is not only the various kinds of behavior which develop in a predictable and describable manner. The very ages themselves can also be characterized and described. Behavior at any age is not simply a sum of the specific things that the child can do. It is almost as if each age had a personality of its own.

To help you see the first ten years in perspective, we are going to describe briefly * what each of the succeeding age levels is like. Not so much what the child can do at each of these ages, but rather what kind of a person he will be like at each age.

Before we do this, however, we shall give you two warnings. The first is this. Do not take the "timetable" which follows too seriously. Do not try to match your own child exactly to it. We are here describing more or less *average* behavior for each age level. That is, when we describe something as being typical 4-year-old behavior, we mean that of any one hundred presumably normal 4-year-olds, approximately half of them will be behaving in the manner described, when they are four years of age. One-quarter of them will already have gone past this kind of behavior. One-quarter will not have reached it as yet.

So that your own child may, quite normally, be a little ahead of or a little behind the behavior discussed in this volume as being typical of his age. Your child will in all probability go through the stages which we describe in the order given, but his rate of going through them will be his own. Do not worry, then, if he is a little faster or a little slower than the given average.

Your task is not so much to compare your child with the "average" as to compare him with himself—as he has been in the past and as he might be in the future. Our age sketches are not absolute "norms" of behavior that every child "ought to" exhibit exactly at a given moment. Rather they aim to help you to know the probable

---

* The ages are described here very briefly. For a fuller description the reader is referred to earlier publications, A. Gesell and F. Ilg, *Infant and Child in the Culture of Today* (New York, Harper & Brothers, 1943) and *The Child from Five to Ten* (New York, Harper & Brothers, 1946).

direction of the changes that you may expect as your child grows older.

A second misunderstanding of our material, which we hope you will avoid, is this. Some people believe that when we describe some unattractive behavior as being typical of a given age (the 4-year-old uses terrible language; the 6-year-old says he hates his mother), we mean that there is nothing you should do about it. They think we are advising them to say, "Oh, that's just a stage," and just to sit back and do nothing.

Far from it! Knowing that an unattractive behavior is in all probability "just a stage" will, we hope, help you to be a little more relaxed about it; help you not to blame too many people for the behavior. But it can also help you face the fact that you may have partly produced this behavior by demanding too much of your child when he "couldn't take it." May the knowledge of what he might do or say bring into operation your own *compassion*.

Knowing what to expect doesn't automatically relieve you of all responsibility for doing something about undesirable behavior. It does, we hope, help you cope with this behavior more successfully than you might have were you shocked and surprised by its appearance. It helps you to handle undesirable behavior more effectively as it occurs. Sometimes you will brush over it. At other times you will substitute other interests. At still other times you will prevent its occurrence. But there will also be times when you will come to grips with it.

2

Ages and Stages

CYCLES OF BEHAVIOR

As we describe succeeding age levels, you will note that the same general kinds of things seem to be happening over and over again. Careful analysis of behavior trends in the first ten years of life —supplemented by later studies * of the years from ten to sixteen— make it apparent that a rather distinctive sequence of behavior stages seems to occur repeatedly as the child matures. Thus the first cycle, and the one we know most about, occurs between two and five years of age, repeats itself from five to ten, and occurs once again between the ages of ten and sixteen.

Some of you may find it helpful to think of behavior in this somewhat abstract and over-all way. Others will find it quite enough to consider one age at a time. For those who prefer the long-range view—here are the cycles of behavior which you may be able to discover if you observe closely the behavior of the child from two to sixteen years of age.

First of all, we have observed that two years of age, five years and ten years all constitute focal points at which behavior seems to be in good equilibrium, the child having relatively little difficulty within himself or with the world about him. Each of these relatively smooth and untroubled ages is followed by a brief period when behavior appears to be very much broken up, disturbed and troubled, and when the child shows himself to be in marked disequilibrium. Thus the smoothness of 2-year-old behavior characteristically breaks up

---

* Data on the years from ten to sixteen will be found in A. Gesell, F. Ilg and L. Ames, *Youth: The Years from Ten to Sixteen* (New York, Harper & Brothers, in press).

10

at two and a half; 5-year-old behavior breaks up at five and a half to six; and ten breaks up at eleven, the 11-year-old child characteristically showing himself to be at definite odds with his environment and with himself.

Each of these ages is followed, once more, by a period of relative equilibrium at three, six and a half and twelve years respectively, when life's forces seem to be in good balance. The child is happy both within himself and in his environment.

These are followed by ages when there is a very pronounced inwardizing or drawing in of outer impressions and experiences, to be mulled over, thought about and digested within. These ages are three and a half, seven and thirteen years. At three and a half this inner process often has disturbing side effects of general emotional instability, a variety of fears, poor spatial orientation, hand tremor, whining and high tremulous voice, stuttering and stumbling. Seven and thirteen are more stable ages and better ready to stand the strain of this inwardizing period of growth. The side effects at these latter ages are more apt to be expressed in marked sensitivity and touchiness, excessive withdrawal and moroseness, and a minor and pessimistic attitude toward life in general.

All three of these ages are followed by periods of extreme expansiveness. Four, eight and fourteen are all times at which the child's behavior is markedly outgoing in most major respects. He is even in danger of expanding too much. He wanders from home and gets lost at four, he demands to ride his bicycle in the street at eight and may get hit, and he gets all tangled in his multiple and conflicting social plans at fourteen.

The next three ages (four and a half years, nine years and fifteen years) are ones about which we perhaps know the least, but we do know enough to recognize certain similarities about the three periods. In each of them, behavior is less outgoing than at the age which directly preceded. In each it is in less good equilibrium. Child specialists have frequently described each of these three ages by the term "neurotic," though they may each represent perfectly normal stages of growth.

And then once more, in each instance, we come to ages of stability and of relatively good equilibrium: five, ten and sixteen.

We have here started this summary of cycles of behavior at two years of age, but actually it could have been begun in infancy, when the same kinds of alternation of ingoing and outgoing periods, periods of equilibrium and disequilibrium, do occur. It is important to note that in early infancy salient changes are very rapid and show up clearly at weekly intervals. As growth progresses, these changes are clearer at two-week intervals. The 6-week-old child smiles spontaneously, but the 8-week-old child smiles in a social response. With increased age (from twelve weeks to one year) monthly increments are readily defined. From one to two years, the intervals of change lengthen to three months, and from two years to seven years, to six months. From seven to ten years (and on to sixteen years) these salient changes appear to take place less frequently—at about yearly intervals. It is probable that this spiral of growth slows down even further during the twenties and thirties, but it seems quite possible that predictable age changes are continuing to take place, though less clearly defined, during these and the succeeding years and probably throughout human life's span.

A brief and rather schematic tabular presentation of the age changes from two years on, as described above, follows:

2 years	5 years	10 years	Smooth, consolidated
2½	5½–6	11	Breaking up
3	6½	12	Rounded—balanced
3½	7	13	Inwardized
4	8	14	Vigorous, expansive
4½	9	15	Inwardized-outwardized, troubled, "neurotic"
5	10	16	Smooth, consolidated

WARNING ABOUT AGE LEVELS

Most of you will realize, without any special warning from us, that any description of age levels such as that which we have just given you is a gross oversimplification. When we describe characteristic behavior for any given age, we do not mean that all children of that age will behave just that way all of the time. In fact, some of them will behave that way scarcely any of the time.

We'll give you specific examples of just what we do and do not mean by our age characterizations. Take four years of age as an example. We describe the child of this age as being characteristically expansive and *out of bounds* in almost every field of behavior— motor, verbal, emotional, personal-social.

And in general, assuming a pretty average child who is developing at an "average" rate, that is the kind of behavior which you will get around the age of four. At about this time, in many children, comes a period of oversecure, overconfident, out-of-bounds behavior which is in marked contrast to the period of general insecurity which just preceded it (at about the age of three and a half), and also in contrast to the period of calm, sunny, good adjustment which came around three years of age.

However it is *the order* in which these stages follow each other which is most important—far more important than the exact age at which any certain child reaches any one of these stages. And each child gives his own individual twist to these age sequences. Also important is the fact that periods of relatively calm equilibrium tend to be followed and preceded by periods when the behavior is less calm, less well adjusted.

Among the many possible exceptions to our suggestion that behavior in general around four years of age tends to be out of bounds, could be the following:

First of all, your child may quite normally reach this 4-year-old out-of-bounds stage a little ahead of time or a little behind time or he may be of such a gentle nature that even at his worst, he does not go far out of bounds. Or he may be of such a vigorous nature that at *every* age he is more or less out of bounds.

Furthermore, even at a rather disorderly stage, there may be times when his environment fits especially well with his own personal needs, when his behavior is quite calm.

And lastly, though four years of age may be in many an age when there is considerable disequilibrium between the child and his environment, some children seem to be relatively in harmony and at peace within themselves even at ages when their behavior is quite disturbing to those around them.

Thus it is more important for you as a parent to recognize the rhythms of growth, the alternations between expansive and inward-ized ages or between harmonious and inharmonious periods, and to recognize that calm is very often followed by storm and vice versa, than to expect your own child to fit exactly into any given timetable or pattern. Each child is an individual, and that you must always keep in mind.

It is also extremely important to keep in mind that every age has its positive as well as its negative aspects, and that there is always a "better" side even to the "worse" ages.

Thus your 4-year-old may often seem overbold, but he at least expresses a self-confidence and an independence which he lacked at three and a half.

Similarly, your 6-year-old may often be rebellious, aggressive, demanding, selfish. But he also shows a tremendous enthusiasm and love of life. Some things may be terrible to him, but others can be equally wonderful. He may hate you one minute but he loves you madly the next.

And Seven, though he may at times be morose and moody, complaining and unhappy, often expresses a great thoughtfulness and restraint which comes as a pleasant change after the boisterousness of Six.

Thus each new age may bring changes for the worse, but it is also quite certain to bring other changes for the better. Try to discover the good while at the same time you smooth over the bad. Here are some of the outstanding characteristics of the first ten years of life.

Four Weeks

What can the 4-week-old infant do in the way of behavior? What can we expect of him?

Very little if we compare him with the sophisticated year-old baby. Certainly he cannot creep, walk, or talk. But compare him with himself a mere three or four weeks earlier, and he can do a very great deal. Never again, in fact—except in the period before birth—will so short a time mark so great an advance in the way of accomplishments.

To begin with, at a purely physiological level, he now breathes with regularity. His heart has steadied its pace. His body temperature has ceased to be erratic. His muscle tonus is already less fluctuant than it was, and he responds with noticeable motor tightening when you pick him up.

He also now sleeps more definitely and wakes more decisively. He opens his eyes widely and does not lapse so often into his earlier shallow, ambiguous drowsing. When awake he tends to have a preferred position—usually lying (when on his back) with his head turned to a preferred side and with the arm on that side extended, the other crooked. He thus may already be giving an indication of what is to be his later preferred handedness, since his preferred hand and arm will likely be the ones most often extended.

Occasionally he will regard his mother's face, but it will be only briefly. Though he may vocalize with small throaty noises, he is not quite ready to smile socially. However, he does react positively to comforts and satisfactions. He reacts negatively to pain and denial. And he can cry. He is already beginning, in his small ways, to impose his wants on the outside world and in turn to respond to that world.

Sixteen Weeks

The 16-week-old infant seems already quite mature, at least in terms of what has gone before. Not only have his motor and verbal abilities increased tremendously, but he has, to some extent, become a social being! He likes the experience of lying on a big bed, and he begins to invade the house more than he did earlier. Feeding is no longer uppermost in his mind, and he can sometimes wait for his feeding.

He is no longer as content to lie on his back as he was when he was younger. Rather, he likes to be held, or propped up for brief periods in a sitting position, so that he can face the world, eyes front.

In fact, there is something which at least hints at the social person he will later become in the way his eyes glisten, his shoulders tense, his breathing quickens, and his face breaks into a smile as he is lifted up to the sitting position.

His motor behavior is much better co-ordinated than it was even four weeks earlier. Twelve weeks, in most fields of behavior, in many children marks a period of definite disequilibrium. Placed on his stomach on the floor or other flat surface, a baby of this age kicks and struggles fruitlessly and awkwardly. (Feeding, too, may raise definite problems around this time of life. And sleeping behavior— particularly getting to sleep—may not go too smoothly. There may also be a very great deal of crying around the twelve-weeks period, especially in the evening.)

Much of this behavior is smoothed out around 16 weeks of age. Feeding goes better. (You probably think you have finally hit upon the right formula if the infant is bottle fed.) Hunger can be very intense at certain times, but he may refuse his 6 P.M. feeding for the very good reason that he is not hungry. He gets to sleep more easily and is more likely to sleep right through the night.

His postural behavior above all may be considered to express the good equilibrium which characterizes the sixteen-week age zone. Put him on the floor, and he no longer struggles helplessly as he did earlier. He may even, for brief moments, be able to maintain the poised position which we know as "swimming." That is, both legs extend at full length, arms flex with fists at shoulders, and (something we ourselves would find difficult to accomplish) lower abdomen lifts well up off the floor.

Eyes now follow a moving object—often through an arc of as much as 180 degrees. Hands reach out for a desired object—even though he cannot as yet do much about grasping such an object.

And, best of all, from the parents' point of view, he is becoming socially responsive. He coos, he chuckles, he laughs aloud. He can even smile back when you smile at him. He is well on the way to becoming a responsive member of the family group.

TWENTY-EIGHT WEEKS

If your 16-week-old infant seemed to you to be delightfully mature, that maturity was, nevertheless, nothing to what he will be able to achieve at 28 weeks of age.

He now not only prefers the sitting position, but he can, under favorable conditions, maintain it for long periods of time.

But by now he is so mature that the mere business of sitting up by no means utilizes all his abilities. He is no longer content just to sit and look. Now he wants to touch as well, and he wants to be held standing and to bounce.

Whether lying on his back or stomach or sitting in his high chair, he must have something in his hands. He now can not only reach out toward desired objects, but can, if they are not placed too far away, pick them up in a crude grasp and finger them. He is most likely to bring them to his mouth. (Even feet are grasped and brought to the mouth as he lies on his back—no mean achievement.)

The baby of this age not only likes to grasp and to finger objects, but he likes to shift them from one hand to the other. This behavior we call "transfer," and he can spend many happy minutes thus engaged. Or he may delight in banging simple objects on the tray of his high chair.

He can, indeed, amuse himself alone for long periods. But this does not mean that he is not interested in people. The baby of this age is an extremely social individual. He likes to smile at onlookers and is usually enthusiastically friendly to both intimates and strangers. In fact, he presents an amiable union between self-sufficiency and sociability. He alternates with ease between self-directed and socially referred activity. He listens to words spoken by others and particularly likes his father's low voice, which frightened him at an earlier age. He listens also to his own private verbalizations.

He gets on well, whatever the situation. For 28 weeks, like 16, represents an age of extremely good equilibrium. Behavior patterns and emotions (which actually are in themselves behavior patterns) are in good focus.

However, as Dr. Gesell has commented, this period of equilibrium, like all such, tends to be short-lived. For the growth complex never fully stabilizes. New thrusts, new tensions of development, soon upset any state of balance, producing unstableness, which is in turn resolved by further temporary stages of equilibrium.

Thus sixteen weeks was, as we suggested, in most a period of excellent equilibrium. New efforts—efforts to do things which he is not able to do—produce at twenty weeks a period of definite disequilibrium. The 20-week-old infant, for example, tries to get his knees under him as he lies on his stomach. He fails. He may try to sit alone. He fails. He reaches out for objects and may try unsuccessfully to grasp them. He cries when his mother leaves him. He is aware of strangers.

All of this produces frustration. Increased abilities coming in at 24 to 28 weeks help to resolve many of these frustrations.

FORTY WEEKS

Forty weeks marks still another temporary stage of equilibrium in the baby's path of growth. At twenty-eight weeks he paused, momentarily, at a delightful point at which his drives and efforts were happily well balanced by his abilities. He was trying many new things—but temporarily he seemed, for the most part, to try only those things at which he could succeed. And to be satisfied with such successes as he could achieve.

All this, in many, changes at thirty-two weeks. New awareness at this age makes for new sensitivity. Thirty-two weeks, for example, marks one of the high points for withdrawing from or even crying at the sight of strangers. This is not a step backward, actually, for it occurs because of an increased ability to tell the difference between the familiar and the unfamiliar.

Posturally, too, the 32-week-old baby may have some difficulty. Unable as yet to get to hands and knees and creep, he nevertheless tries to make progress toward unattainable goals by pivoting in a circular direction. This often leads to confusion and frustration.

For these and other reasons which you may observe in your own infant, thirty-two weeks tends to mark a brief period of considerable disequilibrium. Crying and laughter are very close together and sometimes indistinguishable.

All the more welcome, then, the age range from thirty-six to forty weeks when many babies settle down to a brief period of fine equilibrium.

Socially they are not only well adjusted but often extremely responsive. Many can respond to "bye-bye." Some can pat-a-cake. Vocally most are extremely fluent. Friends and strangers alike are received with warm smiles.

Posturally, too, things are going along excellently. The child of this age can, if in a favorable position, sit alone indefinitely, and can even manipulate objects while sitting unsupported. He can get over to prone from sitting. (In another month he will be able to get to sitting from prone.)

He can get up to hands and knees, which puts him in a position where he can very shortly get about by creeping. A whole new world becomes his when he can actually locomote. He can also pull himself to standing—another new dimension conquered.

Furthermore, his ability to grasp and manipulate objects has advanced, along with other abilities. Grasp is no longer predominantly pawlike. Not only can he poke precisely at tiny objects with extended forefinger, but he can grasp these same tiny objects precisely between thumb and forefinger.

He has become increasingly aware of his social world. Not only may he wave bye-bye and imitate pat-a-cake, but he can now respond to gestures, facial expressions and sounds. He can heed "No, no"—a most useful social accomplishment and one which he will need to use extensively before he in turn becomes a parent. He not only vocalizes spontaneously, but he can imitate such simple syllables as "da-da."

All in all, he adds greatly to the social scene.

FIFTY-TWO WEEKS

Forty weeks of age marks such a peak of infant accomplishment in many fields that you might wonder what next the baby will achieve. Admittedly, he does not change as much between forty and fifty-two weeks as he has changed in any preceding twelve-week period. The rate of growth is slowing down. We shall soon start measuring age changes in larger units of time.

However, there are changes. The greatest, perhaps, is that the baby can now creep about freely on hands and knees. The mobile

1-year-old is thus a quite different person from the 40-weeker who could cover only a small amount of space, if any.

Not only can he get about freely on hands and knees, but he can now "cruise" along beside some object of furniture and can probably take at least a few steps hands supported.

Socially—after going through another period of disequilibrium around forty-four weeks in which he tends to be "strange" with strangers—the infant shows himself serene and self-confident and friendly. He loves to have an audience. He recognizes social approval by repeating performances laughed at. He enjoys the give and take of social games and can imitate simple social actions. He particularly enjoys such games as "peek-a-boo," and he loves to be chased as he creeps.

Increased motor abilities may temporarily, with some, interfere with daily routines. For instance, the baby may prefer standing up as he is fed. Or his love for manipulating the spoon himself may further interfere seriously with eating. But give him scope for his new-found abilities—that is, let him stand up in his high chair supported by an extended harness and let him have a spoon of his own to play with while you feed him—and feeding may go as smoothly as ever.

With a little skill on your part, you can give him opportunity to express growing abilities and at the same time get him through the day's routine without too much difficulty. Because one year of age, though not an age of startling new behavior advancements, tends to be a period of reasonably good, smooth functioning in all fields of behavior.

Fifteen Months

As compared with 1-year-old behavior, that which the baby exhibits at 15 months may be far from smooth. But this is partly because so many new abilities are coming in all at once. He is suddenly trying to do so much, and doing it so vigorously, that it is small wonder if the total behavior pattern loses a little of its earlier harmony.

Fifteen months has been characterized as a dart and dash and fling age. The earlier two-way relationship of give and take has been replaced by one-way behavior (which will become even more one-way at eighteen months). The 15-month-old child is no longer a mere creeping and cruising baby. He can now walk and he strains at the leash with his new-found locomotor abilities. He strains at the leash and he objects to both leash and play pen. A mere verbal "No, no" has little effect on him. There is too much to be done—too much to be seen. Not only is he agile on flat surfaces, but he can (and will, if allowed to) climb stairs endlessly, though this is more common at eighteen months.

He gets into everything. He is ceaselessly active and he knows very little inhibition. He definitely needs to be kept out of the living room and to be restricted to places where he won't get into trouble.

If he is confined to his play pen, he is likely to pick up each toy with which you have provided him and cast it outside. In fact, throwing things is one of his favorite pastimes. He throws things and then shouts for you to bring them back to him. He also loves to put one object after another in and out of any given receptacle, but tends to dump more than to fill. He is more likely to stay willingly in his pen if there are interesting things going on within sight, as traffic going by.

Language is coming in—though it has not as yet progressed very far. However, the 15-monther can often ask for what he wants by vocalizing and sometimes by pointing; can indicate refusal by bodily protest; can respond to a few key words and phrases.

Some rudiments of toilet training are coming in with a few. They can at least remain seated on a toilet receptacle. Some can now allow a dish to stand on their tray without grasping at it. Some may have given up the bottle, and may even be able to hold a cup, though awkwardly, for drinking; or feed themselves, also awkwardly, with a spoon. They may co-operate in dressing by extending an arm or leg when so requested.

Moods are shifting and temper, while quickly aroused and vigorously expressed, tends to be short-lived. Diversion is easy and the child is easily entertained. It is largely a matter of the adult's having energy enough to keep up with him.

EIGHTEEN MONTHS

The 18-monther walks down a one-way street, though this one-way street can be rapidly reversed. And this street more often than not seems to lead in a direction exactly opposite to that which the adult has in mind. Asked to "Come here, dear," he either stands still or runs in the opposite direction. (He may even like to walk backwards.) Ask him to put something in the wastebasket, and he is more likely to empty out what is already in it. Hold out your hand for the cup which he has just drained, he will drop it onto the floor. Give him a second sock to put on, and he will more likely than not remove the one which is already on his foot. His enjoyment of the opposite may be the reason why it works so well, if he is running away from you, to say, "Bye-bye," and walk away from *him*. Then he may come running.

Not only does he not come when called—he seldom obeys any verbal command. "No" is his chief word.

It is not so much that the 18-monther is bad as that there are so many abilities he has not yet mastered. He has not yet reached the place where he is easily motivated by words. He has not yet reached the place where he can wait. "Now" is the one dimension of time important to him. Thus efforts to get him to wait a minute are for the most part doomed to failure, and he cannot stand any frustration. (Unfortunately, no matter how much you try to protect him in the way you set up the environment, he cannot seem to keep from frustrating himself.)

His interpersonal relations are almost completely dominated by ideas of taking—but not of giving. Actually, except for his parents, he may treat other people, especially other children, more as if they were objects than people. He will as likely step on a friend as walk around him. He has not even a beginning concept of sharing.

Eighteen months is not one of the "better" ages if we measure goodness in terms of minding, responding to commands, keeping within reasonable bounds. However, if we can appreciate the immaturity—motorwise, languagewise, and in his emotions—of the 18-monther, it can be fairly easy to keep his behavior within reasonable limits.

Thus, if you would like to have him move from wherever he is to wherever you are—lure him, pick him up and carry him, but for best results, do not call him. He is simply not mature enough to respond, in most instances, to such a verbal command.

If you wish him to stay away from certain areas in the household, for best results make it physically impossible for him to get to those areas. Physical barriers, you will find, work better than does verbal prohibition.

When you do use words, keep them short and simple: "Coat—hat—out" is about as complicated a command as the average 18-monther can follow.

It is important in dealing with an 18-monther to keep in mind at all times that he is an extremely immature little creature. He understands more words than he can say, but even his understanding is extremely limited. He can walk and even run and sometimes climb, but his balance is very unsteady. And with his quick temper and his need to have everything "Now," his emotions are as immature as any other part of him.

If you expect very little, keep your demands that he "mind" at a minimum and give very close and rather constant physical supervision, you may find that you get on very well with and enjoy your 18-monther. However, in many households the phrase "bad boy" is used so commonly that the child may think it is either his own name or perhaps the name of the forbidden activity.

Be sure to give him plenty of outlet for his boundless physical energy—stair climbing is one of the best. And for the rest, it may be a kindness to him to use a harness, especially when he is in new territory.

And don't be above using guile. If he is playing with something that you don't want him to have, try doing something interesting like playing the piano or crumpling some paper in another part of the room. You may be surprised at how quickly he will leave his activity to take part in yours.

Two Years

The child's behavior at two years of age is so much better organized than earlier from the adult's point of view that we sometimes fall into the trap of expecting a steady improvement from here on— and are thus unhappily surprised when the customary difficulties of two and a half make themselves apparent.

At any rate, regardless of what may come after, here at two comes a brief breathing space for child as well as mother. For two is in most children, compared to the ages which immediately precede and follow it, an age of rather marked equilibrium.

Things are much smoother with respect to nearly every field of behavior. Added maturity and a calm willingness to do what he can do and not try too hard to do the things he cannot manage largely account for this greater smoothness.

The 2-year-old is much surer of himself motorwise than he was at 18 months. He is less likely to fall. He runs and climbs more surely. Thus he no longer needs to be so much preoccupied with keeping his balance and getting around, and can turn his attention to other things. Also, the adult does not have to be so much on guard to protect him.

He is also surer of himself languagewise. Not only does he now understand a surprising amount of what is said to him, but he himself can, as a rule, use language with remarkable effectiveness. Being able to make his wants known and being understood by others relieves much of the furious exasperation which he felt earlier when he could only point or cry and hope that someone who knew his ways and wants would be on hand to interpret. At twenty-one months a wrong spoon or a wrong bib could be the cause of a long crying spell.

Emotionally, too, he finds life easier. His demands are not quite as strong as they were. His ability to wait a minute or to suffer slight or temporary frustration if necessary has tremendously increased.

Furthermore, people mean more to him than they did earlier. He likes, on occasion at least, to please others; and he is often pleased by others. Thus he can, as the 18-monther could not, occasionally do things just to please people, can occasionally put another person's wishes above his own. Though he cannot as yet share with other children, he will on occasion, if so directed, be willing to find substitute toys for these other children. This marks a whole new dimension in social relations over those of six months earlier.

Two also is, on many occasions, loving and affectionate. He can be warmly responsive to others. This, along with his increased good nature, makes him, in home or nursery school, a much easier person to deal with than he was when younger. Much can be, and often is, said in praise of the 2-year-old. He is a loving companion and a real joy in many households.

Two and a Half Years

This is an age about which parents may need warning because so much that the child now does naturally, almost inevitably, is directly contrary to what his parents would like to have him do. The 2½-year-old is not, temperamentally, an easy, adaptable member of any social group.

The change in behavior which takes place between two and two and a half can be rather overwhelming, perhaps to child as well as to the adults who surround him. Two-and-a-half is a peak age of disequilibrium. Parents often say that they can't do a thing with the child of this age.

Actually, once they understand a little about the structure of behavior at this time, they often find that, awkward as it may be, it does make sense. Working *around* the behavior characteristics of Two-and-a-half is often much more successful than trying to meet them head on.

We'll list some of these outstanding characteristics:

First of all, Two-and-a-half is rigid and inflexible. He wants exactly what he wants when he wants it. He cannot adapt, give in, wait a little while. Everything has to be done just so. Everything has to be right in the place he considers its proper place. For any domestic routine, he sets up a rigid sequence of events which must follow each other always in exactly the same manner.

Second, he is extremely domineering and demanding. He must give the orders. He must make the decisions. If he decides, "Mummy do," Daddy cannot be accepted as a substitute. If he decides, "Me do it myself," then no one is allowed to help him, no matter how awkward or incapable he himself may be.

Two-and-a-half is an age of violent emotions. There is little modulation to the emotional life of the child of this age.

Furthermore, it is an age of opposite extremes. With no ability to choose between alternatives (it is almost impossible for Two-and-a-half to make a clear-cut choice and stick to it), the child of this age shuttles back and forth endlessly between any two extremes, seeming to be trying to include both in his decision. "I will—I won't," "I want it—I don't want it," "Go out—stay in." If someone doesn't cut into his back-and-forth shuttling, he has been known to go on with it for upwards of an hour or more. The decision of what clothes to wear may usurp a whole morning for a conflict-ridden 2½-year-old girl.

Thus any caretaker of a 2½-year-old will need to streamline all routines, make the decisions herself, try to avoid situations where the child himself takes over.

Another unfortunate characteristic of this age is perseveration— that is, the child wants to go on and on with whatever he is doing. Not only right at the moment but from day to day. If you read him four stories before bedtime yesterday, he wants four stories—and the same ones, too—today. It is very difficult with many a child of this age to introduce new clothes, new pieces of furniture, new things to eat. He wants things to go on just the way they have always been or at least hold on to the old as new things are added.

Total all of these characteristics together and you have a child who is not easy to deal with. Vigorous, enthusiastic, energetic, the typical Two-and-a-half may be. But he is not an easy person to have around the house. However, mothers will find that great patience, a real understanding of the difficulties of the age and a willingness to use endless techniques to get around rigidities and rituals and stubbornness will help get through the time till the difficult Two-and-a-half turns three.

THREE YEARS

Things quiet down, briefly, at three for most children. Two-and-a-half seemed to love to resist. Three seems to love to conform. The typical 3-year-old uses the word "Yes" quite as easily as he formerly used the word "No."

Two-and-a-half seemed to be all "take." Three likes to give as well as take. He likes to share—both objects and experiences. "We" is another word which he uses frequently. It expresses his co-operative, easy-going attitude toward life in general.

Three tends to be in good equilibrium with people and things around him, perhaps because he is in better equilibrium within himself. He no longer seems to need the protection of rituals, of doing everything always the same way. Greater maturity has led him to feel much more secure—secure within himself and secure in his relations to others.

Not only has the need for rituals dropped out, but almost every other aspect of 2½-year-old behavior which made trouble for him and those about him seems to have disappeared, or at least lessened, as well. The child is no longer rigid, inflexible, domineering, grasping. No longer does everything have to be done *his* way. Now he can not only do it *your* way, but can enjoy the doing.

People are important to him. He likes to make friends and will often willingly give up a toy or privilege in order to stay in the good graces of some other person—something of which he was incapable earlier.

Increased motor ability allows daily routines and other necessary activities to be gotten through with minimal difficulty. It also allows him to carry out successfully play activities which earlier baffled and enraged him.

But above all, his increased ability with and interest in language help him to be a delightful companion, an interesting group member. His own vocabulary and ability to use language have increased tremendously in most cases. His own appreciation of the language of others has increased similarly. Now he can not only be controlled by language, but he can be entertained and himself can entertain. He loves new words, and they can often act like magic in influencing him to behave as we would wish. Such words as "new," "different," "big," "surprise," "secret," all suggest his increased awareness in the excitement of new horizons. Such words as "help," "might," "could," "guess," are active motivators to get him to perform necessary tasks.

Two-and-a-half often seemed to resist just as a matter of principle. It was safer. Three goes forward positively to meet each new adventure.

THREE AND A HALF YEARS

Temporarily at three many children reach what most parents and teachers consider to be a delightful stage of equilibrium. The child's wishes and his ability to carry out those wishes seem, for a while, to be in remarkably good balance. Three-year-olds, for the most part, seem to be well pleased with themselves and with those about them, and the feeling tends to be reciprocal. They seem also, so far as their outward behavior shows it at least, to feel secure within themselves.

At three and a half there comes, in many, a tremendous change. It is as though in order to proceed from the equilibrium of the 3-year-old stage to that which is usually attained by five years of age, the child's behavior needs to break up, loosen up, and go through a phase of new integration. All this comes to a head in many at three and a half years of age—a period of marked insecurity, disequilibrium, inco-ordination.

Thus, poor or new co-ordination may express itself in any or all fields of behavior. It may express itself only temporarily and very lightly in some children, for a considerably longer period and much more markedly in others. It is so characteristic of this particular age period that though certainly environmental factors may exaggerate it, in many cases we can fairly consider that it is caused by growth factors alone. Certain by-products of behavior started at this period, such as stuttering, may continue longer than they should within the more usual course of growth.

Thus you may look for inco-ordination in any or in all fields of behavior. Motor inco-ordination, for example, may express itself in stumbling, falling, fear of heights. A child who has previously shown excellent motor co-ordination may go through a period of extreme motor disequilibrium.

Hands alone as well as the total body may be involved. Thus a child whose hand and arm movements have up till now been strong and firm may suddenly draw with a thin, wavery line; may build with a noticeable hand tremor.

Language may be involved. Stuttering very often comes in at this period in children who have never stuttered before.

Eyes and ears may be involved. Parents are often worried by the temporary (or more persistent) crossing of the eyes which comes in here. Or the child may complain that he "can't see," or that he "can't hear."

Tensional outlets are often exaggerated in this 3½-year-old period. Thus the child may blink his eyes, bite his nails, pick his nose, exhibit facial or other tics, masturbate, suck his thumb excessively.

And lastly, along with motor and verbal difficulties often come tremendous difficulties in relations with other people. The 3½-year-old expresses his emotional insecurity in crying, whining and in frequent questioning, especially of his mother: "Do you love me?" Or perhaps in complaints: "You don't love me." He is also extremely demanding with adults: "Don't look," "Don't talk," "Don't laugh." Or he may demand that all attention be focused on himself, and thus becomes extremely jealous of any attention paid by members of the family to each other.

With his friends, too, he shows considerable insecurity and great demand for their exclusive attention. The emotional extremes which he expresses (very shy one minute, overboisterous the next) also make him an uncertain contributor to any social situation.

If the adult in charge knows in advance that all this uncertainty, insecurity, inco-ordination quite normally mark the three and a half age period, it can help considerably. First of all, it can keep you from blaming various aspects of the environment for any or all of the different inco-ordinations. It can stimulate you to improve the environment. And it can help give you patience to show the child the extra affection, the extra understanding which he so desperately needs at this age.

FOUR YEARS

For every age it seems possible to discover a key word or words which describe the structure of behavior at that time. If we can find and remember those words, it often helps us tremendously to understand and appreciate the child of that age.

For Four the key words are "out of bounds." If we can remember those words, and smile sympathetically when we say them, it can be of immeasurable aid in helping us to deal with any 4-year-olds who may come our way. For the 4-year-old is, almost more than the child of any other age, out of bounds—and out of bounds in almost every direction.

Thus he is out of bounds motorwise. He hits, he kicks, he throws stones. He breaks things. He runs away.

He is out of bounds emotionally. Loud silly laughter alternates with fits of rage. "You make me so MAD," he will tell you.

Verbally he is almost more out of bounds than in any other way. The language of a typical 4-year-old can be almost guaranteed to shock anybody except perhaps a hardened nursery-school teacher. Profanity (where did he ever hear such awful language?) is rampant. Bathroom and elimination words come into common use. He uses them not only incidentally or where they might be appropriate, but may dwell on them and rhyme with them—accompanying his rhyming with much silly laughter which shows that he fully appreciates their inappropriateness.

And in interpersonal relations he is quite as out of bounds as anywhere else. He loves to defy parental commands. In fact, he seems to thrive on being just as defiant as he can manage. Even severe punishment may have little chastening effect. A terrible toughness has seemed to come over him—he swaggers, swears, boasts, defies.

His imagination, too, seems at this time to have no "reasonable" limits. This new-found flight through imagination, which often begins at three and a half years, may be a high point for the enjoyment of imaginary companions. These, most parents accept fairly well. Four's tall tales, particularly when they strike the adult as just plain lies, are less well accepted. Yet to the average 4-year-old the line between fact and fiction is a very thin, flexible line. He may not actually be telling falsehoods. It's just more interesting that way, and he may come to believe his own imaginings, which become real to him.

How firm a stand you, as a parent or teacher, take toward all these out-of-bounds behaviors is up to you. Certainly there are limits. Even the very simple social situation of a nursery-school group requires a certain toning down of 4-year-old exuberance. Home life requires perhaps even more.

You will, inevitably, need to use a good deal of firmness in dealing with your 4-year-old. But you will feel less hopeless and less angry as you deal with him if you can keep in mind that behaving in an out-of-bounds manner is not only an almost inevitable, but a probably quite necessary part of development. The 3½-year-old was, certainly, too insecure for practical purposes. Four seems to most of us overly secure and too brashly confident in his own abilities. Nature seems to have this awkward way of going to opposite extremes as the child develops. Eventually the swings of the pendulum become less extreme and settle down to a narrower range as the individual's basic personality is less swayed by age changes.

The 4-year-old needs to be allowed to test himself out. He needs to be allowed to go up the street on his bike in both directions and with expanding limits. We hope there are neighbors whom he can visit and who will receive him and will notify his mother of his visit. He needs to be allowed to run ahead on a walk and to wait at the next street corner. He is surprisingly responsive if he has been allowed some initial expansion. The reins of control can be held loosely, but there are always those moments when they need to be pulled up short and sharp.

FOUR AND A HALF YEARS

The 4½-year-old is beginning to pull in from his out-of-bounds 4-year-old ways. He is on his way to a more focal five, when life is more matter of fact and not so deep.

He is trying to sort out what is real from what is make-believe, and he does not get so lost in his pretending as at three and a half and four years, when he really *was* a cat or a carpenter or Roy Rogers. "Is it real?" is his constant question. Making a *real* drawing of an airplane, he includes a long electric cord so the people can plug it in. He can become quite confused as he tries to straighten out what he pretends, what happens on TV and what is real.

This mixture of reality and imagination can be quite exasperating to parents. Thus when one mother, completely out of patience, threatened that the Sandman would come and get him—we don't recommend this—her 4½-year-old considered and replied, "O.K., well, I think I better take my cowboy boots and shirt—will you get down my suitcase?"

Four-and-a-half-year-olds are a little more self-motivating than they were earlier. They start a job and stay on the same track much better than at four years, and with less need of adult control. When they start to build a farm with blocks, it ends up as a farm—not, as at four years, becoming first a fort, then a truck, then a gas station.

Four-and-a-half-year-olds are great discussers. Reading a book about fires might lead to a long discussion about the pros and cons of fires. They often have a surprising wealth of material and experience to draw on and seem to be prompted by an intellectual, philosophizing sort of interest. They are interested in details and they like to be shown. Their desire for realism is sometimes entirely too stark for adults—they seem sometimes almost too frank as they demand the details about death, for example.

Children of this age are improving their control and perfecting their skills in many ways. Their play is less wild than at four; they are better able to accept frustrations. Their fine motor control as expressed in drawing is markedly improved, and they will often draw on and on. They show a beginning interest in letters and numbers, and may count quite well, though skipping certain numbers.

Four-and-a-half shows a beginning interest, too, in seeing several sides of the picture. He is aware of front and back, of inside and outside. (One child wanted to know what her back looked like.)

He may even draw a man on one side of a paper, then turn it over and draw the back of his head on the other side.

Four-and-a-half, with its increased control and its interest in improving and perfecting skills, is a "catching-up" time with some children, especially with boys who have been slow in motor or language development, or it may be an age of rapid intellectual growth.

FIVE YEARS

Five years of age marks, in many children, a time of extreme and delightful equilibrium. "He's an angel," say many mothers of Fives, in awe and wonderment.

"He's almost too good!" worry others.

Five is indeed a good age. Gone is the out-of-bounds exuberance of the 4-year-old. Gone is the uncertainty and unpredictability of four-and-a-half. The 5-year-old tends to be reliable, stable, well adjusted. Secure within himself, he is calm, friendly, and not too demanding in his relations with others.

Secure and capable he seems, because he is content to stay on or near home base. He does not seem to feel the need to thrust out into the unknown, to attempt that which is too difficult for him. Rather he is content to live here and now. He tries only that which he can accomplish, and therefore he accomplishes that which he tries.

His mother is the center of his world and he likes to be near her. He likes to do things with and for her, likes to obey her commands. He likes to be instructed and to get permission. To be a good boy is not only his intention, but it is something which he usually can accomplish. Therefore he is satisfied with himself, and others are satisfied with him.

Many parents wish, when the customary 5½- to 6-year-old break-up of behavior comes, and when their "good" little 5-year-old turns into an often less-than-good little Six, that they could have their docile 5-year-old back again.

Looking backward in this way is, of course, fruitless. It is like wishing that your 18-monther, when he gets around the house too briskly and gets into too many things, were once again in the pre-creeping stage. Five is, surely, an enjoyable age for everybody while it lasts. But a growing child needs more than 5-year-old equipment to meet the world. He needs to branch out, as he does at six. Unfortunately, in branching out, he often thrusts into areas which cause a good deal of difficulty for all concerned. That is the difficulty of six.

Six Years

By now a certain rhythm of growth will perhaps have made itself apparent to you. You will have noticed that there is a tendency as the child grows older for ages in which he seems to be in relatively good equilibrium—happy, easy-going and secure—to alternate with ages in which this equilibrium breaks up. At the ages of disequilibrium the child is thrusting out or in, trying new things, wanting too much, finding it difficult to adapt to others because his own demands are so strong.

Thus equable Five is followed by tumultuous Six. Actually, the breakup starts around five and a half years of age. By six and a half things have usually smoothed down again. But for a period of six months or so around the age of six, many parents find that their child is extremely difficult to deal with.

Behavior at this time is in many ways reminiscent of that which we have described as typifying the 2½-year-old. The child is, to begin with, violently emotional. And in his emotions, he functions at opposite extremes. He loves one minute—hates the next. Thus he may say, "I love you, Mummy," accompanying his statement with a big bear hug. And the next minute he bursts out, "I hate you!" This outburst may be elicited by nothing worse, on Mother's part, than moving some belonging of his out of its proper place.

What has happened is that Mother is no longer the center of his world, as she was when he was merely five. Now *he* wants to be the center of his world, even though he hasn't yet developed a secure sense of himself. He wants to come first, to be loved best, to have the most of everything. Mother has been removed to second place. And now he takes everything out on her. Whatever is wrong, Mother gets blamed.

And much goes wrong. Because Six, like Two-and-a-half, is very demanding of others and very rigid in his demands. He has to have things just so. He cannot adapt. It is the others who must do the adapting.

Also, he tends to be extremely negative in his response to others. That he has been asked to do something is in his eyes sufficient reason for refusing to do it.

Six is, however, rather delightful in his vigor, in his energy, in his readiness for anything new. This is an expansive age, and the 6-year-old is ready for almost anything. His appetite for new experience is prodigious.

But this leads him to wanting all of everything. It is most difficult for him to choose between any two alternatives because he wants both. It is also most difficult for him to accept criticism, blame, punishment. He has to be right. He has to be praised. He has to win. He is as rigid and as unadaptable in his relations with others as he was earlier at two and a half. Things have to be done his way. The others have to give in to him. If he is winning, everything is fine. If the others win, tears and accusations that the others are cheating!

Thus if all goes well, he can be warm, enthusiastic, eager, ready for anything. But if things go badly, tears and tantrums.

It is difficult to by-pass this age in the child's life, nor should we wish to. We can make it a little easier for him, and for ourselves, by respecting the fact that he is having a difficult time within himself as well as in his relations with others. Use techniques where you can. By-pass as many unhappy incidents as you can. Get outsiders in to help carry through daily routines where you can—for he is at his worst with his mother.

Seven Years

Seven years of age is no exception to the rule that each new age period brings marked changes in behavior (as well as many new accomplishments). The 6-year-old child is typically brash and aggressive, ready for new adventure, falsely sure of himself. He meets new situations head on. Trouble occurs on the playground? He will stay and battle it out. Somebody try to get something away from him? He will fight for his own.

Things are very, very different at seven. Though seven, like any other age, has its moments of exuberance, security and happiness, it is a more withdrawn age. Seven in many ways has calmed down and is easier to live with. But he is more likely to complain than to rejoice. More apt to retreat from the scene muttering than to stay and demand his own. He has, with justice, been described as morose, mopey and moody.

Seven not only withdraws from combat, he just naturally seems to withdraw from other people. He likes to be alone. He wants a room of his own to which he can retreat and protect his own things. He likes to watch, to listen, to stay on the edge of any scene. He is a great television watcher and radio listener and possibly a reader. It is almost as if he is building up his sense of self by watching, observing, ruminating.

But his hands are also very busy touching, exploring, feeling everything he comes in contact with. He has an inordinate love of pencils and prefers the sharp, defined stroke of lead rather than the loose, sloppy stroke of a colored crayon. His intellect is in the ascendancy. He is more discriminating and refined in what he sees and what he does.

He often demands too much of himself. He is aware of the task but not always able to complete it. He is apt to go on too long and then become suddenly exhausted. He needs to be helped to define stopping points. He has his good days and his bad days; his high learning days and his forgetting-everything days. An aware teacher will shift her intellectual fare on these different days. And a wise mother will keep her child at home if his bad day starts the minute he gets out of bed, as it so often does.

For a brief period life for some can be pitched in a definitely minor key. At these times Seven tends to feel that people are against him, that they don't like him, that they are picking on him. The other kids cheat; his teacher picks on him at school. Even his parents are unfair. Though only a few Sevens go so far as to figure that they are adopted, this fantasy does now and then occur, and typifies the "nobody-loves-me" attitude of the 7-year-old. If his family is too "mean" to him, he may threaten to run away. Not from the expansive exuberance which sometimes drove Four out into the world, but simply to get away from the intolerable persecution which he thinks is his lot.

Even the facial expression of some 7-year-olds may express their dissatisfaction with life. Their lips may curl downward in a permanent pout.

Though Seven tends to be less happy and satisfied with life than his parents would like him to be, his good days will steadily increase in number as he gets older, his fatigue will lessen, and he will be ready for most anything by eight years of age.

The parent of the 7-year-old needs to steer a delicate course between being reasonably sympathetic with the many complaints which his child will utter, and yet not taking these complaints too seriously (though headaches do need investigating). His teacher is probably not as unfair as he reports her to be; the other children probably not as nefarious; brothers and sisters not as wicked.

EIGHT YEARS

Seven withdraws from the world, but Eight goes out to meet it. Nothing is too difficult for the 8-year-old, in his own estimation. No task too formidable to be undertaken. No distance too great for him to cover. In fact, to the average 8-year-old, the new and difficult is an exciting challenge which he tends to meet with great zest. He often overestimates his own ability in meeting this challenge.

He will not always follow through in his activities. The burst of energy and enthusiasm with which he tackles each new task may be followed by failure, discouragement and even tears if his failure is mentioned. But this will not stop him from starting something else new—tomorrow.

We often describe the 8-year-old as expansive and speedy. He seems to find it difficult to stay out of touch with any part of his environment. Therefore he is constantly busy and active, constantly enjoying new experiences, constantly trying out new things, making new friends.

In every way, the typical 8-year-old covers a good deal of ground. With his characteristic speed, he covers it rapidly. But alas, with his newly increased powers of evaluation, he may recognize his all-too-frequent failures. Then, tears and self-disparagement! "I always do it wrong!" "I never get anything right!" With his tendency to dramatize everything, we sometimes suspect that he, in a way, relishes even his failures, or he at least makes use of them.

For all his seeming brashness and bravado, he is much more sensitive than one might expect. He needs protection both from trying to do too much and from too excessive self-criticism when he meets with failure.

Thus when his good beginning is followed, as it often will be, by a poor ending, help him from too great a feeling of failure. Plan with him toward a future time when he will carry through better or will not set an almost impossible task for himself.

Seven was most concerned with himself and how other people treated him. Eight has gone further than this in his dealings with others. Now he is interested, not just in how people treat him, but in his *relationships* with others. He is ready for, and wants, a good two-way relationship. Furthermore, it is not just what people do which concerns him, but also what they think. He has more to give to other people than he did earlier, but he expects more of them as well. With his mother, especially, the 8-year-old wants and demands a close, understanding relationship.

The 8-year-old, in his expanding universe, gives us more than a hint of the kind of person he will be later on.

Nine Years

Exuberant! Expansive! Buoyant! Ready for anything! That was your typical 8-year-old. Nine, as many of you will have observed, is again on the quieter strain of five and seven. He lives more within himself, is surer in his contacts with the outside world, is more self-contained and self-sufficient than was the adventurous Eight, who just couldn't keep to himself.

Nine can be, in fact often insists on being, extremely independent. In his own eyes he is quite a man of the world, and he tends to resist too much "bossing" by his parents. In fact, the average 9-year-old tends to be much more interested in friends than in family; and many, briefly, would like to withdraw as much as they can from the family circle. Certainly the opinions of their friends are much more important, to most of them, than are the opinions of their families.

Though the 9-year-old may be interested in adults from the point of view of what they can do with him—expeditions, excursions, shared interests—he is much less interested than he was earlier in the relationship itself. Therefore it is important not to impose yourself on the child of this age. He wants and needs to have his maturity, his independence and his separateness respected.

If left pretty much to himself, if treated as the mature creature he considers himself to be, the 9-year-old usually gets along pretty well and does display a remarkable amount of self-reliance and capability. Nine can be an age of perfecting skills and of real, solid accomplishment. However, there is a disquieting side to the child of this age. He does tend to worry. He takes things hard. He can be extremely anxious and may, in fact, tend to go to pieces over something which would have brought only brief tears a year earlier.

Some people even go so far as to consider Nine a potentially rather neurotic age. Nine not only worries a good deal, but he tends to complain. His complaints may be simply that tasks imposed, at home and at school, are "too hard." Or they may take the form of more serious physical complaints. His eyes smart. His hands hurt. He has a stomach-ache.

These complaints nearly always do represent real physical feelings of discomfort. Nevertheless, it is interesting to note how often they occur in relation to some disliked task. His eyes hurt when he has to do his studying. Hands hurt when he practices. His stomach aches if he has to sweep the floor or rake the yard. He has to go to the bathroom as soon as it's time to wash the dishes. All of these complaints should of course be respected within reason, but should nevertheless be recognized for what they are—Nine's way of meeting an unpleasant situation. Not, as a rule, as really dangerous physical ailments.

Nine may be in some an age of considerable rebellion against authority. Some Nines, however, merely rebel by withdrawing— they can look right through you as you give them a command. Or they rebel by complaining, but actually do carry out your commands. And gradually the complaints and the rebellions and the worries diminish as Nine approaches the peaceful age of ten.

TEN YEARS

If your 9-year-old was something of a problem to you with his worries, his anxieties, his withdrawals, his demands, he will in all probability more than make up for it when he gets to be ten. For ten is, to hear most parents tell it, one of the very nicest ages there is.

Perhaps this is partly true, from the parents' point of view, because of the fact that to the average 10-year-old his parents' word is so utterly law. Ask him a question about almost any phase of his behavior and he will tell you, "Yes, I can do that. Mummy says it is all right for me to." Or he will reply, "No, Mummy says I'm not old enough for that."

He not only obeys easily and naturally, but he seems to expect to obey and gains status in his own eyes by his obedience. "I try to be a good boy," he will tell you honestly.

Not only does he cheerfully obey Mummy (and Daddy), but he is for the most part extremely well pleased with both parents and with the rest of the family as well. Ask him what he loves best of anything in the world and he will tell you, "My mother and father, of course."

Ten is not only satisfied with parents and teacher, but with the world in general. He is pleased with life as he finds it, and he finds it easy to enjoy himself. He is nice, and friendly, to other people, and he expects them to be friendly to him.

He is matter-of-fact and straightforward, and he is also flexible. He doesn't take things too seriously. Ask him a question about some behavior and he will reply easily, casually, "Well, sometimes I do and sometimes I don't."

Ten, more than any age which follows until you get to sixteen, is an age of predictable, comfortable equilibrium. And never again, after ten, will you as a parent get quite the same whole-hearted and unreserved acceptance of you, your actions and your motives as you do from your 10-year-old boy or girl.

3

Individuality

S O FAR we have described the way that behavior changes from age to age and have given you some idea of the general ways in which a 3-year-old differs from a 2-year-old, or a 6-year-old from a 5-year-old. That is, we've illustrated the fact that there are characteristic ways of behaving which tend to occur at each different age.

In chapters which follow we shall describe the way in which the behaviors themselves—eating, sleeping, elimination, getting on with parents and all sorts of other behaviors—change from age to age.

Thus in most of this book we're emphasizing ways of behaving which all children have more or less in common. Before we go on, however, we'd like to discuss, in the present chapter, the ways in which children differ.

That children do differ, and that each child has his own characteristic ways of behaving, is something that all parents know. Thus, in spite of the fact that all children tend to go through the same stages of behavior, you know that each child goes through these stages in his own individual way. You say yourselves, "Oh, Johnny's always been like that. You just have to let him take his time"; or, "He doesn't mix much with the other children, he just likes to play by himself"; or, "She's never been very good at her lessons but she's a wonderful help at home."

Students of human behavior have been observing and studying these personality, or individuality, differences for a long time now. There are many different approaches to the study and classification of individuality. The one which we have found extremely helpful as a basic approach is the one that holds that we behave as we do (that is, our personality is what it is) because of the way our bodies are built.

This way of studying individuality is called "constitutional psychology." We shall explain it briefly. If the technical terms we use seem confusing to you, or if at this point you'd rather proceed directly to finding out more about how children *in general* behave, and what solutions you may try for the everyday problems which confront you, you may prefer to skip this chapter or to come back to it later.

PHYSICAL APPROACH TO THE UNDERSTANDING OF INDIVIDUALITY

"Looks don't matter," some people tell us. And if by "looks" they mean superficial regularity of the facial features, they may be right. But if by "looks" they mean bodily structure—the way in which head, neck, trunk, arms, legs and extremities are fashioned—we suspect that they are wrong. Because the way in which the body is structured appears to be the first and most important clue (for those who know how to interpret it) to what the human being is and will be.

One of the most important things that a parent can do if he wants to know more about his child's personality is to familiarize himself, if not with the details, at least with the more basic aspects of the known differences in human structure. Because if he understands these differences in structure, it will help him to understand differences in human behavior—that is, personality differences—as well.

This study of personality assessment based on measurement of bodily structure actually covers every aspect of human behavior. From the way a human being is built, many scientists believe that they can predict how he might act—his eating, sleeping, social behavior, what kinds of situations he will seek or avoid, the possibility or impossibility of his being a success in activities requiring physical skill.

They can also get an idea as to whether or not he will be interested in competition, how and to what extent he will express his emotions, how much courage he will have for combat and how brave he will be in the face of physical pain. The individual who shows stoicism and indifference in the face of pain is not merely exercising more "will power" than the one who flinches at physical pain. He may be responding differently largely because, being built differently, he actually is less physically sensitive to pain.

Understanding all these differences and respecting the fact that they are the result of basic and deep-seated differences in actual physical structure and not merely the result of the way the individual has been treated by his parents or by the world around him can help parents in their efforts to understand their children. It can also help them to understand themselves.

All of this does not mean that human behavior is *entirely* determined by hereditary factors. What it does mean is that the body structure provides the raw material out of which personality is formed: that it is the instrument upon which the life forces, both internal and external, play. Tendencies to behave in certain ways are to a large extent predetermined, and these tendencies are then either reinforced or modified by the environment. So the same individual might develop along very different lines in contrasting environments—but certain behaviors would be less possible for him than others.

THREE PHYSICAL TYPES

Though there do not actually exist different distinct "types" of body build, there can be identified three chief physical components.* Each person actually represents a combination of these three different components, but in most people one or the other tends to predominate. Thus we often loosely speak as if there were three different types of individual. These three components are: endomorphy, mesomorphy, ectomorphy.

These three kinds of individuals may be described as follows:

The person in whom endomorphy predominates is referred to as an endomorph. These individuals have large stomachs and livers,

* These different kinds of physiques are discussed in full in the following books by Dr. William H. Sheldon, *Varieties of Physique* (New York, Harper & Brothers, 1940) and *Varieties of Temperament* (New York, Harper & Brothers, 1942).

that is, large digestive viscera. They float high in water and are usually fat. They are soft and spherical in shape. Their behavior is characterized by extreme relaxation and love of comfort. They are sociable, love food, love people and are gluttons for affection.

The mesomorph, in contrast, has big bones, a well-developed heart and circulatory system, and heavy muscles. He is hard, firm, upright, and relatively strong. Blood vessels are large and the skin is relatively thick, with large pores. In his behavior, muscular activity and vigorous bodily assertion predominate. He loves exercise and activity, loves to dominate.

The ectomorph, in extreme contrast, is the thin, fragile, linear person, flat of chest and with long, slender, poorly muscled or "pipe-stem" arms and legs. His behavior shows restraint, inhibition, over-sensitiveness and a desire for concealment. He shrinks from even ordinary social occasions.

In the pages which follow we shall expand these brief character-izations and bring you further detail about each of these kinds of people. Reading these descriptions, or even reading Sheldon's books, will not turn you into a constitutional psychologist. But it may help you to understand and appreciate the personalities of your children better than you perhaps now do.

The names of these three types may seem rather technical and specialized, but we believe that once you have mastered them, they will be extremely useful to you. Increasingly they are becoming a part of the common vocabulary.

Each of these three types of individual, because of his own special physical structure, has different drives, different responses, different interests, from each of the others. Sheldon sums up these differences by saying that the endomorph exercises and attends in order to eat; the mesomorph eats and attends in order to exercise; and the ecto-morph eats and exercises in order to attend.

(It is very important to keep in mind that no one individual is *purely* one thing or another. In most individuals, one component or the other predominates and largely determines behavior, but we are each a combination of each of these three elements.)

The differences in the ways in which the endomorph, the mesomorph and the ectomorph behave show up in eating, sleeping, emotional behavior—in fact, in every life situation.

SLEEPING

Take sleeping behavior, for instance. You all know that in spite of tables and charts which tell you how much sleep a child of any age "ought" to get, children vary tremendously in the amount of sleep they do get and require; in the deepness of their sleep; in how quietly or restlessly they sleep; how easily and quickly they get to sleep and how easily they waken. Some sleep so quietly that the bedclothes are hardly disturbed in the morning; others leave bedclothes completely rumpled.

According to Sheldon, the endomorph loves to sleep, in marked contrast to the mesomorph who loves to wake up and be active, and also in contrast with the ectomorph who hates to go to sleep but who, once asleep, hates to wake up and be severed from his dreams.

The sleep of the endomorph is deep, easy and undisturbed. There is complete relaxation in sleep. He goes to sleep easily and quickly. He can sleep comfortably in any position and usually snores. He loves sleep—frequently becoming a "sleep glutton." It is difficult to wake such a person during the night.

The mesomorph has a low sleep requirement. It is important to remember this. He is the voluntary early riser. A mesomorph may sleep no more than six hours nightly and still retain boundless energy. He goes to sleep readily and generally sleeps well. But he sleeps "vigorously," tossing and thrashing about. He seldom dreams but often snores loudly.

Things are very different with the ectomorph. Insomnia occurs in adult life, and even in childhood habits of going to sleep are irregular and erratic. It is hard to get a child of this type to sleep unless he is close to physical exhaustion. He wakens easily, but it is hard for him to get up. He sleeps lightly, does not fully relax, seldom snores, often dreams, is abnormally fatigued. He needs more sleep than do the other two types of individual.

Thus you will see that it is not practical to make hard and fast

rules about how much sleep your child needs—since sleep requirements vary so tremendously from one "morph" to another "morph"
and from child to child.

EATING

There are certain children (and adults)—the slender, sensitive,
fragile ectomorphs—who eat very little, seem never to gain weight.
Their parents worry that they will be ill if they don't eat and constantly try to force on them "just one more" piece of bread or one
more helping of potato. And yet, despite his lack of interest in food
and the lack of "flesh on his bones," the child of this type is often
among the healthiest in any given group.

In the supervision of the child's feeding behavior, almost more
than in any other sphere, it is important during the preschool years
for mothers to recognize and respect the fact that different types of
children have widely differing needs.

Many so-called "feeding problems" arise simply from the fact
that the parent is trying to overfeed the child, especially the ectomorph who simply "hasn't room" for two tall glasses of milk and a
second helping of meat and potatoes and a dish of good, nourishing
rice pudding.

We often find that the thin, "scrawny" or petite child who seems
to care very little for food does better on four or five small meals a
day than on three big ones. A child of this kind, when he does become hungry, becomes suddenly and sharply hungry. But his hunger
does not last, and if you refuse him the snack he asked for "because
it is almost mealtime and it would spoil your dinner," you may find
that by mealtime that little spark of hunger is gone.

As to type of food needed, the ectomorph particularly needs pro-
tein, especially meat, and the easily digested carbohydrates. As to
speed of eating, the ectomorphic child tends to eat very rapidly.
Sheldon has commented that children of this type are often "mis-
understood" and sometimes badly bullied by well-meaning relatives
who try to normalize them and to make them not only eat as much
as they "should," but sit patiently through a long, deliberate meal

when, with their speed, they have finished—or could finish if allowed —in five minutes' time.

The fat, soft, roly-poly endomorph is, in contrast, almost never a feeding problem. This kind of child seems almost to live in order to eat. He is characterized by "a love of food and a warm appreciation of eating for its own sake. This is not to be confused with a mere voracious appetite. There is deep joy in eating."

The endomorphic child is not fat simply *because* he eats. But he is almost invariably a "good" eater. He loves to eat—it is a primary pleasure, and even when not eating, he loves to talk about and to think about food. As he approaches the stage of preadolescence, a child of this type may seem to do almost nothing but eat, and, if a girl, will find that she needs to resort to those dresses termed appropriately by the manufacturer "Chubbies." Such a child will often be interested in watching his mother cook and, boy or girl, will often take great pleasure in being allowed to cook.

Digestion is usually excellent in the child of endomorphic build— all sorts of indigestible foods such as pickles, mince pies, cucumbers and the like can be eaten with no embarrassment. "Roughage" is handled with no difficulty—and constipation, colic and stomach-aches are seldom experienced.

In fact, eating constitutes such a primary pleasure for individuals of this type that, from infancy on, their mothers have little trouble in getting them to eat and drink all they "should."

Eating is such a pleasure, in fact, that to deprive an endomorph of his supper (children seem hardly ever to be punished by being made to go without breakfast or lunch) is a really harsh punishment. The ectomorph, on the other hand, might hardly notice such punishment. Sheldon has noted that adult endomorphs probably never go on hunger strikes and that Gandhi was an extreme ectomorph.

The mesomorphs, to complete this story, are hearty eaters, like "good plain food," and often eat too much. They like to "wolf" a large quantity of food at one sitting and, if permitted, may gorge themselves.

So, in general (though excess eating can produce a problem too), it is as a rule the ectomorph who tends to be classed as a "feeding problem," and a clearer understanding of his real food needs can often take him out of the "problem" class.

EMOTIONS

"That child just doesn't feel a thing, she's so unloving," complains grandmother to mother. (Skinny little Rosalie, a child of typically ectomorphic build, has just rejected Grandmother's efforts to give her a welcoming kiss as she came home from school.) "Really, I don't think she'd shed a tear if the whole family was killed all at once. She just looks so stony and secretive. I think she likes us all well enough in her way, but I don't believe I remember her ever showing any affection. Even as a tiny baby she wasn't cuddly the way the other children were.

"And it's so hard for her to thank anyone for anything. You can feel that she is pleased, but she certainly doesn't let herself go to any extent.

"Sometimes I think we ought to take her to a psychologist or something. She seems like such a normal child in so many ways. But she just seems to lack warmth and affection."

Such a lack could indeed, in a certain type of child, be a sign that something might be going wrong. But in the child of typically ectomorphic physique, as was Rosalie, such behavior may be considered not only quite normal, but to be expected. (This does not mean, however, that with shifting growth forces, effort and experience that some changes cannot and do not occur.)

According to Sheldon, the ectomorphic individual is normally characterized by secretiveness of feeling and emotional restraint. These people are tight-lipped and do their suffering in silence. They do not "let go" and reveal their emotions or feelings in the presence of others. "External expression of feeling is powerfully inhibited though there may actually be great intensity of feeling. Signs of emotional weakness are choked back as if subject to great shame."

Quite the opposite is the case with the fat, jolly endomorph. Rosalie's sister, Dorothy, was a typical endomorph, and her grand-

mother had no complaints to make of her. Warm, loving, friendly—
she was, the family felt, satisfactorily responsive.

This too, we could have predicted from one look at Dorothy. It
isn't necessarily that she loves her family more, or appreciates them
more than does Rosalie. It is just easier for her to express her feelings. Having the temperament which characteristically accompanies
an endomorphic build, Dorothy finds it easy and natural to express
her emotions freely. The endomorphic individual characteristically
"gives way naturally and easily at all times to a free communication
of feeling. Nothing is ever choked up or held back. There is no
emotional inhibition. Feeling is smoothly and naturally communi-
cated to whomsoever may be available as recipient. Whether the
individual is pleased, grieved, disappointed or shocked, his feelings
are to be read like an open book. . . . He conceals nothing. . . .
Such a person 'registers' delight or sobs and cries convincingly at the
time when it will do the most good. He 'wears his heart on his
sleeve.' " *

So, whether you have a Rosalie or a Dorothy, try to keep in mind
that it is quite normal for different kinds of people to express their
emotions differently, and to a different degree.

STAND UP STRAIGHT

"Stand up straight, Mary!"

How many children's lives are made miserable by this oft-
repeated command.

Some parents limit their efforts to improve their children's posture to verbal nagging. Others make their children take exercises.
Still others may even go so far as to buy elastic harness affairs which
their poor children are forced to wear, in the hope that their posture
can be improved and their stooping shoulders straightened.

It is natural, in our society, to try to improve the child's posture. Most of us feel that a straight back and square shoulders are
desirable and "look better" than do other postures.

Yet, according to Sheldon, there is actually little to be said for
the perfectly upright posture except that it is the preference of the

---

* Sheldon, William H., *Varieties of Temperament,* pp. 44, 45.

predominantly mesomorphic individual and that it is often associated with high blood pressure.

Thus, if your son or daughter is of a primarily mesomorphic build, he will very likely prefer to sit and stand straight. And even if he does not, your directions to him to do so may prove very effective.

Not so with your thin, wiry ectomorph. According to Sheldon, the round shoulder of the ectomorph is probably as normal and characteristic for him as is the round belly of the endomorph.

For the ectomorphic individual, the favorite posture is usually round shouldered. Also, he likes to sit on one foot, or to wind one leg around the other. He is most comfortable when he tips his chair back on its back legs. (And may be much happier with his hands clenched and in his pockets.)

Sheldon suggests that there may be nothing more unkind in all of education than forcing all children, regardless of their body build, to sit in the same kind of chair and in the same posture. And since it is the kind of chair (long and with a level seat) and the kind of posture (straight back and square shoulders) which best fits the mesomorph, it is the ectomorph who suffers most.

So regardless of your own postural preference, if your son or daughter is an extreme ectomorph and seems most comfortable when sitting or standing with his shoulders rounded over, think twice before you torture him with, "Stand up straight." There may come a time, however, when the little mesomorphy he possesses may come to his rescue, may blossom even though slightly, enough to afford him a "better" posture.

THE OVER-AWARENESS OF THE ECTOMORPH

"Mamma, make him stop rattling the paper." Janice is practicing at the piano. In the next room her brother is reading the funny papers. The sounds he is making with these papers are barely audible, but Janice notices them and they interfere with her practicing.

"Janice," commands her mother firmly, "you just concentrate on your practicing. You're a regular fuss budget. You just let your brother alone. He isn't bothering you."

Mother may be right from the point of view of harmony in the home. Everyone in the household, obviously, can't keep perfectly still just because some one member is playing the piano.

However, she is wrong in her statement that, "Your brother isn't bothering you." Because in making this remark she is reckoning without the fact that Janice is of an extremely ectomorphic body build (and temperament). And the ectomorphic individual is perhaps supersensitive to any little disturbance of sight or sound, even those which he can just barely see or hear. As Sheldon says, "He is overaware, has a low threshold of attention, notices everything." (Though he can, if completely absorbed in something which really interests him as an interesting book, be almost deaf to what goes on around.)

Thus in school, an ectomorphic boy or girl may be terribly distracted by a classmate who is drumming on his desk with his fingers, even several seats away. He will be particularly distracted if he is in a classroom where half the group is supposed to be studying, half reciting.

If doing his homework, he may feel that he is unable to concentrate if someone else in the family is making even a small noise in some other part of the house. He may be unable to read unless there is perfect quiet in the room.

The tapping of a shutter, or any small, rhythmic sound (particularly if unidentified) may be so distracting that he just can't seem to go on with any concentrated activity.

What do parents usually do when an oversensitive, overaware son or daughter complains of such noises or distractions? The child says that these noises bother him, make him nervous, that he can't concentrate.

Far too often his parents simply tell him to get on with what he is doing and not make so much fuss. Just put his mind on his work and forget about the distractions. That they won't bother him if he will just ignore them.

Kinder and wiser to recognize that your child, if an ectomorph, will in all probability throughout life be of a supersensitive temperament, overly alert to and aware of his environment, easily bothered by little sights, little sounds. Help him to find, so far as possible, quiet surroundings for study and practice. When such surroundings are not available, sympathize with his need for them but help him gradually to adapt to less than perfect quiet. If he must, as most have to, put up with some minor distractions, at least don't make things worse for him by telling him that he is foolish to be distracted.

THE NOISY MESOMORPH

"Joe! Come back into the house again and then go out and shut the door quietly. Don't slam it! There's no need of your knocking the house down every time you go in or out."

Or, "Joe! Don't shout so! Do you think we are all deaf? Honestly, everything you say can be heard at least three blocks away. Talk in a normal tone. There's no need of shouting."

Well, in a way there's no need of shouting. And in a way there's no need of slamming the door when you could shut it quietly.

But if your boy or girl is of a basically mesomorphic physique (that is, if he has the vigorous, well-muscled, posturally alert body which we classify as mesomorphic), it will be natural for him to behave in these ways. For the mesomorph is just naturally noisy, vigorous, assertive and dominating. The person of this build (whether child or adult) just naturally makes a lot of noise.

To speak softly, to shut a door gently, to work quietly, to move a chair by lifting it and then quietly putting it down somewhere else —all these are unnatural ways of behaving. He would have to remind himself, on each occasion, to behave thus.

In public, as well as at home, this characteristic noisiness of the mesomorph makes itself felt. On the school bus, in the school cafeteria, at the movies—he (or she) shouts the loudest, laughs the most noisily.

His behavior is, therefore, in direct contrast to that of the ectomorph (the thin, bony, characteristically shy person). The ectomorph sits in the corner, speaks quietly, tries to avoid attracting attention.

Nobody taught the ectomorph to be so unobtrusive and quiet. He just naturally behaves this way. But just as the ectomorph almost automatically behaves in a way which will avoid attracting attention, the mesomorph acts in a way that will call attention to himself.

You can, within very narrow limits, help your ectomorphic child to feel enough confidence in himself that he will speak up above a whisper. But it is unlikely that he will ever become conspicuously noisy. Conversely, you can encourage a mesomorph to tone down his voice and his movements a little, especially if you choose certain specific situations and work on them. But he will remain a basically noisy, unrestrained individual.

FUNCTIONAL APPROACH TO INDIVIDUALITY

A second, though not contradictory, approach to an understanding of individuality is to note how the individual behaves under certain circumstances and to determine the ways in which his behavior shows certain predictable qualities. Does he concentrate well? Does he shift rapidly from one thing to the next? Is he more interested in people or things? These and other behaviors will be considered, a bit at random, in the following pages. These particular personality characteristics we are about to discuss have not as yet been related specifically to physical structure, though we have little doubt that such a relation does exist and that with further research we shall some day be ready to correlate these different factors.

You may be interested to think over your children and the children you know to see if any of the following functional items will help you to identify each child in his separate right. And to discover at least in part what distinguishes each child from other children.

PERIPHERAL AND FOCAL

Peter sits in a corner of the nursery-school playroom, his back to the group, building a house. Steadily, busily, ignoring the other children, he builds. Larger and fancier rises his structure. The morning goes by. Still he builds on this one building and still he ignores the other children.

Robert started out the morning sharing Peter's block play, but he soon tired of this quiet pursuit. So he rode a bike for a while, running into or over people and things which crossed his path. Then he joined the group in the doll corner for a minute or two. He talked to the teacher. He fooled with the turtle. He made some biscuits out of clay. He had a conversation with one of the girls.

Their mothers were watching them from the sidelines. "If only Peter were friendly like Robert," complained Peter's mother to Robert's mother. "If only he would stir out of that corner and join into things. He ought to mix more with other children."

"If only Robert would stick to one thing better. He's so all over the place. He never stays still a minute and never accomplishes a thing. I wish he could learn to concentrate the way Peter does," replied Robert's mother.

And so, for as long as we have been observing children, we have seen these two sharply contrasting types. And nearly always their mothers are trying to change them. Trying to bring Peter out and to pull Robert in. Trying to broaden out Peter, who sits in the corner, and to make him more sociable. Trying to make Robert settle down, stick to one thing, concentrate and accomplish more.

Some children are of course mixtures of these two, but many more are of one temperament *or* the other. The name we use to describe these two kinds of children are *focal* (the one who focalizes or concentrates always on the one thing close at hand) and *peripheral* (the one who is all over the place, responding to many different things, quickly changing, flexible, versatile).

It is important for the parent of either kind of child to keep in mind two things: First, that neither type of child will change basically through the years, though each may become "better" or "worse" at certain ages. Each will in all likelihood go on as he started, concentrating or spreading out. However, with increased age and environmental influences, growth tends to cut down the extremes of behavior. Though the peripheral child remains peripheral as he grows older, he can often learn to concentrate at crucial moments. And though the focal child is still focal, he can sometimes be pulled out into the periphery as needed.

Second, it should be remembered that there are many solid advantages to either one of these kinds of personality. If your child is extreme in either of these ways, it will be easier for you in the long run if you can adjust to and reconcile yourself to the kind your child is, since you cannot in all probability make him over—even though time and experience tend to produce their mellowing effects.

As we earlier emphasized in our description of body types, we are each of us a combination of all three physical components—endomorphy, mesomorphy and ectomorphy—in varying amounts. We are not just one or the other. The same is true of tendencies to peripheral and focal behavior. We each have some of both in varying amounts. We will also express these ways of behaving differently at different ages. Think of the focal attention and concentration of the 7-year-old, and the spread and peripheral interests of the 8-year-old. The 9- and 10-year-olds try to combine these two forces so that less extreme behavior and modulation is possible. Age determines, as well as individuality.

INABILITY TO SHIFT

"There are no problem children. There are only children with problems," say some people who work with delinquent youth. But delinquent children are not the only ones who have problems. Perfectly "good" children, as they grow up, have many problems too.

One of the major problems any child has to deal with, because it is a problem always with him, is the problem of his own personality. And of all the problem personalities we have encountered, one of the most troublesome is the kind which cannot make shifts, which is poor at transitions. (That is, he cannot move easily from one thing to another or from one stage of behavior to the next.) The child who suffers this personality difficulty may be quite normal in all respects except that he is simply unable, without help, to move easily from one type of activity to another, from one situation to another, or from one stage of behavior to another. He gets stuck wherever he happens to be and cannot, without help, move on to the next thing.

Such a child usually ends up by being called "bad." "He is a bad eater, a bad sleeper, bad in his play, bad with people—in fact, I can say that he's just an all round bad boy," one mother told us when she brought her attractive and intelligent but cross-looking little 3-year-old to the Gesell Institute.

A thorough psychological examination and a detailed interview with his mother brought out the fact that this boy was in reality a good eater. He had a good hearty appetite and could feed himself nicely. But he tended to get stuck with one kind of food and did not like to shift (that is, to make the transition) to new foods. So he always made a fuss whenever a new food was added to his menu. He just wanted to go on and on eating the same thing for every meal.

He was also a good sleeper. He slept soundly for the "proper" number of hours each night. But he found it hard to get to sleep each night (that is to make the shift from waking to sleep) and he also found it hard to come awake in the morning (that is, to make the shift back to wakefulness).

As to play—he actually played very nicely. He could entertain himself for long periods alone. But he found it difficult to shift within his play. That is, if he was playing with his wagon, he did not want to shift and play with blocks. And he found it hard to shift from play to any other type of activity. For instance, he found it hard to leave his play to come to dinner.

As to his relation with other people, he was "good" with one person at a time, but found it hard to shift from one person to another —for instance, from mother to baby-sitter. He had trouble both in separating from his mother at nursery school and separating from nursery school to go home with his mother.

So it turned out that this boy was not really *bad* after all. He was merely bad at making transitions and this was not, we believe, real badness, but a definite characteristic of constitutional individuality. What he needed, then, was not scolding or punishment when he failed to make some necessary transition desired by his parents.

What he needed was real and specific help from his parents whenever there was a transition to be made.

If a child does not see as well as he should, we help him in various ways. Sometimes he needs special visual stimulation. At other times he may need glasses. Similarly, if he cannot by himself make the necessary shifts from one thing to another, we should help him here too by providing the transitions which he needs and cannot arrange for himself. (When leaving nursery school, running to find his mother in her car rather than being met on the playground may well facilitate leave-taking. Or being given a new pair of pajamas may break into that going-to-bed ritual which has lasted all too long. These and many similar techniques will smooth the way for the poor shifter.)

CHILDREN WHO ARE GOOD IN A NEW SITUATION AND THEN DETERIORATE

Some children, however, have just the opposite response to change. "He's so much better since he went to this new school. The teacher says she just can't understand why that other school had so much trouble with him," explained Danny's fond mother to her husband.

He was bad in the old setup, but a change of environment has fixed him up and he's wonderful in the new. How many times we hear this theme repeated!

Two social workers were discussing one of their charges. "That little Davis boy—you know, he was getting along just terribly. But we put him in a new foster home and it's done wonders for him. The new foster mother says she can't understand why anyone couldn't get on with him. He's one of the best children we ever gave her."

The same story. He was bad in the old, but he is good in the new. Just a matter of taking a little pains and finding the right setup.

. . . We could go on indefinitely with similar examples, but let us instead return, after a six-month interval, to **Danny** and to the little Davis boy.

Danny isn't doing so well in his new school. In fact, his new teacher is now making the same complaints that his old one did. Danny is rude, disobedient, uninterested, careless and he makes trouble with the other children.

And the new foster mother has completely given up on the little Davis boy. She says he is disrupting the entire household and has asked the social worker to find him a new foster home.

What has happened? What went wrong? Danny seemed so happy and good in his new school. The Davis boy's foster home placement seemed like such a favorable one.

A careful psychological evaluation of the personalities of either of these two boys might have allowed us to predict how things would turn out. It is likely that both of them belonged to that deceptive group of children who almost inevitably do well in a *new* situation.

Things going badly? Give them a new home, a new school, a new teacher, a visit to grandmother's, even a new bed (in case they have had trouble with sleeping) and, briefly, the change will work wonders. They behave beautifully. The new teacher, or foster parent, or relative takes credit for the improvement in behavior and blames the former caretaker for the former bad behavior.

And then the new wears off and the old patterns reappear. Then you can make another dramatic change of environment and temporarily improve the behavior. Or you can decide to stay where you are and work on the problems from there.

(However, all of this does go to show that newness and change often do give the child a pick-up even though it may be temporary. Let us hope that eventually the child himself will develop sticking power, some learning from experience, however slow it is. We as parents and caretakers may sometimes be guilty of accelerating a downhill pattern by anticipating too much, expecting too much too soon. We need rather to support the child, and to protect him from himself.)

THE DESTRUCTIVE CHILD

"We've got to have some help with Teddy," explained Teddy's mother. "He is without question the worst child in the neighborhood. Why right while I'm phoning, he is climbing up the living-room curtains. We absolutely have no control over him."

An abbreviated list of 3-year-old Teddy's bad behaviors, which she later related to us during their visit to the Institute, included the following:

Teddy breaks everything he can get his hands on, even the handles of hammers. He especially likes to break windows.

He is "into everything," and he is so quick you can't stop him.

He ran away one Sunday at 6 A.M. without any clothes on and was brought back home, an hour later by the police.

He is rough with children and adults. He hit his aunt over the head one day and knocked her out.

He constantly destroys neighbors' property.

He messes up stores if his mother lets go of him even long enough to pay for and accept purchases.

A careful psychological examination ruled out a first possible explanation of Teddy's behavior—that he might be "bad" because he was defective and unable to understand the normal demands of socialized living.

A second possibility was that his bad behavior was due to bad handling on the part of his parents. However, Teddy in our own hands behaved little better than with his mother. After two hours of his company we and the Institute were considerably the worse for wear.

The most likely conclusion, therefore, and the one which our tests indicated, was that this boy's personality was the thing at fault and the source of his difficulty. We found him to be a boy who had absolutely no ability to modulate or restrain his impulses. His drive to touch, to grab, to climb, to act, was very strong, and he himself had no ability to control or modify it.

Therefore, as we explained to his mother, the environment will need, for the time being, to be very firm and to provide the control that is necessary. It also needs to provide outlets for his desire to destroy and tear apart so that destruction can have its legitimate though temporary outlet. We need to remind ourselves that in life's dualities the *negative* usually precedes the *positive, no* comes before *yes, taking out* comes before *putting in, destruction* before *construction*. Some of the most destructive children we have known have later grown up to be among the most creatively constructive.

But when a child is destructive for destruction's sake, without moving into any constructive expressions, then we have to seek out deeper causes. We then need a more thorough examination with a brain-wave test, if possible, to see if anything is more seriously wrong and what, if anything, can be done about it.

THE AUTISTIC CHILD

Another example—a special kind of personality which in its extreme form is described by child specialists as "autistic." This kind of child is characterized chiefly by his marked lack of warmth in personal relations.

Dr. Leo Kanner was the first to describe the autistic child, and we refer any serious students of personality deviation to his *Child Psychiatry* (C. C. Thomas), for the best description and treatment of the subject.

Briefly, the autistic child is one who does not relate himself in the ordinary way to people and situations, from the beginning of life on. People say of him, "He is in a shell." . . . "Happiest when left alone." . . . "Acts as if other people were not there."

These children often treat people as if the people were merely objects. They also seem to have little defined sense of self or of who they are. One autistic boy we know, when asked if he could write his name (usually one of the first words a child can write), replied in the typically hollow voice of the autistic child, "I don't know that word. That's just a middle-sized word and I only know big words and little words."

Their language, in the early years, often does not convey much meaning to other people, and their wish to communicate with others may be very mild.

They often repeat things just as you say them. Thus if you say, "Say good-by to Mrs. Jones," they will repeat, "Say good-by to Mrs. Jones."

Their surprising rote-memory often encourages their parents, but their rigid demand that things be done always the same way (like the 2½-year-old) is often extremely trying.

With such children relation to objects is nearly always stronger than relation to persons.

If you have a child of this type, it is important to recognize the fact that he was, in our opinion at least, born that way. Too many parents of autistic children have been counseled that the child acts as coldly and impersonally as he does because they, the parents, have rejected him. Too many are told that he is withdrawing from their own cold treatment of him. This is not, in our opinion, the case. We do not believe that you "make" your child autistic, no matter how coldly you might treat him. Your cold treatment—which he himself inspires in you—may exaggerate, but it does not cause, his coldness.

Your warmth, conversely, can help to "thaw him out," but it cannot change his basic personality.

If you have a child of this type, you will probably want to seek specialized help for him. However, it will encourage you to know that many autistic children do grow up to lead relatively normal lives.

THE FEMININE BOY

"A perfect little lady!" Or, "A regular boy!" Fortunately, from the parents' point of view, the majority of little girls, even at a very early age, show signs of femininity. And vice versa. Even in nursery school, girls in general seem to show a preference for dolls and domestic play—boys for trucks and cars and building blocks.

Some people believe that the culture, even at the earliest ages, is imposing these preferences. Others believe that these basic differences of taste and behavior are largely inborn.

Inborn or not, and in spite of many exceptions, marked differences do in general occur between the ways in which young girls and boys behave. Exceptions are usually slight and not too worrisome. Betsy is something of a tomboy. Jackie isn't too good at rough-and-tumble play and seems to prefer the quieter, gentler games.

As a rule these exceptions are slight enough not to cause too much concern. However, there is one exception which occurs over and over again and which causes grave concern to parents, particularly to fathers.

This is the boy who from the beginning prefers feminine activities and shuns anything rough and tumble. He prefers to play with girls. He favors such activities as painting, singing, play-acting, dressing dolls. He himself loves to dress up in girls' clothes.

Such behavior to most parents seems to be a sign that something is definitely wrong. Some scold, some punish, some ridicule, some worry in silence. But nearly all are concerned.

It has been our experience that ridicule and punishment not only do not improve matters, but can do much harm in making a boy like this feel inferior or peculiar.

As a rule the best treatment seems to be to permit these favored activities within certain bounds. Thus one mother we know rules, "No lipstick and no flowers in the hat *outside the house*." Permit the artistic, creative activities which the child enjoys, but try also to encourage him to play with boys. Even though he may not get far as an athlete, provide plenty of gross motor equipment so that he can at least climb, swing, perhaps do trapeze stunts.

Keep firmly in mind that many of these boys grow up to lead perfectly normal personal lives, and at the same time may eventually become outstanding as artists, musicians, or as actors, costume designers, playwrights. The very activities which worried their parents may be indications of giftedness in perfectly acceptable fields.

Frequently a boy "grows out of" such behavior in its extreme by the time he is seven or eight, or ten or eleven. But if he doesn't, combating his natural tendencies or fighting against them will only make him uncomfortable and may do him more harm than does his own behavior.

Our best recommendation would thus be not to combat his own inclinations, but rather to try, within reason, to encourage other kinds of activities. If the worrisome behavior is excessive and long-continued, a thorough personality evaluation by a competent psychologist can help you to a better understanding of such a child. It can also help you to plan in what areas you may try to direct and rechannelize his interests and activities.

Then What Can You Do?

Behavior is a function of structure. That is to say, the human organism seems to act as it does largely because of the way it is built. Whether we approach an understanding of individuality from measuring the way that the body is built, or from an observation of the way that the individual behaves, we come to the conclusion that individuality is largely inborn.

A favorable environment (home or otherwise) can, it appears, permit each individual to develop his most positive assets for living. An unfavorable environment may inhibit and depress his natural potentials. But no environment, good or bad, can so far as we know change him from one kind of individual to another.

Some people don't like such ideas. They want to feel that it's all up to them. That their child's individuality is not predetermined, but that they can produce in him, by their own treatment of him, either a favorable or an unfavorable individuality.

They object to the idea that individuality is inborn, with such comments as, "You mean there's nothing I can do? I have to just sit back and accept the personality my child is born with? He won't benefit at all by a happy home and good loving care?"

Our answer is that there is plenty you can do about it. First of all, recognize your child's individuality for what it is and give up the notion that you either produce (except through inheritance) or that you can basically change it. Recognize it, understand it, accept it.

Accept the fact that no matter how "well adjusted" he is, your thin, wiry ectomorph will probably be at heart a shy, quiet individual who prefers to remain relatively inconspicuous. That your well-built, heavily-muscled mesomorph will be active, competitive, noisy, relatively insensitive. That your plump, pear-shaped endomorph will be jolly, friendly, sociable, easy-going, but will have little desire to compete and dominate.

Realize that your basically focal child will always be able to focalize and concentrate better than the more peripherally oriented person. That some children will always find it difficult to make transitions. That others will always have a tendency to put their best foot forward in a new situation and then gradually do worse as time goes on.

Understand your child's basic and inescapable endowments. Help him to understand himself. Then try to provide, so far as you can, the kind of situation in which each kind of child can feel comfortable and can do well. But don't try to change him and make him over.

Try to recognize and respect your child's basic, inborn individuality.

Part Two

4

Eating Behavior

E ACH culture has developed its own specific eating patterns. The kind of food to be eaten, the way it should be prepared, the methods of eating, are all to a large extent culturally determined. All of these factors vary widely from country to country.

A child slowly grows into the adult cultural eating patterns, whatever they may be. Often we do not realize how slowly this process takes place, with its backward as well as its forward steps—and sometimes even its standing still. When the child is pushed, then there may also be the resistant steps.

There was a period in our own culture in these United States when science in its most sterile and dogmatic form took over the control of eating behavior. Everything was known; everything was ordered. The child was to eat certain quantities at certain times. Ounces, calories and the clock became absolute tyrants, and the poor child was too often lost sight of. Some children succumbed by giving in and adjusting, but others could not or would not. They became our feeding problems, which were multiple in the 1920's and 1930's.

With failure in the guise of all these feeding problems staring us in the face, we slowly came to realize that something was radically wrong. We realized that the cultural demands must at least to some extent be modified to meet the child's demands, and must adapt to what he can accept. More recently we have become aware that a regulation of feeding behavior needs to include both the demands and needs of the child and the demands of the culture. This realization, put into practice, has resulted in a marked reduction in feeding problems.

The greatest problem that exists at present is that since we live in a land of plenty where food is easily available in ready-to-use forms, we are still apt to think that if a little food is good for the child, more would be better. We are too much inclined to serve large helpings of food and drink. We haven't scaled quantities of food down to the child's size the way we have his furniture and play equipment. However, this fault is gradually being corrected, for there is no one more eager to learn about the welfare of his children than the American parent.

DEVELOPMENTAL SEQUENCES

INFANCY IS THE HEYDAY OF EATING

Infancy is a time for its own special feeding problems; but on the whole appetites are good. In the first four months, they can be so excellent that the infant seems perpetually hungry. Fortunately, especially for boy infants, the earlier introduction of solid foods has satisfied appetites as milk alone seemed unable to do.

But it is not enough to make general rules about feeding. We can and should get down to the specific demands of each individual infant. Our present individualized method of feeding, which allows the baby to eat when he is hungry rather than by a schedule, is called "self-regulation," and it includes both a response on the part of the parents to the infant's demands and an adaptation on the part of the infant to the demands of the parents. It is an adjustment of take and give, of demand and acceptance. At some ages the demand is high, at others the acceptance is high, and at still others there is equilibrium between these two forces.

Not all children thrive on this method of feeding, though the majority do. It takes a well-integrated infant who is capable of knowing when he is hungry and when he is satisfied to profit by this freer schedule. (Your pediatrician can help you here.) There are some infants, however, who do not know when they are hungry and who do not demand. There are others who tend to overdemand and thus do not come into balance. These two extremes of infants thrive best on a more controlled and regular schedule.

Those infants who are on self-regulation usually organize more quickly than those who are on a strict schedule. They may demand as many as seven to eight feedings per day shortly after birth. This reduces to five to six by four weeks of age, and often settles down into the rather unusually advanced pattern of three feedings a day even as early as twelve to sixteen weeks of age. Such a reduction is possible only when the infant is capable of taking large quantities of food at one time.

With the coming of greater satiety by sixteen weeks of age, there is often a noticeable reduction in appetite. Occasionally refusals of the early afternoon or early evening feeding are in evidence. With the poor feeders, vomiting may increase if excessive intake of food is urged.

By 16 weeks most infants are accepting some form of solid foods. (Boys are often so hungry that they will accept and relish solid foods as early as six to eight weeks.) Mashed banana is a uniformly preferred solid.

Cup feeding may be started as early as sixteen weeks. The approximation of the infant's lips to the rim of the cup is at this age still very inadequate and much spilling results. But in spite of this, the infant often enjoys the process of drinking water or fruit juices from a cup.

By twenty-eight weeks he shows new awareness of the cup and spontaneously makes demands to be fed from it. However, he is incapable of taking more than one or two swallows. He prefers water and juice to milk and may refuse milk from a cup.

In the second half of the first year, feeding is usually well regulated and is an activity of great enjoyment for the infant. In most things he is now an adjustable member of the household, though he may grow impatient at thirty-two to thirty-six weeks as he watches his meal being prepared. He just can't wait. It would be wise to have his food all ready before he is brought into the kitchen if he is fed there.

The first year of life can go very smoothly in the feeding realm if the parent is aware of the fluctuations of appetite and behavior which occur from meal to meal, from age to age, from individual to individual. The infant speaks out very clearly both in his demands and his refusals. If the parent is aware of and sensitive to these shifts in infancy, then he is more ready for the new demands and influences that are almost certain to show up in the succeeding years.

APPETITE RETARDED

In the second year of life appetites often falter. The generally smooth course of infant feeding seems to be broken by new interfering forces. For example, the gross motor drive at one year of age may make it difficult for the child to sit long enough to eat his meals. Standing in his high chair or carriage supported by a harness may be the preferred posture for eating while this gross motor drive is strong, between twelve and fifteen months.

Another interference stems from the child wanting to feed himself but being unable to do so. This occurs most frequently from fifteen to eighteen months. Help in filling the spoon may solve the problem. Giving the child food that can easily be finger fed may be an even better solution. Those who still require puréed food may accept being fed, but like to have some activity of their own, at least a dish or spoon to play with.

Drinking from a cup may be at its lowest ebb in this second year, especially for the consumption of milk. Small cups that the child can handle and small portions can make this activity a continued interest. A colorful small paper cup, enticing the child's eye, easily handled and not in danger of breaking, is to be recommended. Whenever the 18-monther has completed a task such as drinking from a cup, he extends the cup forthwith to his mother as he says, "All gone." If she is not there to receive it, what else can he do but drop it?

New interferences hamper the appetite of the more aware 21-monther. His taste may be so discriminating that he will accept only one brand of baby foods. He also becomes dependent upon a certain bib, a certain spoon, a certain dish, and these become a necessary part of a successful meal. If the parent is unaware of these demands, the child may cry until the parent finally guesses the right answer. The child doesn't yet have adequate words to express his desires.

Because of the 21-monther's heightened awareness, he is sensitive to all kinds of distracting stimuli. Mealtime is no time for father to burst into the house. Even the kitchen may be too stimulating and the meal may be more readily eaten in the seclusion of the child's room. Some 21-monthers even need to be served one food at a time, because they are distracted by multiplicity. Mixing all the foods together and then not wishing to eat the new concoction is a characteristic trick of the child at this age.

FINICKY—FUSSY—FOOD FADS

The child's poor eating habits in the third year of life can be most distressing to the parent. The second year may have brought a reduction in appetite, but the third year brings all the exasperation of indecision and finicky choices. Preferences are high and may be related to taste, form, consistency or even color. The child may want foods to be served very separately, without having one food touch another on his plate. Small helpings, even teaspoon size, are often best. This is the time for food jags, which had best be respected. What is wrong about stewed apricots night after night? But it is also important to introduce new foods under new and pleasant situations so that the child will have something to fall back on when the food jag suddenly wears itself out.

This ritual demand of the same thing time after time reaches its height at two and a half years of age and not only includes repetition of foods but also of dishes and arrangement of dishes, and even repetition of time when a certain food can be given. A soft-boiled egg may be accepted for supper but never for lunch.

It must be kept in mind with children of this age that appetites fluctuate markedly from very good to very bad. This type of fluctuation is characteristic of the age period and needs to be allowed to swing, within reason. As the child becomes surer of his own likes and is able to feed himself more adequately, the swings will lessen. Pouring his own milk from a little pitcher into a small cup may motivate his drinking his milk more than if it is poured for him.

Though he desires to feed himself, the child of this age may continue to spill considerably. Some children don't mind this. Others judge it as failure and wish to be fed. The child may feed himself part of the meal—the part he likes—and the parent feed him the rest of the meal.

CALM

The 3-year-old is, in feeding as in all his behavior, much easier to handle than the child just younger. His eating is definitely better. His appetite fluctuates less. He has become a good chewer. He pours more deftly from a pitcher and handles a cup with ease and dexterity. He does best with a small cup and pitcher, and if given a choice of color, might well prefer a blue one in contrast to an earlier choice of red or yellow. He feeds himself more efficiently and even demands a fork to spear his meat. He is in fact often judged to be more capable than he really is. Surely if he acts so well, he is ready for the family table, parents think.

But with this added burden of the family table, the child may demand everyone's attention, want everything in sight, and wind up with endless dawdling. By demanding too much, the parent has now put himself in a fix. Should he coax the child to eat; should he feed him; or should he leave him to finish by himself? Too often a vicious circle is set up which would not have been started in the first place if meals had continued to be solitary, or at least apart from the total family group.

SPEED AND INCENTIVE

Four is an age of speed, of new expansion and of incentives. Four feels his age and wants to graduate to new demands and new activities. He wants to help set the table or even to help prepare the meal. Joining the family group, at least for one or two of his meals, may be the incentive he needs. His chief difficulties at this age are that he talks too much, has trouble sitting still and quite frequently has to interrupt the meal by going to the bathroom.

Rather than joining the family group for dinner, he may enjoy and profit by the following incentives which are more easily carried out in the kitchen. He might desire to eat to get big, to race with the baby, to finish within a certain time allotment or to work toward a dessert goal. What Four does, he does with speed, including the drinking of his milk.

APPETITE RISE

With many children there is a distinct appetite rise at four and a half to five years of age. The child of this age is more on his own. He can handle more meals with the family and is beginning to listen as well as to talk. His choices and acceptance of foods are wider and may even be influenced by radio, television or the man across the street. He is even branching out in his use of utensils and may use a knife for spreading, though not to cut his meat.

Five may again need help in being fed the last part of his meal, or he may monopolize the conversation. It may therefore work out best to have him eat the main part of his meal in advance of the family and then join them for dessert.

PERPETUAL MOTION

Six, in eating as in everything he does, is all over the place, both predictable and unpredictable. His appetite may be tremendous and he may wish to eat all day long. He may eat better between meals than at meals. Breakfast is usually his most difficult meal, especially if it precedes some demand such as going to school. He (or especially she) may complain of a stomach-ache or nausea, and may even vomit. In such cases a light breakfast which he can accept should be given, with the plan that he will have a ten o'clock snack at school. He makes up for his low intake in the morning by a rising intake during the day and often demands a sizable snack just before he goes to bed. Six may awaken in the middle of the night and ask for food.

Six-year-olds are, however, not good finishers, in food any more than in other things. Their eyes are bigger than their appetites and they will often ask for larger helpings than they can eat. Though they are interested in sweets, they may not be able to eat their dessert.

Six's perpetual activity does not make it practical to include him in the family evening meal. In fact, he is a menace both to himself and those around him. He simply can't sit still. He wiggles in his chair; he teeters back on one chair leg; he swings his feet vigorously; he spills his milk; he talks with his mouth full; he eats with his fingers—until finally Father in exasperation sends him from the table. Far better that he had not come at all and had been allowed to have a tray in his room, possibly in bed, listening to a favorite radio program.

RAVENOUS APPETITE

Seven consolidates his appetite and may eat less than he did at six. But Eight, with all his new inclusions and expansiveness, usually becomes an excellent eater. Foods he would not eat earlier, he now tackles. He is so hungry he even wolfs his food. He belches spontaneously. He feels so full he has to loosen his belt for comfort. He no longer is interested in listening to the family conversation as he did at seven. He wants no delay between main course and dessert, and he then wishes to leave the table and to go on about his 8-year-old business.

Even those who have earlier been very poor eaters are less of a worry to parents at eight. They don't necessarily have a very good appetite, but it is at least passable and they begin to show an interest in food.

In general, from eight years on, appetites and quantities consumed increase steadily, or even alarmingly. By eleven the child feels definitely full after eating and knows he has overeaten. But there is no further mention of feeling full at twelve, and it sometimes seems as though twelve has a bottomless pit for a stomach. Appetite begins to come into better control by thirteen; but it is not until fifteen that a semblance of adult balance is reached. This is also true of table manners. The course is up and down. The down course is especially marked at eleven, when behavior is reminiscent of the 6-year-old. Eleven even refers to his own *terrible manners*. Thirteen is the turning point toward better manners, and Fifteen is the conclusion and entrance into a capacity to accept adult standards.

APPETITE AND PREFERENCES

It is an odd commentary that the parent all too often spends the first eight years of a child's life urging him to eat and the next eight years urging him not to eat. If the appetite were respected, it would be allowed to function as a part of growth. In the previous section on the development of eating, the fluctuating appetite has been noted. The good appetite of infancy is often followed by a very low intake in the second year of life. (Though milk intake in the second year may be very low, its substitutes in the form of butter and cheese may be very high. This is the age when butter may even be eaten in handfuls.)

Appetites continue to be low from two to three years, but definite preferences for food are coming to the surface. Carrots and beets may be the preferred vegetables for both color and sweetness. With the stronger advent of chewing at two and a half, meat becomes a real favorite. Certain foods may be so desired that the child wants them repeated day after day (*e.g.* lamb chops, fruits, jelly sandwiches, ice cream). These food jags are very prevalent at two and a half years of age.

By three, with a more stable appetite, the range of food choices is increasing. Green vegetables are now accepted often for the first time. Raw vegetables are preferred. Desserts and sweets are more desired.

With a reduction in appetite at four years there is often a return to food jags, or the child goes on strike about certain foods which he has previously liked.

From four and a half to five years there often is an improved appetite which may steadily rise into the excellent appetite of eight. Throughout this age period of four and a half to eight and older, though appetites are good, the demand is for plain cooking and there is a real antipathy to all casserole dishes, gravies and fancy sauces.

Six's preferences and refusals are often very strong. One unfortunate experience with a certain food which has a stringy texture, or a rim of fat on his meat, might "put him off" that food for some time. He is often off dessert, especially rice pudding and custards. His new-found passion in life is peanut butter. Children can almost be placed in two different groups, those who love peanut butter and those who don't. This craze reaches new heights for those who do at seven and eight years of age and recurs in periods throughout the early teens.

Eight, with his definitely increased appetite, is ready to tackle new foods. He is often quite venturesome. And yet he is a sensitive being and may refuse to eat chicken if he has seen one killed. He also continues to renege at fat on his meat.

Acceptance of all foods is steadily increasing from eight on. Food is definitely on the minds of 10- and 11-year-olds, even to the extent of dreaming about it. By twelve some like everything and in general there are many more likes than dislikes. Some favorites stand out at different ages, *e.g.* mashed potatoes with gravy at twelve, and ice cream and steak at fourteen.

Since appetites are excellent and intakes are high in these early teen years, rapid gain in weight may be expected. It is unfortunate when too much time and thought are given to restriction of food and dieting. True, there is such a thing as moderation. But this is no time for strict dieting. By fourteen to sixteen there usually comes a slimming down and a sense of the relationship of food eaten and weight gained.

INDIVIDUAL DIFFERENCES

Some children live to eat. They are the round, often plump children. They are rarely feeding problems. But there are others who rarely think of eating. They are the small, petite, or even scrawny children. Hunger may come often to them but it is usually sharp and short-lived. These children often do better on small, frequent meals, even five or six a day. Such children often become feeding problems. With forcing of food upon them, they lose any little appetite they have and may be pushed into vomiting. They gain weight very slowly but are active and healthy, more healthy, often, than the larger robust children. If the parent can be guided by the child's slim appetite and keep portions small, usually no feeding problem will develop. In due course these children, too, may eat with a ravenous appetite, especially in their teens.

SPECIAL PROBLEMS

INFANTILE COLIC

An all too common accompaniment of feeding in the early months is infantile colic. Orange juice is one of the worst offenders and can fortunately be easily replaced in the diet by some other fruit high in vitamin C or vitamin C substitute which your doctor may recommend. If the infant is bottle fed, a change in formula may be indicated. Prepared milk substitutes now available are more easily digested, but in some infants, food is not the primary offender. Since the colic seems usually to be limited to the first twelve to sixteen weeks of life, there is undoubtedly a growth factor involved. But how to live through it is still a problem. Initially the infant responds best to soothing protection from further stimulation. He quiets when rocked, held, or taken for a ride in the car. But as he grows older, he responds best to stimulation of light and sounds and to the watching of movement around him.

VOMITING

Regurgitation, or spitting up, may also be an early accompaniment of feeding. Just as the young reader in the first grade doesn't know which way the letters go, the gastro-intestinal tract in some infants doesn't seem to be sure in which direction it is operating. "Should the food go down or come up?" By 28 weeks, growth has taken over, and the downward direction is usually established.

Some infants, however, continue to vomit into the second year and as late as 21 months. By this age they may know in advance that they are going to vomit and may reach a container in time. They will also be forewarned and will refuse food at the meal when they feel that their gastro-intestinal tract is in indecision. Before this period of greater self-awareness, it is for the parent to judge at what time the gastro-intestinal tract is most unstable. Is vomiting most apt to occur at the noon or evening meal? Whenever it is most apt to occur is the time for a reduced feeding or a "split bottle," with an hour between the two halves. There should be no alarm over this behavior. This is a part of growing up for this kind of child.

HOLDING ONTO THE BOTTLE

And then there is the problem of holding onto the bottle. Most infants give up their bottle at about the same time they would have given up the breast—in the last quarter of the first year. They may even go so far as to fling their bottle out of their crib. But there are some who cling tenaciously. Parents often continue bottle feeding because they fear the child will not otherwise receive his quota of milk. Actually, this is not necessary. Ten to sixteen ounces is adequate, and this can be given on cereals, in puddings, and so forth, as well as sipped in small amounts by cup feeding.

Some drastic change in the nipple at fifteen to eighteen months will often help the child to give up his bottle. A new nipple, especially in color or style, or an enlargement of the holes or cutting off the tip to induce drinking rather than sucking, may help in giving up of the bottle.

However, some children are so attached to the bottle that it is wise to continue possibly one night bottle until two or even three years of age. A bottle is often sleep inducive and insures the milk intake without anyone's having to think about it. As they approach three years of age, if they still are clinging to the bottle, you often can plan with them that *when they are three* they won't need the bottle any longer.

With those children who refuse milk completely when taken off the bottle, the provision of bright-colored cups or glasses with a small pitcher for them to pour from may produce an interest in drinking. The use of a straw may help. Serving milk at a "tea party" may give it a new value to the child. And, of course, disguise of milk as chocolate milk may make it more pleasing to the palate.

REFUSAL OF SOLIDS

Some infants are slow to accept any form of puréed or mashed foods in the first place and then will only accept this consistency and will not go further. They choke on chopped foods. They chew poorly. They will accept only extremes—the puréed foods that slip down easily or the crispy foods like bacon or melba toast that must be chewed first. Such children are often found to have a very small throat opening and one which gags readily. They are not ready for in-between consistencies before three years of age and may delay until five years. Some experience away from home, such as a birthday party, may give them the courage and incentive to eat the same kinds of food as their contemporaries.

REFUSAL TO FEED SELF

The same child who clings to puréed foods may be the very one who will not feed himself. Often these children have shown poor hand-to-mouth responses earlier. They may have refused to feed themselves a cookie at eight to ten months. They do not suck their thumbs. Some, on the other hand, have tried to feed themselves and have failed. They are the ones who dislike spilling. These children may delay any attempt to feed themselves until five to six years of age. Their fine motor behavior improves at four and a half. But the motor movement of filling a spoon and bringing it to the mouth is more complicated than we sometimes realize. Feeding a younger sibling may be easier and will give this child a feeling of success. Then he will more likely attempt to feed himself.

"SPICY" APPETITES

Why all children's diets should be bland is a very real question. There is a certain group of petite girls (and sometimes boys) with high emotional tone who may hit real eating snags at two years of age unless their parents recognize their peculiar preferences. Even as early as one year of age a little onion juice may make bland mashed potatoes acceptable to such a child. This is the kind of child who accepts and seems to need salty foods, strong cheeses, olives, salami, lobster, mushrooms, avocado pears and spicy sauces on their spaghetti. They crave this more stimulating diet, which can be given at least in moderation.

REFUSAL OF VEGETABLES

Refusal of vegetables is a child problem as well as an adult male problem. Many children do not eat vegetables to amount to anything before three years of age. The sweeter vegetables such as carrots, beets and tomatoes are usually accepted first and some of these are preferred raw. (Dentists now tell us that there is less decay in teeth that have received the good strong pressure of chewing.) Green vegetables are more often accepted by three, and there is no reason why a raw pea or string bean isn't as good or even better than a cooked one.

General Rules to Help Children Enjoy Food

1. Serve food attractively.
2. Give small helpings.
3. Serve food without comment.
4. Do not stress amount of food to be eaten. Many children who have small appetites to begin with absolutely revolt at any mention of how much food they are expected to eat.
5. Try to maintain a calm, unworried attitude toward the child's eating. Nothing creates a feeding problem more quickly than an overanxious attitude on the part of the parents.
6. Don't stress table manners with young children. Manners can come later when a positive attitude toward eating has been established.
7. Allow finger feeding until the child has become fairly proficient at eating and is interested in food.
8. Do not have the child eat at the family table until you find that he is ready to do so.

5

Sleeping and Dreams

GETTING THE CHILD TO SLEEP

GETTING the child to sleep and keeping him asleep can be one of the most trying and exasperating tasks in a parent's day.

Of course there are those children who fall asleep the minute their heads touch the pillow and who sleep soundly all night long. If your child is one of these, you are indeed fortunate. There are such children.

But there are many others who from infancy on have sleeping difficulties. Particularly do they find the transition from waking to sleep to be a difficult one. If you have such a baby or such a child, it is most important to keep in mind that his inability to fall asleep easily is a real inability, and not just perverseness or badness. Since it is a real inability, your best role is to help him to make this difficult transition, not to punish him for not making it.

The best ways for getting a child to sleep vary of course from child to child and from age to age. There are none which can be guaranteed to work. And we know of no extremely new and surprising ones. However, we shall tell you about some of the common methods which other parents have found useful.

IN INFANCY

In infancy, release into sleep is not as a rule as difficult as in later years. To some extent the self-demand and self-regulation schedules which many pediatricians nowadays recommend approximate the conditions of a more primitive culture, and the child eats when he is hungry and sleeps when he is sleepy.

But if your baby is following a stricter schedule, he may need some help from you in getting to sleep. In that case, modern culture has, so far as we know, found nothing superior to rocking (in someone's arms or in a bassinet or carriage) for getting a baby to sleep. Rocking accompanied by singing will as a rule be especially successful.

From eight to twelve weeks of age, the baby who cries and cannot seem to fall asleep may be helped to sleepiness by being given a light to look at or even by being brought out into the lighted kitchen or living room. He is hungry for lights, movement and for people as well as for food. With satiety he sleeps more readily.

At any age, giving the child a presleep breast or bottle feeding is a trusty method of inducing sleep. Music is successful with some. And often a baby will go to sleep more quickly for someone other than his mother.

However, if in the first year of life there is an undue amount of resistance to bedtime and fussing for the mother, many pediatricians feel that firmness is best. Dr. Benjamin Spock believes that you should give the child what he *needs,* not what he cries for. Thus he recommends putting the baby to bed at a sensible hour and with usual signs of affection. And saying, cheerfully but firmly, "And now it's time for you to have your sleep and for me to have a rest." (The tone of voice, Dr. Spock believes, is probably more important than your exact words.)

If the child has been a colicky baby and you have been giving him lots of necessary pampering, he may be outraged and may set up a big howl. Harden your heart and let him cry it out. As a rule this crying does not last for more than three nights, and its duration decreases rapidly even during that time (though there are exceptions when the crying increases and this method has to be abandoned). The most important rule, and the hardest, Dr. Spock feels, is *not* to go back.

Whether you can go this far or not is of course up to you. But whatever you do, remember that firmness on your part is important. It is also important to establish a bedtime pattern and to hold to it. If for any reason you have to shift your pattern, then do so, but let this new routine become the pattern. Don't let the child decide.

As the baby develops through his first year, he will often devise methods of his own to help him fall asleep. He may suck his thumb or rock in his crib. But as he goes on into the preschool years, being rocked or sung to, or even his own devices may not suffice, and parents may need to vary their techniques and to become considerably more ingenious. Letting the preschooler cry it out may have to be resorted to, but it is not usually recommended. Here are some methods which sometimes help to induce sleep in the 2- to 7-year-old.

THE TWO-YEAR-OLD'S BEDTIME DEMANDS

"It must be Heaven, it must be Heaven, to hear a baby cry!" was the refrain of a song popular in the late 1920's.

Well, maybe! But a lot of young parents certainly think otherwise.

And similarly, to the sentimentalist, the 2-year-old's bedtime request for "just one more kiss, Mummy," might seem a sweet and lovely thing.

But to the average long-suffering parent of the 2-year-old it is a dismal sound. Because "just one more" is the call with which the young child, reluctant to leave his family and the joys of being awake, puts off his final lapsing into sleep.

"One more kiss," "A drink of water," "A hankie," "Go to the bathroom." These are only a few of the demands which the 2-year-old makes to get just a little more time and attention from his mother before she finally leaves for the night.

Parents soon come to realize that such requests—real needs or not —are in the nature of a racket. It is not simply the things he requests that the child actually wants, but his mother's continued presence. How you will deal with these demands is of course up to you. Some parents are more patient than others. Some children are more demanding than others.

With many children around the age of two years, you can shorten and simplify the bedtime scene by anticipating as many of the bedtime demands as possible. Be sure that you provide the child with a drink of water, and a handkerchief, and his favorite toy or toys. Be sure that he has been toileted. Give him his good-night kiss. Then leave, with a firm, "Good night," and if necessary, state that you are not coming back.

If you have an extremely docile or a very sleepy child, or if your past history of firmness has led the child to know that you really mean what you say, he may settle down at once to sleep, and there may be no further demands. Or he may call out once or twice, and, getting no response, may give up and go to sleep.

He may! But what if he doesn't? What if the demands go on?

We know of no one solution to the problem which is guaranteed to work—but here are some things you might try.

First, remember that your child's demands for continued company and attention represent a real need. But, since it is a need that you cannot reasonably be expected to answer, you are going to have to help him get over it, for his sake as well as for yours.

Added age will be the surest remedy, but in the meantime, if his demands of Mother are too excessive, get Father to step in. A final kiss, a firm admonition from Father, "Now I'm not coming back again," will quiet many a 2-year-old who is too demanding of his mother.

Or, if neither Mother nor Father can stem the flow of demands, it may be wise, for a short time and if it can be arranged, to have both of them be out of the house at bedtime for a few nights at least. Let a helpful grandmother or aunt or maid, or an experienced baby-sitter take over putting the child to bed. Bedtime demands may be much less when someone other than Mother and Father is managing things.

Of course, there is another solution. If instead of a determined child and a gentle parent you have the combination of a gentle child and a determined parent, you may find that simply ignoring his repeated calls may (once you have gone back a "reasonable" number of times) work.

TWO-AND-A-HALF BEDTIME RITUALS

Two-and-a-half is an age of rituals. The child of this age doesn't like change. He doesn't like variety. He likes everything to be in its place, and what he did yesterday he wants to do again today.

Bedtime is no exception. The going-to-bed rituals of the typical 2½-year-old can be the despair of an entire household. Before you have realized what is going on, the child can build up a ritual about every single part of the going-to-bed activity.

Saying good night to the people downstairs will have to be done in just a certain way, and these good nights will have to be said in a certain order. A certain number of kisses. The exact same words to be said by everyone.

Then there can be a going upstairs ritual. The getting undressed, being bathed, having teeth brushed rituals can be long and elaborate.

And then the pre-bedtime play! If on even one occasion you have rashly read three stories, played two phonograph records, allowed a little athletic activity, woe to you! Every night from now on (till this ritual age is over) your 2½-year-old may demand just these same activities in just the same order.

Then he may want to arrange all his belongings in a certain standard manner. One girl we know had to put her thirty-eight dolls to bed in just a certain way before she herself would get into bed. Another child had to have a hat on each bed post, each one turned just right.

And even after the child is once in bed, you may not have come to the end of his ritualistic demands. Many have to take certain special things to bed with them. One boy we know required a hammer, a green pepper and a sharp pencil. This of course was rather unusual. Most are content with a favorite doll or soft animal. But often it has to be just the right one. Not any old doll or any old soft animal!

The possibilities are endless and formidable! But here as elsewhere, advance knowledge on your part, though it will not change the child, can help you manage the situation.

First, knowing in advance how strong the rituals of the 2½-year-old can be, you will try at all times to keep bedtime activities as simple as possible. Try to avoid building up a too complicated ritual which the child will then insist on following.

Second, you can be more patient with Two-and-a-half's rituals when you know that they are perfectly natural for children of this age and that they act like bridges for him to cross when a shift of activity is demanded of him. It is easier for him to get to sleep if he is allowed the transition from waking to sleep which the ritual provides.

BEDTIME—THREE TO TEN YEARS

Bedtime problems usually become less severe and less exasperating, or at least different, in the ages which follow two and a half years. At any of these ages a quiet period of music or reading can be one of the best ways to induce sleep. Roughhousing should in general be avoided at bedtime. It can overstimulate the child and leave him in no condition to go to sleep. (Although in some cases a physical workout, if held within limits, can result in the child falling to sleep more quickly. It is the child who can't stop, who gets wound up further and further, who especially needs to be protected from roughhousing.)

By three years of age, bedtime problems are often much less troublesome than at two and a half. Many 5-year-olds go to bed quite willingly, fall asleep with relative ease. (Their sleep problems may come later in the night.)

At four, it may simplify things to allow the child to read (some book he can look at by himself, such as the *Golden Dictionary*) and then to turn out his own light. He may behave much better than if you turn out the light for him.

The 5- and 6-year-old may like to have a little time to himself to read and to color. By six, many enjoy a brief chatting time with Mother or Father alone. At such a time they not only like to play favored games—boys especially like number games—but this may provide a good opportunity for talking over and smoothing out any of the day's tangles.

By seven and in the years which follow, the bedtime hour is improved for many by letting them have a small bedside radio. Then they may hurry through their undressing and into bed so as to be on time for a favorite program. The length of listening can usually be regulated by the number of programs you decide to let them enjoy.

These, and many other similar things which you will undoubtedly work out yourself, all can help the child to end his day happily and to avoid the difficulties which sometimes accompany the business of getting to sleep.

However, by eight and more strongly at nine, the problem of bedtime becomes again, in many, as it was in the preschool years, a real disciplinary problem. This in a way seems to have less to do with sleep as such than with a whole new attitude which the child may have toward his parents and toward any parent-imposed task.

Even with children who have hitherto showed no resistance to bed, going to bed may suddenly become a sharp problem of discipline. The child tries by every means to put off bedtime as long as possible, and seems to feel that going to bed is something that his parents are trying to impose on him.

A later bedtime can help here—recognizing that the child does not need quite as much sleep as he did earlier and letting him feel that you respect his new grownupness.

But let the later bedtime depend on the smoothness of his bedtime performance. Let him feel that if he is ready for a later bedtime, then he is also ready to go to bed without stalling and without complaints.

Also let him realize that you mean what you say when you announce bedtime. You may help him out by giving him a little warning in advance, but try to make him feel that when you finally do say, "Bedtime," you really mean it.

Sleep Problems

Some children are by nature "good sleepers." Unfortunately, there are many others who are by nature light, fitful, restless sleepers. Who resist going to sleep. Who wake easily and often during the night. Who are disturbed by fears, by dreams, by physical pains.

Not only are there certain *individuals* in whom sleeping difficulties abound, but there are some *ages* at which even "good sleepers" may have difficulties. As in all things, a knowledge of some of the more common difficulties may help you in dealing with your own child's sleeping difficulties when they do arise.

WAKING AND CRYING IN THE NIGHT

More usually than not, with a stable child whose routines have not been unduly upset by illness or visiting, night sleep is relatively undisturbed during the first months of life. This is particularly true if the mother dresses the baby warmly (as in a Dr. Denton and perhaps later, when he is more active, in a bathrobe as well), and sees to it that his room is reasonably warm so that no covers are needed. Then if he wakes, as many do, and plays around in his crib, he can fall back to sleep when he is ready without his mother needing to go in to cover him up.

If the mother does not go into the baby when she knows him to be awake, most will play happily by themselves for a bit and then go back to sleep again. Many can, if necessary, lull themselves to sleep with their thumb, a blanket to be sucked or a favorite toy.

A few can only relate themselves to some person, and can only be comforted by some person. With such children, the sooner you go to them, the more easily they can be quieted. A little food, a bottle, changing their diaper or perhaps holding and rocking them a bit, may be all that is needed.

Normally, waking several times in the night and crying for attention—or crying and refusing to be comforted—do not occur. If things have gone wrong to the extent that they do, great ingenuity on the part of parent or pediatrician will need to be exercised. Or you may need, for a while, to get some outside person to take over.

MIDDLE OF THE NIGHT ACTIVITY AT THREE

Many 2-year-olds, once you have gotten them to sleep, do sleep right through the night without giving you, or themselves, much trouble. But at three, with many children, an active night life begins. They go to bed nicely. To sleep nicely. And then, often after all the rest of the family is in bed and sound asleep, up gets our hero and starts his middle of the night activities.

These activities often surprise and worry parents. It seems so strange to them for a small child to go wandering around the house in the middle of the night. Yet that is what some of them like to do!

Some get out of their crib easily by themselves, go to the bathroom, go downstairs and get some food out of the refrigerator, "read" a magazine after turning on the light in the living room, and may even be found asleep on the living-room couch next morning. Others go even farther afield and wander outdoors. Some merely play happily in their own rooms for an hour or two.

Such activity probably does very little harm *if* you see that outer doors are securely locked and if dangerous or valuable things inside the house are locked up. And if the child is not one who just naturally harms himself and things around him when left to his own devices.

Many children go directly to their parents' room. With others to their parents' room is the one place they do not think of going. They want to set about their own activity, doing what they please. There is most probably the spirit of adventure in them. A few can contain their adventure within bounds, but the majority of these adventurous children need to be checked. Tying the child's door loosely with a bell attached will give the necessary warning that he is up as he attempts to open his door.

Such a child should be allowed his excursion to the icebox, to the bathroom or wherever he had planned to go. He may wish to look at a book for a while. He will settle down much more quickly after his needs have been satisfied.

We do not recommend spanking for this behavior. This wakefulness and need for night activity is a quite natural behavior for many children. This period of night waking often disappears when the child is around four years of age.

GETTING INTO MOTHER'S BED

Even when your child wakes in the night, you may not be *too* much disturbed if he is one of those who can enjoy, and will be satisfied with, a *solitary* night life.

But, alas, not all children are so constituted. Not all are happy to be in their beds and to talk and play or even to wander about the house *entertaining themselves* for an hour or so. Some when they wake up in the night want their mothers. And what's more, they want to get into their mother's bed. This is in many no passing fancy or half-hearted notion. It is a real, strong demand, and they insist on it.

How you deal with this situation and whether you give in or not will depend on many things, but chiefly on three: on you, on your husband and on the kind of child you are dealing with.

In most cases, parents find that it does little harm and seems to do the child a lot of good to let him get into bed with them when he wakes and makes a strong demand. Usually you can put him back into his own bed as soon as he becomes drowsy again or when he falls asleep. If he wakes and objects, some parents find that it creates less confusion just to let the child spend the whole night with them. (A king-size bed would be big enough for the whole family, and with the protection of rubber pants, no wetting accidents need to be coped with.)

As a rule this demand does not persist for long, and you can speed its end by suggesting at bedtime after a few nights—or a few weeks, depending on your stamina—that he is not going to get out of bed *any more*. This suggestion can, if necessary, be strengthened by the explanation that if he does get up, and does wake mother and father, everyone will be too tired next morning to carry out whatever may be his favorite morning activity.

With most children, as we say, we have found it fairly safe to give in to what is usually only a temporary demand.

But with the child who is a strong perseverator, who holds onto patterns once established and will not give them up, it is wiser not to start anything that you don't want to continue. Such children can sometimes be discouraged from starting such a habit as getting into their parents' bed by a clear-cut refusal and a show of real firmness from Father.

This may mean having to let the child "cry it out" for a few nights, but you may consider that preferable to letting him get into a habit which he will later have difficulty in breaking.

Or, if you have gotten into the habit of letting him sleep in your bed and he holds onto this privilege too long and simply refuses to start the night in his own bed, you may let him go to sleep in your bed but tell him that you will put him down in his own after he is asleep. Or you may plan so many nights a week with Mother, so many by himself.

THE BIG BED AT FOUR

Sometimes, if he has not already made the shift from a crib to a big bed of his own, the promise of a big bed (at four) will get him back into the habit of sleeping alone. Four is an ideal age to shift to a big bed. At four the child is ready to try new experiences and to give up old patterns. Planning ahead with him about his new bed may include the giving up of some of his undesirable sleep habits or other undesirable behaviors.

"When you're four and have your big bed, you won't get out of bed in the night *any more!*" "When you get your big bed, then you won't need to get into Mummy's bed *any more.*" "When you're four and are sleeping in your big new bed, you won't suck your thumb [or wet the bed, or whatever thing you are currently concerned about] *any more.*"

The power of suggestion, the excitement of this dramatic new event, the importance of being four, can for many children be the necessary stimuli to bring about the desired behavior. Plus the fact that by the time the child is four years of age, many of the earlier pre-school sleep difficulties are often about ready to iron themselves out anyway.

But let us warn you, don't overuse this technique. Give the child the idea well in advance of the shift, as you would plant a seed, and then watch it sprout when the proper time and situation come around. Also, be ready to judge whether this type of planning will work with your child. If he is still too immature, better not to use this method, or at least be ready to backtrack when it doesn't work, and tell him he'll be ready when he's older. The extremely immature are often not ready for improvements before eight years of age.

BAD DREAMS

"I had a bad dream!" This is a common complaint among young children. But it varies in severity from a quietly voiced objection to loud screams of terror which waken a whole household and which can be quieted only with the greatest difficulty.

How common are such complaints? How early do they begin? How can they best be dealt with?—parents ask us.

Even by three years of age, and sometimes earlier, children begin to report that they have been dreaming. Some 3-year-olds are wakened by their dreams, but as a rule these dreams are not particularly disturbing. The 3½-year-old may do quite a bit of dreaming, and may be disturbed by it, but as a rule he merely calls out and is easily quieted.

At four there may be less dreaming, but by four and a half to five years it frequently increases in amount and severity. And it is the 5-year-old who perhaps is oftenest really disturbed, and disturbs others, by his bad dreams or night terrors. For dreams and nightmares definitely invade the sleep of many 5-year-olds.

It is interesting to follow the shift in the content of some of these dreams. One of the youngest dreams that a child reports may be about a train. A 2½-year-old child is often suddenly frightened by this large moving object as it pulls into or often roars into a station. It may invade his dreams. Three-year-olds may dream of pigs under their beds. Three-and-a-halfs may dream of fish swimming around in their beds, and Fours often dream of wolves. The wilder animals, wolves, bears and snakes, often appear from four to six years.

Many a child of five awakens screaming and has difficulty coming out of his dreams and in coming awake even when his mother is right by his side. Some, even when quieted and comforted, do not fully awaken and cannot report their dreams or tell what is bothering them. These are probably the ones who have severe nightmares.

Others, who may simply have dreamed of dangerous wild animals which seem to chase them or of strange, bad people who appear at their windows, can usually wake up fairly quickly and are usually quieted fairly easily. They often can tell their dreams, either on the spot or the next morning. (Some children tell us of such elaborate dreams that we suspect a little fiction is getting mixed up with the dream.)

As a rule, no matter how terrified the child may be when he first calls out, you will shortly be able to quiet him. Especially if you remain calm and confident and do not let yourself be disturbed lest there is "something wrong." Those who have trouble coming out of their nightmare may respond more quickly if they are taken into another room or have their face washed with cold water.

The 5-year-old may have considerable difficulty in going back to sleep after such an episode, and may need considerable soothing and his mother's continued presence until he is safely asleep again.

Five may be the worst age for this sort of episode. By five and a half or six many can wake up and run into Mother's room, where in many cases they can tell their dream and, after a short, reassuring snuggle, go back to their own bed. Others may need a longer visit with Mother—but the terror is usually much less intense and more easily quieted when the child is six years old than when he is five. Still others may not wish to return to their beds, and prefer to remain in their parents' bed. A wise parent will know when the child's fear is real and when he needs to remain. If he does stay, the parent may enjoy a less disturbed sleep by moving into the child's bed, which it is hoped is a big, comfortable one. This period won't last too long. But it is intense as long as it does last.

Bad dreams persist, though diminishing steadily to a low peak at eight years, often with a return rise at nine.

Six shows his extremes in his dream world as well as in his real world. First he may be frightened to death by the appearance of ghosts and skeletons in his dreams. Next he is soothed by angels. Animals do bite and chase him, but friendly dogs lie under the table. Dreaming about fire is one of the commonest dreams of boys. Dreaming about some injury or harm to their mother is commonest among girls.

Pleasant dreams are steadily making their inroad—dreams about playmates, dreams of parties or of play at the seashore. Seven really enjoys himself in his dreams, swimming with the greatest of ease or flying through the air. But an ominous note of drowning or of danger to his father may invade his dream life.

By eight all can be fairly quiet in the dream world and scary dreams can usually be traced to their origin of stimulation through books, movies, radio or television programs. Whereas Seven cannot protect himself against these forces, Eight usually knows when to shut the book, hide his eyes at a movie or switch the knob of his radio to stop the vicarious experience that he knows will invade his dreams. Parents need to be alert to these dream producers and to control them when necessary.

Nine can protect himself even further than Eight from scary dreams. He has his own ways of getting around this close relationship of his experiences and dreams. He knows that if he reads a scary book in the light of day, he will be protected from its influence which might occur if he read the same book in the darkness of bedtime. But he does have odd whirling dreams, dreams of standing on his head, dreams of odd rhythmic patterns which can only be understood in relation to inner growth forces. This type of dream is especially significant since it occurs more often with boys.

By ten, nightmarish dreams may be decreasing, though at this age dreams are sometimes good and sometimes bad.

FEARS RELATED TO SLEEP

"But I'm afraid of the dark! Please don't turn the light off!"

"I think there's somebody hiding in the closet."

"I can't put my feet down. My bed's full of little bugs crawling all around!"

These are but a few of the bedtime fears experienced at one time or another by many perfectly normal children. The number and intensity of such fears, of course, varies considerably from child to child.

If your child does have such fears, no matter how silly they may seem to you, it is always important to treat them sympathetically and respectfully, and above all not to make fun of him or of them.

If it is the dark he fears, and in many this fear is especially strong around three and a half, leaving a low light on in the hall or in the next room may give him the confidence he needs. Or a faint light placed in the baseboard of his room may give the needed illumination without throwing shadows to frighten him. Attractive luminous pictures are now available which will glow softly in the dark for some hours, usually till long after the child has fallen asleep.

Another excellent way to help him get over his fear of the dark, especially when he is four, is to let him keep a small flashlight under his pillow. Then he can turn it on whenever he feels he needs it. Often just having the flashlight there is enough. The child may not actually find it necessary to use it.

Margaret Wise Brown's *Night and Day,* a story about a white cat who liked the day and a black cat who liked the night, has helped many a preschooler to get over his fear of the dark.

As the child grows older, it may not be so much the dark that he fears as the shadows. Shadows on the wall or ceiling may look to him like ghosts or burglars or other threatening figures. Such fears should never be ridiculed and preferably should not be belittled. Rather, if possible, by curtaining or otherwise, arrange that lights from outside, especially from car headlights, will not throw scary shadows. Or shift the child's bed so that he is less disturbed by the shadows. Or if shadows absolutely cannot be avoided, take the trouble to show your child just how they are cast and convince him of their harmlessness.

The child who feared the dark at three and little bugs at three and a half, may very likely have moved on to wild animals by five and a half. To men under the bed by six (girls especially express this fear). To burglars and ghosts at seven.

Parents differ tremendously in the amount of sympathy and help they are willing to give to the child who is fearful at bedtime. Some, in spite of the specialist's advice, believe that all fears are nonsense, and will have none of them. The light is turned off, the door shut, and the frightened child ordered to behave himself and not be so silly.

Others, more imaginative themselves and the parents of imaginaive children, go along with the child's fears and brush the "bugs" onto the floor, shoo the "wild animals" out of the room, exorcise the ghosts from the closet.

Both types of parents may notice that these bugs, wild animals, men and ghosts exist only in the child's room. The parents' room may be miraculously free from all these frightening things. The child may go to sleep readily in the parents' bed and accept being transferred to his own bed after he has fallen asleep.

But, whichever path you follow, it will help the child if you recognize these two facts: (1) The child's fear is very real to him while it lasts; (2) with a little ingenious help and patience from you, most such fears can usually be dispelled after a short time.

NAPS

The afternoon nap! Perhaps not a world-shaking topic to those of you whose children are past the age of naps. But a very important part of the day's schedule of both mother and child for those whose children are still preschoolers.

Here are a few general facts about nap behavior at the different ages through five and a half years.

4 weeks: The four to five nap periods which occur in each twenty-four hours represent a reduction from the seven or eight which characterized the earliest weeks. Individual differences as to their exact time and duration are marked.

16 weeks: Generally there are now three nap periods in each twenty-four hours. Naps occur in the early morning, late morning, afternoon or evening. The early morning nap may merge with night sleep. The late morning nap may alternate with the afternoon nap. An evening nap is unusual.

28 weeks: Here there is a wide variety of nap patterns. There are usually two to three naps a day. The midmorning and afternoon naps are the most stable. Many children have a consistent pattern of a long morning and a short afternoon nap, or vice versa.

40 weeks: The most usual pattern now is a long midmorning and an unstable afternoon nap which comes and goes.

52 weeks: Now usually only one nap in midday, from eleven or eleven-thirty to twelve-thirty or two.

15 to 18 months: The nap usually follows the noon meal, and though the child may take favorite toys to bed with him, he often falls right to sleep. The nap lasts for around one and a half to two hours, and the child usually wakes happy and wants to get right up.

21 months: Now there may be difficulty in release of consciousness, but most children play well by themselves till they do finally go to sleep. As they gradually become drowsy, Mother may need to go in and once more put them under the covers. They may now sleep longer (two to two and a half hours), and many are fussy upon awakening.

2 years: Most are able to let the adult leave them, without making any demands, more easily at nap time than at nighttime. Some no longer sleep every single day, but even if they do not sleep, most will play contentedly in their rooms for an hour or more. If they do get to sleep, they often sleep for as much as two hours.

Many awaken slowly, and unless the nap is so prolonged that it interferes with night sleep, it may be better to let them wake up by themselves, rather than waking them.

2½ years: The nap is often a real problem at this age. Many are slow getting to sleep and are by no means willing to remain in their cribs till they do fall asleep. In fact, many just refuse to nap in their cribs at this age.

One solution is to let them nap in another room on somebody else's bed, but usually it is better to keep them in their own room. Tie the door to, if necessary, and be sure that the windows are very safe. An active 2½-year-old is likely to climb on the window ledge.

When they have tired themselves out in play around the room, many are ready for sleep. Do not be too surprised if the child prefers to sleep in a bureau drawer, on the floor, or in a blanket bed on the floor, or under the bed or on top of a (cold) radiator, or on a window seat. We do not fully understand some of these strange but definite demands of the child of this age—but we usually feel that it works out best to give in to him whenever we reasonably can do so.

The time of waking is apt to be stormy. The child may feel miserable and often cries harder the more his mother tries to quiet him. He responds best if his mother pays little attention to him, pulls up the shades, goes about her own activities. Then he will wish to approach her, and calms down as he does so.

3 years: Now he may merely take a "play nap." If he sleeps, he usually goes to sleep more quickly and wakes more pleasantly than he did at two and a half.

4 to 5½ years: Though some children in this age range still have naps and really sleep, the majority have merely play naps or no naps at all. (If the child still naps at six years, he may well not be ready for an all-day first-grade session and might better remain in kindergarten.)

There are a few common problems which arise with regard to napping which we would like to discuss briefly. One is the problem of the too long nap which interferes with night sleep. Some children, around the age of two and a half or so, go to sleep so late and sleep so soundly and so long that, unless aroused, they do not wake up till five or even six o'clock. Then, obviously, they aren't going to be ready for bed at the customary six o'clock bedtime.

Here, of course, mothers have to make their own individual decisions as to when it best suits them to have the child asleep. If they welcome a long, uninterrupted afternoon and do not mind the delayed bedtime, there is no reason they should not arrange the schedule that way. But if Mother and Father both like to have their preschooler nicely out of the way by six o'clock or so, it will be necessary to wake him before he has had his afternoon sleep out in order for him to get back to bed again in time. Or you may prefer to help him give up his nap altogether.

However, if, as often happens, you find that omitting the nap altogether produces extremely bad behavior in the late afternoon or during dinnertime, you may prefer to continue it, even though it does delay night sleep.

Wakening the child from his nap may be easy or very difficult, according to his temperament. Some children wake easily and pleasantly. Others are extremely cross, irritable with their mothers and often tearful when awakened. If your child is of this latter type, some indirect method of awakening him may work best.

Children vary tremendously in the age at which they give up their naps. Some are really through napping by two or two and a half years of age. Others cling to an afternoon nap till they are five or six. But whether he gives his nap up early, or clings to it late, the child's own rest requirements may well be the factor which determines how long and how late he naps. By requirements, we don't mean just what he *says*. "Don't want to take my nap" may express only a normal resistance to routine.

You judge more by his behavior than by his remarks. Does he sleep, or at least rest, during his nap period? Is his general behavior improved by this intermission? Or does insistence that he nap do little good and cause lots of trouble? These are the kinds of indications that will help you decide. In many cases the child will profit by a play nap after he has given up his regular nap.

Waking Behavior

Getting to bed, getting to sleep, staying asleep and waking. Each phase of the sleep process brings its own problems as most of you, except the most fortunate, know all too well.

Morning waking is no exception. In infancy, it is true, it does not create too much difficulty. The infant wakes, usually wet and hungry, and as often as not cries for attention. You give him the attention and all is well. He expects a more or less immediate response. You expect to give such a response. So there is no trouble except that you perhaps aren't able to sleep quite as late as you might like to.

Trouble starts, usually, at whatever age you decide the child should be able to lie quietly in his crib and entertain himself and not disturb you till you are ready.

Most preschoolers just aren't made that way. Most, in the years from say two to five, wake very early indeed, often as early at 6:00 A.M. Most demand toileting at once and, as a rule, after this refuse to get back into their own beds and play quietly. They often insist on playing in the parents' room, and even if they will agree to remain in their own rooms, their demands are numerous. As a rule, some one member of the family finds it necessary to give up the idea of further sleep once the 18-month to 2½-year-old child is awake.

With some, however, even around 18 months to 2½ years of age, if you provide toys and a little food, either where they can reach it from the crib (or in the room if they can get out of the crib), they will entertain themselves for some time before becoming restless and crying for you.

(It is perhaps important for you to keep in mind that, contrary to what one might expect, usually keeping a child up late at night does not result in making him sleep later in the morning.)

By five or even earlier, some can take care of their own morning toileting and can play in their own room without bothering their parents. This is by no means the rule, however, and many parents find that their children need to be as much as eight or ten years of age before they can manage entirely by themselves in the morning. And before they can grasp the important concept that their parents' morning sleep should not be disturbed.

In the teens, through one of the many seeming paradoxes of growth, the child who earlier disrupted the entire family by his early waking and rising now seems to find it virtually impossible to get out of bed at all in the morning. Similarly, this same child who as a preschooler "ate like a bird," may in the teens be an absolute glutton for food. Remember that for many children both (morning) sleep and food requirements are very high when they reach their teens.

INDIVIDUAL DIFFERENCES

Sleep requirements and sleep patterns thus change conspicuously from age to age, but it is always important to remember that they also vary tremendously from child to child. We have discussed this fact in detail earlier (p. 46).

Suffice it to say here that some children consistently sleep better, go to sleep more easily and need less sleep than do others. Try to adjust the amount of sleep you require from your child to the amount he really needs—not simply to some arbitrary figure which you may have found somewhere in a sleep chart, or to the amount that other children in the neighborhood are getting.

Be as flexible as you can be. Remember that eating and sleeping are not only necessary for the human organism but can be real pleasures. Try not to spoil these natural pleasures for your children by making an unnecessary fuss over them.

6

Elimination

How soon shall I begin toilet-training? The answer to this question varies with the society you live in. Some primitive tribes are notoriously carefree about the whole business. It also varies from decade to decade. There was a while, back in the 1920's and 1930's, when many experts thought that the sooner you got started the better. Some pediatricians even held out the shining goal that if you started in early enough, and firmly enough, you could hope for a completely "trained" child as early as eight, twelve, twenty or thirty-two weeks (depending on the optimism of the pediatrician).

Actually the delay between feeding and the occurrence of a bowel movement, even in the early weeks (eight to twelve weeks), can often result in temporary "success" if a mother is quick enough to get her baby onto some receptable before evacuation takes place. Similarly, by forty weeks and often earlier, a lucky mother may on occasion manage to get her baby onto his potty at the time when he is going to urinate, especially when he wakes dry from a nap or after he returns from a carriage ride. Or in this last quarter of the first year he may give a warning, by grunting, that he is about to have a bowel movement. He usually accepts being placed on the toilet seat, or preferably a potty chair, and functions with success.

Such "successes" do often occur, but when they do, it should be kept in mind that they are more the successes of the mother than of the baby. The baby is not, in these early instances, learning to stay clean and dry. Bowel and bladder release are, in the first year of life, basically "involuntary" functions. That is, they are not under conscious control. The baby is not "learning" to do anything—it is simply that his mother has responded to his clues and has caught him at the right time. (This is true in the majority of cases. However, some conditioning response may be set up at these early ages. But unconditioning responses are as important as conditioning responses. It is as important for the child to break or give up old habits so that he may develop new ones at an older age. The infant who is trained early and remains trained is most often the good learner but one who lacks inner spontaneous growth forces.)

As we have come to realize all of this, the fashion has swung (and we believe wisely so) to almost the opposite extreme. Most pediatricians now recommend letting the child make his own timetable. We can tell you some of the stages through which the child normally proceeds as he develops toward the ability to keep himself clean and dry. But we cannot predict in advance how slowly or rapidly he will go through these stages.

Carefully controlled research studies have shown that training in any ability is not effective until the child is almost ready to do the thing in question. Training the child to perform toilet functions at a suitable time and place is not really effective until the child's organism is almost ready to succeed.

The important thing to keep in mind is that success in toilet-training depends, with most children, not on the repeated experience of being placed on the toilet, nor on the child's "will power," but upon nerve connections which must mature. And these nerve connections develop more rapidly in some children than in others. All toilet training must wait for a certain amount of maturity in the child's central nervous system.

The danger of starting training too young, even by the last quarter of the first year, is that success is taken too seriously and is expected to continue. We may well ask ourselves: Should we bother about these short success periods, when they lead us to the danger of expecting too much too consistently?

Really consistent success does not as a rule occur much before two years of age. Mothers who have made little effort to train their children (these mothers are fortunately growing more numerous) often report that their children "trained themselves" around two years of age.

BLADDER CONTROL

The following timetable will help to familiarize you with some of the steps your child will go through as he develops the ability to keep himself dry.

4 weeks: Infant may cry during sleep when wetting and there may be a glimmer of wakefulness.

16 weeks: Number of daily micturitions has decreased and volume of any one has increased.

28 weeks: Soaking wet diapers. Intervals of dryness from one to two hours in length.

40 weeks: May be dry after a nap or after a carriage ride. Mother may have temporary "successes" placing child on pot.

1 year: Dryness after nap. Intolerance of wetness at certain times of day. Fusses until changed.

15 months: Postural difficulties (insistence on standing) have lessened. Likes to sit on toilet and responds at best times. At other times may resist. Retention span has lengthened to two or three hours. Placement on toilet may stimulate child to withhold urine. May release urine as soon as removed from toilet. Points with pride to puddles and may pat them.

18 months: Can respond with nod of head or "No" if asked if he wants toilet. May even ask, saying, "Uh," etc. May feel shame at puddles (if any) and may report accidents by pulling at his pants.

21 months: Reports accidents by pointing at puddles. Tells after wetting and sometimes before. Pleased with successes. But number of urinations increases and lapses may multiply.

2 years: Better control. No resistance to routines. Verbalizes his toilet needs fairly consistently. May go into bathroom and pull down own pants. May express verbal pride in achievement. "Good boy." May be dry at night if taken up, though picking up may disturb his sleep.

2½ years: Retention span lengthening. May be as much as five hours. Child may stop and then resume in the act of micturition. May have difficulty initiating release.

3 years: Well routinized. Accepts assistance if needed. Few accidents. May be dry all night; may wake up by himself and ask to be taken to toilet. Girls may attempt standing up.

4 years: Still routinized, but may insist on taking over routine himself. Curiosity about strange bathrooms.

5 years: Takes fair responsibility but may need reminding during day. Few daytime and only occasional nighttime accidents. Less reporting to Mother, though desires Mother's permission to go to the bathroom. May waken for night toileting and report to parent.

6 years: Mostly takes responsibility, though may have to dash. Accidents are rare, and if they occur, child is disturbed by them. May need reminder before going out to play. Some giggling at sound of urine stream, and may mention this function in humorous or angry attack on others. Some require night toileting, but these can usually attend to themselves.

INDIVIDUAL DIFFERENCES IN TOILET-TRAINING

This timetable for toilet-training tells you that the child at two years of age may be "dry at night if taken up" and should be able to "verbalize his toilet needs fairly consistently." If you are fortunate, your child may live up to these standards, or may even do better than this.

But do not be disappointed if he lags behind this schedule. Probably in no field of child behavior are individual differences greater than with regard to toilet-training. Probably in no field are parents more impatient.

Children do not always develop all of a piece. Not all of their abilities develop at the same rate. Thus we have children who are "early" talkers but "late" walkers. Others are "toilet-trained" almost before you start thinking about it, but their social behavior may develop late. Still others are advanced (for their age) in every field of behavior except elimination.

If your child should be one who is developing slowly in this respect, and as so often happens a medical check-up has shown that there is nothing physically or medically wrong with him, we would chiefly advise patience and an unworried attitude on your part. We have seen many normal children who literally do not seem to know what goes on below their waists. This unawareness of their own "accidents," of which others are usually all too aware, may go on through five or even six years of age. Then suddenly everything may be all right almost overnight.

It is often a long wait, but in this as in other fields, patience is nearly always rewarded. It may help to remember that there is no "proper" age for staying dry. Practically all children go through the same stages which lead up to this desired ability, but each one makes his own timetable.

BOWEL MOVEMENT CONTROL

Training the child for bowel control is one of the less attractive but most necessary tasks of early parenthood. We would like, if we could, to lighten this task by recommending that you do not start in too soon, and that you take neither early "successes" or early "failures" too seriously.

Even as early as twelve to sixteen weeks of age the delay between feeding and the occurrence of a bowel movement may result in a temporary "success" if the mother is quick enough to get her baby onto a receptacle in time. Such a success means very little, except in terms of saving laundry.

Similarly, from nine to twelve months some babies make vigorous sounds just prior to defecation, turn red in the face and regard their mother as they defecate. This potential for success means little so far as consistent and sustained "good" performance is concerned. Because around one year of age many children no longer give these warning signs. Many go through a stage when they function best alone and standing up, at the crib rail or in their play pen.

At this time and for months thereafter they may function preferably while standing and may even resist being placed on the toilet seat. Or they may accept such placement but respond to it by withholding—releasing as soon as they are removed. Still others are apt to function during sleep, especially during naptime.

By eighteen months many can associate some appropriate word with the function, thus increasing voluntary control. Many have few "accidents" after this age.

A temporary diarrhea comes in with many around eighteen to twenty-one months (followed by a period of constipation around two and a half years).

By two years or shortly thereafter, many are able, if the mother removes their training pants for them and leaves them near the toilet facilities which they can use by themselves, to take care of their own needs. Some, however, do best if divested of all clothes, even their socks and shoes.

Around two and a half years, many develop a spirit of intense privacy about all toilet functions. "Mommy go way," they say, and even insist that the bathroom door be securely closed. Their demand for privacy, like other strong common growth stages, should of course be respected.

From then on, with most children, there are as a rule relatively few problems in this connection. However, it is important to keep in mind that expecting the child to have his bowel movement regularly every morning is somewhat unrealistic. From three years of age on there is a tendency in many to have it after lunch or after their nap, and this shift if it occurs should be respected.

"When Can I Expect Him to Be Dry All Night?"

"How long do you think I'll have to wait before Danny will be able to stay dry all night?" Danny's mother asked us. "He's almost three now, and he's nearly always wet in the mornings. I've been hoping that if I just waited patiently, things would improve, but they don't seem to."

"Is Danny usually dry after his nap?" we asked her.

"Well, no, he isn't, most days. Why—does that have anything to do with it?"

Unfortunately it does, we told her, and went on to explain the relation. Almost invariably we find that children are able to stay dry for the, obviously, shorter duration of naptime considerably before they are able to stay dry all night.

In the normal course of events, many babies wake dry from their naps as early as one year of age. By eighteen months, many are reasonably well regulated in the daytime so far as toileting is concerned, though the responsibility for keeping the child dry is still the mother's. He does not yet indicate his toilet needs, but will wait a reasonable length of time for an opportunity to use the toilet.

By two years the average child of those we have studied will be dry in the morning on waking if he is taken up during the night. (But this is often disturbing to the child of this age and we do not as a rule advocate it.) By three years of age, many are dry all night without being taken up. (Remember that boys are usually slower than girls in this respect.)

But this is only on the average. So we know that for many children it will be long past two or even long past three years of age before they can stay dry all night. And, as we have indicated, before you can even begin to hope that your child will be able to stay dry all night, he will in all probability need to have reached the stage of staying dry after his nap.

The child's awareness or concern over wet pants usually means that there will soon be no more wet pants. Dryness after nap means that you can at least start hoping for dry nights. But until these two preliminary steps have been taken, it is largely useless to look for the final control.

"Shall I Pick Him Up at Night?"

"Do you believe that picking a child up at night does any good? And if so, should he always be wakened thoroughly, or is it all right to toilet him without waking him up?"

These two questions usually go hand in hand, and they are usually asked, at some time or other, by nearly every young parent—

except, of course, the extremely lucky ones whose children are "dry" almost from the moment of their arrival.

There is no one answer to the first of these two questions. As with so many problems of child rearing—it all depends.

If your child, regardless of his age, has come to the place where he is customarily dry after his nap, dry during the day (even though with some assistance from you), and if by being taken up once or even twice during the night he can manage to be dry in the morning, then your efforts are certainly being rewarded. You will probably feel that it is worth your while to take him up in the night.

If, however, you take him up, say at ten o'clock and again at midnight, finding him dry on each occasion, but nevertheless he is sopping wet when you go in to him at six or seven in the morning, you have not really saved much by your efforts. It might be just as well to see to it that he is arranged in sufficient rubber pants and pads to protect the sheets, and let him sleep through the night.

And if he is already wet an hour after he goes to sleep, or even when you first pick him up at ten o'clock, you have so far to go that you might just as well give up and wait till he can at least stay dry for the first two or three hours of the night. Or pick him up an hour or so after he goes to sleep to insure his comfort and save on the laundry, but don't expect him to be dry in the morning.

Not his chronological age, but how he is actually functioning is the thing that should chiefly determine whether you pick him up or not.

As to waking him thoroughly when you pick him up, opinions differ considerably about this. We ourselves advise, in most instances, that you do not wake him. Carry him to the bathroom if he is small and easy to pick up. Let him function in a bottle if he is a boy. Remember that picking him up is merely palliative. You pick him up in order to keep him dry and warm and to reduce the laundry. Picking him up does not *teach* him to stay dry. Therefore waking him does little good and may do serious damage in that once wakened, he may not be able to get back to sleep. A sleepless child may be more trouble to himself and others than a wet child.

However, the problem of picking up and waking is different at different ages. Even up through two or three years of age, many children are better off if not picked up during the night. In some, even being picked up more than once does not insure a dry night. In many picking up disturbs sleep to such an extent that the child cannot get back to sleep.

The situation is different by four or five years of age. Then very often (assuming that the child is not entirely and consistently dry at night, as many are) picking the child up once two or three hours after he goes to sleep may insure dryness and is obviously well worth while. Some children are dry some nights without being picked up and tend to wet only after an especially exciting day. You may find that you need to pick them up only on such nights.

If your child is six or seven years old and still wetting at night, then you judge by whether or not he has ever had any dry nights even with the help of being picked up. If there is no past history of dryness and he still wets within an hour after bedtime and is never dry in the morning, then you have a long way to go. You may still want to pick him up before he is apt to wet, usually one to two hours after he has gone to sleep, and again when you go to bed to make him feel more comfortable. But don't expect him necessarily to be dry in the morning.

However, if his span has even increased to two or, better, three hours after bedtime, the prospects are better, and just one pick-up during the night may insure dryness. Remember that many perfectly normal children are as much as 8 years of age before they reach this stage.

Snags in Toilet-Training

There are many snags in toilet-training, as there are in training the child in any other kind of behavior. We shall tell you about a few of the more common ones.

If you work hard at it, you can often "catch" a baby of sixteen to forty weeks, or in the last half of this first year, and can combine him and a suitable receptacle often enough and quickly enough that he stays dry most of the day, and you may have the illusion that he is toilet-trained. When he is just a little older, increased frequency and greater irregularity of urination along with changing motor patterns may result in "failures" and may dispel your illusion. Then if you have been priding yourself on your early success, you will be disappointed and may feel that he is not doing as well as he did when he was younger. Yet actually the early "success" was your success, not his. Later on he will arrive at real success of his own, so don't be discouraged.

Especially discouraging is the reaction of some children, often seen around fifteen months of age. Placement on the toilet seat for many children around this age results in sphincter contraction or withholding of urine. They simply refuse to function so long as they sit there, releasing only after they have been removed and their diapers put on. This seems like deliberate badness to parents and is often punished. It will still be a nuisance, but you will be calmer about it if you recognize it for what it is—a stage of development which appears to be an immaturity. Actually it is an advance in that the child learns to inhibit, or to control, his sphincter by contraction. This more often occurs in the seated position and especially on the toilet, where he is expected to function. He often functions as soon as he is taken off the toilet and his diaper is put on. Part of the ease of release is because he is taken out of the demanding situation. Another part is that he functions best when he is extended in posture, either standing up or lying down. If this demand to function standing persists, it is wise to place a newspaper in a corner of the bathroom and allow the child to release his bowel movement on it. We need to recognize the wide distance between the cultural level and demands of our bathrooms and the level at which the little runabout is functioning. He is happier to be treated like a lovable creature who still needs to be literally harnessed and curbed, though at a human level, than to be expected to participate fully in what we think of as being civilized.

BED-WETTING

Bed-wetting is an especially discouraging behavior, and "what to do about the problem of bed-wetting" is a question that parents ask and ask again. More often than not the answer is, "Wait awhile."

In other words, more often than not the child in question, regardless of his chronological age, is not yet mature enough in regard to this particular function to remain dry all night. If this is the case, you have no "problem" insofar as that nothing has really gone wrong, and that there is no special thing that you can do to improve matters.

Some children are not ready to read at the conventional age. Some children do not begin to lose their baby teeth, like the majority, around five or six years of age. And some are not yet ready to stay dry at the age when, norms show us, the average child has reached that desired goal—or even for years thereafter. Boys are more apt to be slow in developing control than are girls.

Check on your family history. Often you will find, or remember, that there is a history of belated bladder control somewhere in the family.

And the child's own elimination history will give you good clues. Was he much later than the average child in showing awareness of his own functioning or in staying dry after his nap? Is his span for dryness still short in the daytime? Is he already wet at eleven o'clock or even an hour after he falls asleep? Has he ever had periods, short or long, of being dry at night?

If, after making all these checks and after checking with your pediatrician, you then conclude that his inability to stay dry is just a matter of late development, pad him thoroughly at night (a folded diaper slung into his pants and pinned both front and back to waistband affords a good absorbing surface), add rubber pants, and—if you can—forget the whole matter for a while. There is a certain group of children who do not even show glimmers of control before six or seven years of age, and finally do stay dry at eight years either by being picked up or without help. Besides the more obvious evidence of occasional dry nights or of staying dry until picked up at eleven or midnight, the child's own feeling response to wetting can be very telling. If he isn't disturbed and hardly gives it a thought, then the necessary structure for control is not yet there. If he boasts about his "soaking wet bed," then he is at least responding, but in the wrong direction and will have to reverse his course before he will grasp the situation. But if he distracts his mother's attention and talks about the birds he sees outside or about other things as she comes to greet him in the morning, then she may know that this wetting is not congenial to him. For good shame comes with new awareness, and without shame the effort of a change cannot be made. It is for the mother to know that the child is most vulnerable at this stage and needs most help. The wetting child doesn't want the other members of the family to know that he has wet his bed. This can therefore be a secret between himself and his mother. Then mother and child can work out ways and means by which he can learn control. If he still needs padded and rubber pants, he needs to be made to feel emotionally comfortable in them and to realize that these are used for his physical comfort and also to save on the laundry. The other children of the family must not be allowed to shame him.

If he achieved bladder control at two years and then, as can sometimes happen, lost this control at four years (when tensional overflow is more often in the pelvic region of his body), he needs to be helped to know that this happens to a lot of children. Then he needs to be treated like a younger child until he regains control.

Also the increased wetting that occurs during the turmoil period of five and a half to six years and also on the cold nights of the fall of the year or just after a too exciting day or a frightening television program—all of these need to be understood and circumvented if possible by the parents. A half-day in first grade which cuts down fatigue or a happy chatting time with his mother after he is in bed may be all that is needed to break into a 6-year-old's tendency to wet his bed. An overnight visit to grandmother's where he is happy and is given a lot of individual loving care may result in a dry bed and give him a real emotional uplift. (But don't let him stay for two nights. If he is a wetter, he's sure to wet the second night.)

Many psychiatrists feel that emotional factors alone are at the basis of bed-wetting. We feel they are a definite part, especially operative in this 5- to 7-year-old period, but if control is not achieved by the outer limit of eight years, then we feel that there has been definite failure in learning to control.

It is then that we recommend a conditioning device, after the usual methods of control have been tried and found wanting. (It is always safest to use such a device with the help and advice of your pediatrician.) There are a number of these devices on the market, but fathers or even boys themselves can rig up their own contraptions. The important thing to realize is that in bed-wetters there is a lack of relaying the simple message to the brain that the bladder is about to be emptied by the release of the bladder sphincter. Something needs to be devised to warn the child of this thing that is happening to him which he knows nothing of until he awakens later in a cold, wet bed. The children who are close to developing their own control are the ones who respond to being picked up or having an alarm clock set at some special time. But it is the quality of the more usual bed-wetter that he doesn't respond to the usual preventive methods, that he sleeps too soundly to be awakened by his own inner activities and that he needs some strong stimulus to give him a warning at the time he is wetting.

Dr. O. Hobart Mowrer worked on various devices of conditioning. He at first used the more drastic method of having the mattress suddenly drop to a lower level as the child began to wet. Then the concept of setting a bell to ringing superseded this method.

The method of producing this needed stimulus at the time of wetting is quite simple. All that is needed is some device by which the salt in the urine will produce a short-circuit and thus set up an electric current to ring a warning bell, turn on a light or set in motion any other means of stimulation that may be chosen. In one such device simple wire window screening is used as the pad the child lies on, two bound pieces with an absorbent type of cloth between and a tight sheet on top. These screens are connected by wires to a dry cell with a bell attached. This bell device should be placed across the room so that the child will have to get out of bed and go across the room to turn it off. Then when he is awakened in the midst of emptying his bladder, he can complete this function on the toilet and then start all over again with a dry cloth between the screening, a dry sheet on top, and the bell switched to "on."

At first the child will be slow to respond and may have made a sizable puddle before he is awakened. But as his response is quickened, the size of his puddle grows smaller and smaller until it is finally no bigger than a dime. It is then that he comes to the final stage of "beating the bell." He receives the warning from his bladder before the sphincter relaxes. This conditioning usually is accomplished within a period of two weeks at this 8- or 9-year-old stage with a co-operative child.

The parent should be warned that the child should be in a room by himself so that he won't disturb the other children. Also the parent should be willing to get up and help the child freshen his bed and give him courage that it won't be long before he can do without this device. The intensity of the sound of the bell should be just enough to wake up the child, but not enough to wake up the rest of the family.

If this method is not working and is too hard for the child to accept, try it and then put it away until a later time when he is more ready. Sometimes the child responds well but has a relapse later. Then an extra session of conditioning may be needed. As for using this device before eight years of age, this is up to the discretion of the parents. We often find that parents tend to be too eager to try things before the child is ready. Be sure that he both needs such a device and that he is ready to work with it and through it before you try it. (If you are not mechanically minded, your pediatrician can tell you where to purchase such a conditioning device.)

NOT DRY IN DAYTIME BY THREE OF FOUR YEARS OF AGE

Rarer than bed-wetting but sometimes even more discouraging is the inability to stay dry in the daytime at an age when most children are fully "trained."

If a medical examination shows that there is nothing physically wrong, and if your pediatrician has no better suggestion, we would recommend the following. First, try to forget that your child is "old enough to be doing better." Just start in all over again as if dealing with a much younger child.

Find the time of day when he is most apt to be dry and see if you can get him to the toilet successfully at that time. Perhaps he will be dry right after his nap and you can "catch" him then. Then perhaps he will have a short dry spell following that, and you can "catch" him again.

At other times of day, keep him in diapers and rubber pants, using training pants only at the times when you are hoping to have success.

As a rule, if you treat even the older child this way, you will find that he will run a course, even though slowly, quite similar to that of the younger child. If you start slowly and don't expect too much, the rapidity of his progress may surprise you.

CAN'T STAY DRY AT PLAY

Another related, though usually quite temporary, problem is that of the child (usually three to four years of age, and usually a boy) who cannot stay dry while out at play. When out with his mother, shopping or visiting, he never has an "accident." But almost every day when out playing, he comes in wet. And the mother usually finds that warning, scolding, spanking or even keeping him in the house for a few days does no good at all.

The reason that spanking and punishment do not help is because such a child's difficulty is not badness—it is a real inability.

The complex task of stopping his enjoyable play, leaving his friends and getting into the house in time is just too much for him. And so his mother will need to work with him, not against him. She needs to help him, not to punish him. He needs practical help. And so, his mother will need to plan with him about getting into the house.

She may, for instance, plan with him that she is going to call him in at intervals. She may be able to figure out what his time span is and call him accordingly. If she can't figure this out, and if his timing is very irregular, she can just call him in every hour, or half hour, or as often as she thinks necessary. A police whistle which he has helped to purchase may work better than just the human voice. And some surprise for him after he has gone to the bathroom will make his coming in more enjoyable.

Soon his span may increase so that preventive toileting before he goes out to play may do the trick. Later he may reach the point where he can remember to come in without help—though he may wait till the last minute.

WETTING IN SCHOOL

Wetting in school, which occurs in a few first-graders, is usually a sign that the child is immature for his age. It is often a warning that the child is not quite ready for first grade.

For any first-grader, ideally, toilets should be adjacent to the classroom, and children should be free to come and go as they need to. Until such architectural arrangements can be made universal, however, teacher and parent will have to help the immature child as best they can.

First of all, question his readiness for daily all-day attendance, and for being in first grade at all, for that matter. If he must so continue, then be sure that he takes the time to go to the bathroom just before and just after the class session. The teacher must recognize that she needs to take over a mother's responsibility—that the child is unable to take care of himself.

Scolding and shaming are of course to be entirely avoided. Most of these children are doing the very best they can.

ODD OR BIZARRE TOILETING BEHAVIORS

The following are not really "snags" in toilet training, but should simply be mentioned so that they will not worry you when and if they occur.

The 2-year-old's inordinate interest in bowel movements as you take him out for a walk shows his own level of development. His eyes seem to spot every dog's defecation in sight. Then he goes to these, points to them, exclaims over them and all too often embarrasses his mother beyond words. We have often wondered if it isn't the very child who has been made too aware of his own functioning at home who is so conscious of the functioning of others, especially animals.

Many little girls around the age of three attempt to urinate standing up. This is a perfectly normal experiment and not in our opinion a sign that they have "penis envy" or have been overexposed to little boys. It may rather suggest their powers of observation.

Many children around four express an excessive interest in other people's bathrooms. Take them visiting and they are almost certain to say that they have to go to the toilet. A good hostess could perfectly well say to her 4-year-old visitor—who loves in any case to go exploring in another's house—"Would you like to see the rest of the house—the bedrooms, bathrooms and everything?"

Throughout the preschool years some children exhibit rather bizarre toilet behaviors. Thus they may void in unusual or unsuitable places, or may save products or even store them away in bureau drawers. Such behaviors often occur in children who have slightly atypical personality patterns; but if these particular behaviors are the only atypical signs, as a rule a parent should not be too much concerned, though he will probably wish to prevent the behavior if he can. If this kind of response is part of a whole group of unusual and atypical responses, he will probably wish to consult a child specialist.

Another thing which occurs especially around four is an excessive expression of need for privacy for their own toilet functions, but a tremendous interest in watching other people in the bathroom.

And lastly, also around four (and again at six), many indulge in a good deal of name-calling related to toilet functions. "You old wee-wee pants," or, "You old bowel movement" are favorite epithets. You may wish to prohibit this, but you should not be too much concerned when it occurs, as it is extremely common. Rather should you consider the circumstances that brought about this name calling. This may be the child's method of swearing in anger. If, however, this name calling is in silly play, it should and can be restricted in time and place and other more enticing activities of play that need to be adult stimulated can be substituted.

BOWEL MOVEMENT DIFFICULTIES

Most children have less difficulty with regard to bowel movements than with regard to urination. Many children are easily "trained" in this respect and a great many have no difficulties and no accidents after eighteen months of age.

There are, however, a few snags which you may run into in this department. First of all, many children, especially boys, around fifteen months to two and a half years of age may insist on standing up to have their bowel movements, even though they may have earlier been perfectly good about sitting on the toilet seat. It is usually best to permit them to function standing while this demand lasts.

Stool smearing occurs transiently in many children around the age of fifteen to twenty-one months. It occurs probably most often at the end of the nap if you do not go to the child quickly enough. He simply has a bowel movement in his diaper and then plays with the product.

Aside from being messy, this is not usually a serious problem. Preventive measures chiefly involve getting to him sooner or seeing that his training pants fit more securely. If this behavior occurs frequently, excessively and consistently, you may need to put on such securely fitting night clothes that he can't get them off. Prevention is the secret here.

A more worrisome problem is that which arises when a child (usually a boy) as old as three or four years of age absolutely rejects any efforts to train him so far as his bowel movements are concerned. He refuses to sit on the potty chair or toilet and has his bowel movement in his diapers.

When this is the case, a mother will need to start in at the very beginning. Give up the idea of having him use the toilet at first. Simply try to localize the behavior as to the time and place.

Try to determine at about what time of day he usually functions. (Unless it has narrowed down to some approximately regular time, you may just have to wait till it does.)

Then, at this time, let him play in the bathroom, nude or at least with his pants and underpants off. Have a newspaper on the floor, preferably in a corner behind the door, and indicate to him that when he is ready to function, he may do so on the paper.

Success is usually obtained within a remarkably short time. Once it has been established, you can gradually introduce a potty chair onto the scene and then can eventually shift from that to the regular toilet at such a time as he tells you he is "ready" for it.

Related to this refusal to function on the toilet, or sometimes not so related, is the problem of constipation, which may become quite severe in the preschool years.

There are several things you can do about this problem. First, as in other fields, be sure that you really have a problem. Remember that some children quite normally do not have a bowel movement every twenty-four hours. Also, there are ages when the child quite normally is a little more constipated than usual. Particularly is this true around two and a half years of age, especially with girls.

In other instances it turns out that the parents simply are not giving the child the privacy during elimination which he demands and needs. Added privacy often quickly solves the problem.

Equally simple is the giving of canned prune juice or a good non-abrasive laxative such, for example, as Patch's Kondremal. Reasonable experimentation with laxatives and experimenting with a relaxing diet should certainly be tried before you conclude that your child's constipation is an "emotional" problem.

But if you have tried all reasonable methods which you and your pediatrician can devise and your child's constipation continues to be excessive and chronic, then you will probably want to consult a psychologist or psychiatrist and get some specialized help. You will probably then find that the child's excessive constipation is just his organism's way of telling you that something is wrong, for him, in his daily family life.

Another problem which may also require professional help for its solution is that which arises when a preschooler attempts to "control" his mother's actions by having bowel movements in his pants to get her attention. She may be entertaining company; she may be attending to Father, or the new baby—whatever it is, she is not paying as much attention to him as he thinks he should have. So he has a bowel movement and she has to stop whatever she is doing and clean him up.

Here, obviously, the problem is as much one of mother-child relations as one of elimination. And unless the mother can herself figure out ways of making the child's life more harmonious and satisfactory, she may well wish to get a little professional help with the problem.

Two last problems in this realm.

Around five to six years of age many children again go through a period of increased withholding, as at two and a half. It often takes them so long to function that they simply do not bother. This difficulty can usually be controlled by careful checking by Mother and the use of prune juice or mineral oil.

Just the opposite difficulty comes in around six years of age with some, when there is tendency to overrelease. The child functions almost without warning to himself—on his way home from school in the afternoon, or at school also in the afternoon, or in Sunday school, or out at play. Children may be terribly embarrassed when this happens—and most parents are either embarrassed, worried or angry. They think that the child is "old enough to know better." Actually, this represents a real developmental problem and should be treated as such.

What the child needs here is a little more supervision and help. He should never be scolded or frightened. See that he functions before he goes back to school in the afternoon. If he is a 6-year-old, try to arrange that he attend only a morning session at school. Or if necessary, call for him at school and drive him home, since this behavior most often occurs on the way home from school. Or after school, be sure that he functions before he goes out to play. A little planning on the parent's part can usually overcome this temporary difficulty.

7

Tensional Outlets

STOPPING THEM

"MY 3-YEAR-OLD daughter seems to be awfully jealous of the baby, who was born when she was just under two. In addition to demanding an unreasonable amount of attention from all members of the family, she also sucks her thumb. How can I stop her?" writes the mother of a 3-year-old.

Another asks us: "My 2½-year-old son is very aggressive and destructive in the daytime, and at night he rocks his crib. If I try to stop him, he gets very angry and bangs his head against the crib rail. What can I do to stop his rocking?"

These questions are typical of dozens of others which parents bring to us: "My child sucks his thumb, rocks his bed, bites his nails, stutters, pulls out his hair, masturbates, etc., etc. How can I stop him?"

Such questions are so numerous that we believe it may be useful for us to discuss our concept of *tensional outlets*.

Many children have some behavior (and some children have many behaviors) in which their parents and other adults do not like to see them indulge. As suggested above, these children suck their thumbs or rock their beds or bite their fingernails. And they do these things not just once in a while, but more or less habitually.

Many parents think of these behaviors as "bad habits" and consider them to be a sign that the child is insecure, unhappy or maladjusted. They often seem to think that if the child were "all right," he wouldn't do these things—that is, he would "give up his bad habits"—or better still, he wouldn't have gotten into them in the first place. A well-adjusted child just wouldn't do such things.

Many parents even go so far as to feel that if their child does indulge in such behaviors, it is because they have failed to make him feel secure.

Our own attitude toward all these kinds of behavior is quite different. We think of all these tension-relieving behaviors which we have just mentioned as *tensional outlets*. That is, we believe that many children, like many adults, feel at times certain normal tensions. The adult has many ways of relieving these tensions—smoking is one of the most common. The child, too, has ways of relieving his tensions—and among these are the so-called bad habits which we are discussing.

We believe that your attitude as a parent toward these behaviors can significantly affect the situation. If you can think of them as devices for helping a child live with his tensions rather than as vices which must be cured, your own greater calmness and relaxation and acceptance of them will definitely benefit your child.

Nine times out of ten a child will grow out of these behaviors of his own accord. You not only will not find it necessary to break him of his "bad habits," but often the less you say about them, the less you call them to his attention, the sooner he will get over them.

In fact, the nagging (well-meant correction) of a tense parent may often increase rather than decrease the child's thumb sucking or nail biting or whatever it is he is doing that you object to.

And so, as we say, perhaps the most help we can give parents is to try to help you to take a calm, relaxed attitude toward these behaviors. Our best way of doing this may be simply to give you a timetable which shows the ages when we have found that the most common tensional outlets appear and the ages when they usually drop out.

You will note as you read this timetable that some behaviors such as temper tantrums drop out and then later reappear. Others, once they have finally dropped out, do not as a rule recur.

1 year: *Thumb sucking* strong, with or without an accessory object; occurs in daytime, just before sleep and during the night.

Transient and somewhat accidental *stool smearing.*

Presleep *rocking* in crib, *bed shaking, head banging* or *head rolling.*

Handling genitals and possibly some *masturbation.*
Crying.

18 months: *Thumb sucking* reaches a peak. May go on for several hours a day as well as just before sleep, or even all night.

Rocking, bed shaking, head banging or *head rolling* may occur.

Occasional episodes of *stool smearing.*

Furniture moving. Takes objects out of bureau drawers.

Sit down *temper tantrums.*

Tears books or wallpaper.

21 months: Tears bed apart.

Removes clothes and runs around unclothed.

2 years: *Thumb sucking* less during the day. Has a positive association with hunger, frustration, fatigue.

May be some *stool smearing.*

Rocking, bed shaking, bouncing, *head banging* or *head rolling.*

Many presleep demands.

Fewer tensional outlets at this age.

Left alone in a room, removes everything from drawers and cupboards.

2½ years: *Thumb sucking* less during day. At night strongly associated with accessory object. Some sucking in daytime, often with accessory object.

Rocking, head banging in some.

Some *masturbation.*

Stuttering may come in with high-language children.

Tears wallpaper, digs into the plaster.

Completely disrupts playroom, both large and small objects.

Sudden aggressive attacks—may "sock" a stranger.
Temper tantrums.

3 years: *Thumb sucking,* often associated with accessory object,
at night or occasionally in the daytime. Can tolerate
having thumb removed from mouth during sleep.
Fewer tensional outlets.
May wander around house during night.

3½ years: An increase in tensional outlets here.
Thumb sucking at night with accessory object. Can suck
in daytime without object.
Spitting.
Considerable *stuttering.*
Nose picking, fingernail biting.
Hands may tremble and child may stumble and fall.
Much *whining.*

4 years: *Thumb sucking* only as goes to sleep.
Out-of-bounds behavior: Motor—runs away, kicks,
spits, bites fingernails, picks nose, grimaces. Verbal—
calls names, boasts and brags, silly use of language.
Nightmares and fears.
Needs to urinate in moments of emotional excitement.
Pain in stomach and may *vomit* at times of stress.

5 years: Not much tensional overflow. Often not more than one
type in any one child.
Hand to face: *nose picking, nail biting.*
Thumb sucking, before sleep or with fatigue, often
without accessory object.
Eye blinking, head shaking, throat clearing, especially
toward end of day—peak at dinnertime.
Sniffling and twitching nose.

5½ years: Number and severity of tensional outlets increasing.
One child may show several types of overflow.
Hand to mouth: *nose picking, nail biting* increasing.
Some *throat clearing,* sometimes ticlike.
Mouthing of tongue and lips, tongue projection.
Less presleep *thumb sucking.*

School entrance may cause increase in *stuttering, nail biting* and *thumb sucking.*

6 years: General restlessness.
Clumsy. "Falls over a piece of string."
Kicks at table legs and piano as swings legs.
Sits on edge of chair, nearly falls off chair, pushes chair back.
Temper tantrums may return.
Makes faces with some relation to others, somewhat for fun.
Throat noises.
Heavy breathing, gasping with excitement.
Nail biting, tongue extension, *spitting.*
Stuttering.
Thumb sucking only in those with prolonged history, and may show an increased intensity.

7 years: Very few tensional outlets reported. Old ones dropping out. Those who still *suck thumbs, bite nails* or *stutter* are usually attempting to control.
Some *blinking* or reference to eyes hurting. Scowling.
Spontaneous undulating movements similar to St. Vitus's dance.
Headaches.
Things go "round and round" in head.

8 years: Very diffuse. Any of the earlier patterns may reappear; *eye blinking, nail biting, eye rubbing*—but all are less persistent.
A few persistent *thumb suckers,* especially boys, still suck during reading or listening or during illness or fatigue.
Picking at fingers.
Crying with fatigue.
Making faces when given unwelcome command.
Stomach-ache.
Need to urinate before unpleasant task.

9 years: Stamping feet, rubbing hands through hair.
　　　　Fiddling, pulling off button.
　　　　Drops and breaks things, picks at self.
　　　　Growling and muttering.
　　　　Feels dizzy.

TENSE AGES

Just a word should be said about the fact that not only may any given child have a favorite and characteristic method (or methods) of releasing his tension, characteristic of him and liable to occur at any age, but also that at some ages any child is apt to be notably more tense than at others.

Thus two and a half, three and a half, and five and a half to six are, as the preceding table suggests, even more than others, ages of tension. This means two things. First, that at these ages you should particularly go out of your way to prevent, or break into, situations which are likely to arouse tensions in your child. Second, that you may normally expect an increase in tensional outlets at these ages and should try not to worry too much about this increase.

TEMPER TANTRUMS

Daniel, aged two and a half, was having a full-fledged temper tantrum. He flung himself onto the floor and kicked and screamed. He drummed his feet and howled with rage.

His mother, in the best current tradition, observed him calmly. Most mothers find that if they can walk out on a child or remain calm and unemotional themselves while the child is having a tantrum, it is over much sooner and is somewhat less likely to be repeated. If having a tantrum gets them nowhere, many children give up this way of expressing themselves after only a few trials.

But Daniel's grandmother was also present. (The apartment was so small that no member of the family could be very far absent.) And she did something more than watch him calmly. For she had, like other grandmothers, brought up a family of her own and she knew that handling a temper tantrum skillfully was only a first step. A second and even more important step was, if possible, finding out what had caused the tantrum and what set of circumstances was thus to be avoided in the future to prevent further tantrums.

"I know just how he feels," sympathized Grandma. "And I suspect that he needs a lot more space to move around in. This summer when you all come to visit us, we'll fence in the yard, and then he'll have all the room he needs. I think he won't get frustrated so often."

This is one of the most important things that the adult can do when dealing with a child who is bothered with (and bothers others with) tantrums. Try to find out what things, or what kinds of situations, cause these tantrums. Even more important than treating them calmly is trying to prevent their occurrence.

Temper tantrums most often occur when the child is tired or when he is frustrated. Some frustration is inevitable and perhaps necessary as a child grows up—but frustration is most apt to end in tantrums when a child is tired.

If you will take the trouble to keep a record of the situations when your child has tantrums, you will often find that they occur at a time of day when he is particularly fatigued. At such times you will find that his tolerance for frustration is low. The same refusals and denials which he might be able to stand early in the day or after a nap often bring on a tantrum when they occur just before lunch or suppertime, for instance. A snack before suppertime may help to break into his fatigue.

But not only fatigue brings on a tantrum. Sometimes some very simple incident will bring it on. That is why it is important for you to try to discover *why* your child explodes and *how* you can prevent a recurrence.

Normal Course of Thumb Sucking

Your baby, if he is going to be a thumb sucker, may possibly be one of those who gets such an early start that already at birth his thumb bears guilty traces of having been sucked. More likely, however, thumb sucking will start, if it is going to at all, around three to four months of age.

At this time the behavior most frequently occurs right after feeding. The baby has been sucking (at bottle or breast), and just keeps right on after the source of food has been removed. Later on, as you may have noted, this urge to suck spreads to the period before feeding, and then finally to other times of day as well.

By six months, with some, putting an object to the mouth may take the place of thumb sucking. But around seven months, when hand to mouth is such a favorite gesture—and posture—thumb sucking will be very strong in many. In fact, it may reach such a peak that sucking may take place during a good part of the day and for at least much of the night. If you remove the thumb forcibly from the child's mouth, it is likely to come out with a loud pop and to go back in again at once unless forcibly restrained.

It is usually when sucking has reached such a peak that parents worry the most and are most anxious to do something about it. Unfortunately, this is probably the very worst time to interfere. Your efforts during such a period will have the least effect. It usually proves much more effective if you can wait till the behavior is on the wane before you make any definite attempt to stop it.

(Here let's say a good word for this behavior which is looked upon askance by so many parents: The baby who sucks his thumb may cry less and may get through teething much more easily than the baby who doesn't. He is also likely to go to sleep more easily and to get along better in many other ways.)

After this seven-months period there may be a repeated rise and fall in the amount of sucking. First you think it's dropping out, and then you fear that it's getting worse. Then around eighteen months, with many, such a peak is reached that many mothers become not only discouraged but worried, too.

It may encourage these mothers to know that there is a good chance (though by no means a certainty) that sucking may decrease, during the daytime at least, by the time the child is two years old.

Not only does it (usually) reduce in amount around this time, but it often has a more positive association with hunger, sleep, frustration or fatigue. If this does happen, it gives you something to go by. You can note the situations when it is most apt to occur and can try to prevent these situations or to reduce their difficulty for the child.

By two and a half to three years of age, sucking in many is much less during the day and at night may be associated with a certain (accessory) object held in the free hand. If the child needs to suck in the daytime, he may have to go and get this object before he can enjoy his sucking.

By three and a half many can do their daytime sucking without the object, even though they use it at night. At this age, daytime sucking is often stimulated by such excitements as being read to, watching television or looking up at an airplane.

And in the majority of children, if it has not already disappeared earlier somewhere along the way, by four or five thumb sucking will be associated only with sleep, and may then drop out of its own accord or with just a little help from Mother or Father.

Thus perhaps the most practical suggestion we can give parents when they ask what to do about their child's thumb sucking is the following: We can suggest that they familiarize themselves with the more or less usual course which thumb sucking takes (in our children, in our time) and then check to see how far their own child has gone along this course.

If, as we have noted above, the thumb sucking is merely on its way in or has about reached its peak, efforts to stop it in all likelihood not only will be ineffective but may actually be harmful, since thumb sucking, if it occurs, seems to need to run its course.

If it is nearing its end, you can either wait till it has taken its normal course or you may take such direct measures as seem fitting to you to hurry a little this natural ending of the behavior. The gift of a kitten might be the necessary stimulus to stop thumb sucking in a 3-year-old. But in a 5-year-old the thumb itself needs to be attacked. Various means can be used with the child's co-operation. One method might be a nightly Band-Aid with a projecting tab that he can chew on. This may shift him out of his sucking habit.

Sucking with Accessory Object

"He not only sucks his thumb, but he rubs his nose with his forefinger at the same time!"

"He pulls the fuzz of his blanket with his left hand while he sucks his right thumb!"

"She twists her hair—or pulls her ear—all the time that she sucks her thumb!"

"He can only suck his thumb if he has his 'pretty' (or his 'cuddler,' or whatever name the individual child may have for his soft blanket, or sweater, or soft piece of his mother's clothing) clutched in his other hand!"

These very customary statements are usually made to us prefaced or followed by the question, "Did you ever hear of such a thing?"

And we note that most parents report these things with a combination of pride and discouragement. Pride that their child could have worked up something so complex and "unusual." Discouragement because they have a feeling that he has a pretty bad habit and that it may even be a sign that something is "wrong" with him.

Though it may occur at most any age, we have found this sucking with an accessory object or gesture to be most common around two and a half or three years of age, when it occurs mostly at bedtime. (Yet some at this age cannot suck even in the daytime without their treasured blanket, or whatever they may have chosen.)

At this age, as a rule, if their desired objects are denied them, they usually cry or scream and become very much upset. This is not, in most, a good age to withhold the object or even to suggest withholding it.

Even by three and a half, when many have gone back to being able to suck in the daytime without their special object, they still are not able to give it up at night.

But by four or five years of age with many you can successfully attack the thumb sucking itself through this accessory object. With some you can merely say that the blanket (or whatever it is) is in the wash. Some will accept the story that it is lost. (If they do, the probability is that their thumb sucking has nearly run its course.)

With others you can frankly plan a giving up. A fuzz-puller may agree to buy chintz and help cover a fuzzy blanket so that the fuzz will not be a temptation. Another child may agree to *try* going to sleep without his blanket. Or he may allow Mother to sit by his bed and hold his hand in place of his sucking his thumb and holding his blanket. ("It isn't working, Mother," one little girl said after several nights of this. "I guess I'm not ready to give it up yet.")

Whatever specific plan you yourself may find successful—getting the child to give up his accessory object or habit is one of the best ways to help him over thumb sucking—*if* you do not start in too soon.

Tongue Sucking

A behavior less common than thumb sucking but equally worrisome to parents is tongue sucking. Tongue sucking, obviously, is harder to get at than thumb sucking. Many of the simple things which we can at least try to do to break into thumb sucking are of no avail here.

In general, with tongue sucking, it is more important to handle general behavior than to attack the sucking problem directly. That is, you do not make an issue of the sucking or try specifically to get the child to stop.

Rather, you attempt to improve his total life situation so that, perhaps, the tensions which get relief in the sucking will no longer be felt, or no longer felt so strongly. Nursery school or any similar activity which gives the child happy, pleasant experiences can be a great help. Or more time alone with Mother, or a satisfactory baby-sitter.

Some parents have found that gum chewing (even though not a very attractive behavior in itself) cuts into tongue sucking.

Does Thumb Sucking Do Harm?

Do thumb sucking and tongue sucking actually distort the shape of the child's mouth?

This problem is perhaps one which concerns the parents of thumb suckers more than any other. Even if parents do not like to see their child sucking his thumb, many of them would have no major objection to the behavior if they were sure that it was not deforming his mouth. Conversely, even parents who do not object to the behavior as such feel that they ought to stop it because it may be interfering with the child's later looks.

The answers given by different specialists to this question are extremely varied. The nature of the answer seems to depend largely on who is doing the answering.

Some, though by no means all, dentists do seem to feel that thumb sucking definitely mars the shape of the mouth and is thus specifically harmful. Most psychologists and psychiatrists, and many pediatricians, consider that it is basically not a harmful habit and that it does not in most cases alter the shape of the mouth. Particularly do they feel that it is harmless in this respect if it ceases before the second teeth come in, as it usually does.

These two points of view are pretty much opposed, obviously, and thus cause parents no end of worry. If the so-called authorities disagree, what is a parent to do? How is he to know whether thumb sucking actually is, or is not, harmful to the child?

Dentists who really believe that sucking is harmful state flatly that it "directly displaces teeth" and should be stopped as quickly as possible. To stop it, some of them suggest a really horrid-looking device known as a "hay-rake," a metal device which can be cemented to the teeth and which, with its vicious looking (and probably feeling) prongs, quickly deters the child from putting his thumb into his mouth. Merely looking at a picture of such a device would prevent most tender-minded parents from dreaming of using such a thing.

Fortunately, many qualified dentists agree with the psychologist and psychiatrist (and with us) that in most cases thumb sucking does not permanently impair the shape of the mouth. A recent authoritative source (J. H. Silliman, writing in the *Journal of Pediatrics,* Vol. 39, 1951) reports a fourteen-year follow-up study based on serial dental casts taken at least once a year on a group of children from birth through fourteen years of age.

This author—and his findings are typical of many—states clearly that in his opinion thumb sucking may affect the oral structure of children with "poor bites," but has little or no effect on those with "good bites." That is, if the child's mouth was well shaped to start with, thumb sucking did not distort it. Only in those cases where there was a poorly shaped structure to start with did the sucking possibly distort it further.

Specific Things to Do (and Not Do) about Thumb Sucking

Does all this mean that we must just sit by and do nothing about thumb sucking? you may well ask.

Not entirely! Some people can, of course. They are calm and patient enough, or objective enough, to wait and watch till thumb sucking has run its natural course.

Most parents, however, assuming that they basically dislike having a thumb sucker around the house, want to *do* something about it.

Here are some of the things you can do.

Around two years of age, with many children, thumb sucking occurs less during the day than formerly, and when it does occur, it tends to be brought on by hunger, fatigue, frustration or boredom.

Thus it is not too difficult for a mother to check up, to see in what situations and at what times it occurs. And having done that, she can often prevent the sucking *before* it starts. Arrange for an earlier nap to prevent fatigue. Provide a little snack to prevent hunger. Give a little more attention and help if your child is lonesome or frustrated.

Substituting another object for the thumb—that is, giving him a toy to hold so that he cannot suck his thumb—works less effectively than many parents hope and expect. Especially if the desire to suck is still at its height.

Sometimes, oddly enough, going to nursery school will cut down thumb sucking. The new interest of nursery school has been known to work in this field as well as to cut down wakeful nights and to improve poor appetites, as it often does.

Just keeping a record of when and to what extent the thumb sucking occurs has been known to help many mothers, even though it does not actually keep the thumb out of the mouth. Keeping a record helps you to view the behavior more objectively and allows you to see the progress and improvement which are usually brought about by time.

As a rule, the more you try to stop sucking in the early stages, that is, during the first three years or so, the stronger it may become and the harder it may be to stop later. If you tackle it before it has run its course, you are likely to get into trouble. But by the time the child is four or five, if you haven't made too much fuss earlier, the behavior will usually drop out by itself or with just a little help from you. (It may get worse briefly around five and a half to six, when tensional outlets normally do increase.) You can plan with the child as to what he can try. Often something fairly simple such as putting adhesive tape around his thumb with an extra tab to chew on may do the trick. It is important to remember that there can be no lapses of forgetting to put on the adhesive tape or there will be a return of thumb sucking. It may take as long as three months of nightly application to finally stop this habit.

BITING

"What do you do to stop a child from biting? Bite him back? That's what some people advise us." Many a parent has asked this question, phrased in just this way.

Our answer is that biting back is one of the least desirable and often one of the least effective ways of preventing biting.

Biting is in many children an extremely temporary way of behaving, expressed only when the child is in a social situation which is too difficult for him. Frustrated and unable to express himself more effectively, he resorts to biting. Two simple remedies, then, are: (a) First simplify the play situation. Don't have him play with so many, or such difficult (for him) companions. And don't have him play for so long. (b) Give more adult supervision. Step in, not just to punish biting after it has taken place, but to prevent the need for it. Help the child to express himself in more satisfactory ways.

Just these two steps can often prevent any need for biting. And time itself takes care of things in most children. Behavior proceeds (or develops) from head to foot, scientists have learned. The child who bites in September may hit in December and kick in June.

So in most cases, if you can keep him out of too difficult situations for a brief while, the urge to bite disappears.

But suppose it doesn't? We have found in a nursery school situation that if you have a biter on your hands, it often helps to have one teacher delegated to follow him or her around for a morning or two. Then every time such a child opens his mouth to bite, the teacher just cups her hand under his chin and gives a quick upward push. This, repeated every time he starts to bite for a few days, as a rule quickly discourages future biting.

More often we have found that biting can be "cured" by some such simple trick, by added age or by just a little simplifying of the play situation. Or by a little extra supervision. Or by isolating the child from the group or from his playmates each time he bites.

If these things don't work, the biting, like any other aggressive behavior, may be considered a sign at least that something deeper is amiss. In such a case you may want to call in outside help. Play therapy for the child, or even help for the parent in smoothing out the whole home situation may be needed. We definitely do not recommend such drastic measures as biting the child back or washing his mouth out with soap.

Biting may be one special manifestation of a certain type of personality. It may eventually become significant in an individual's whole sweep of development. But—and this is our advice not only where biting is the problem—never seek the complicated explanation or remedy when a simple one will do. Biting is not necessarily a sign that something is deeply and ominously "wrong" with a pre-schooler.

NAIL BITING

Nail biting is a slightly discouraging topic—in that nail biting, unlike most of the other early tensional outlets (head banging, rocking, thumb sucking), does not normally run its course and disappear by the end of the preschool years or shortly thereafter. Research into the tensional outlets of adolescents has shown us that nail biting is the most common and the most persistent of the specific ways in which teen-agers release their tension. Many continue this behavior till they are fifteen or sixteen or even, as many of you realize, right into adulthood.

Some children bite their nails only under extreme tension (nervousness about exams, excitement at the movies). Others just bite their nails.

Nail biting often seems to be a quite different kind of response from thumb sucking (though a few children are thumb suckers first and nail biters later). Nail biting is a pressure type of response and certainly is effective in releasing a good deal of nervous energy. With some children we do get the feeling that they need to do this.

Three of the possible courses of action which parents may follow in the case of nail biting are:

First, consider that the biting may be an indication that some specific thing is bothering the child. (We know, for instance, of a little girl who stopped it when she was moved to a different school.) Try to find out if this is the case.

Second, it may have started as a necessity, but may have moved on into the "habit" realm. In this case, mere cosmetic arguments may suffice to break it up. (Point out to the child—if a girl—how nice her nails will look when long and polished. Or even, in the teens, let her wear artificial nails.)

Third, it may be something, like smoking (though actually less harmful) which the individual seems to need to do (or feels that he needs to do) and which may just go on without stopping until the individual is ready to exert the necessary controls himself.

ROCKING

"My little boy gets up on his hands and knees in his crib and rocks back and forth. He rocks so hard that you can hear him all over the house, and he actually moves his crib from one side of the room to another. Did you ever hear of such a thing?"

Yes, we have.

"My little girl rocks herself to sleep every night of her life, and sometimes we even hear her rocking in her sleep. Do you think this is a sign that something is wrong with her?"

No! We don't.

We repeat: We have often heard of it. And we don't think it is a sign that anything is necessarily wrong with the rocker.

Rocking, like many other outlets for tension, starts out as a perfectly natural and normal stage of development. Around forty weeks of age many babies, able to get up onto their hands and knees but not yet quite ready to creep, rock their bodies backward and forward without actually moving from their original location. Hands and knees remain firmly on the floor (or mattress), but trunk moves forward and backward.

More often than not, this behavior drops out after the infant learns to creep. But sometimes it doesn't. In those cases this actually quite normal behavior may continue to express itself, particularly at bedtime or during sleep, long after the second birthday.

In such cases it often reaches its peak at two and a half to three and a half years of age, and then gradually drops out. Only in a minority of children does it persist after four.

As with most such tensional outlets, it is usually best, if you can, to let this behavior alone till it runs its course. However, some of the things which you can try, which may cut it down a bit, are:

Pad the child's crib heavily, be sure that the crib is screwed tightly together so that it does not creak unduly and put a soft rug under the crib. This reduces the noise and movement, which are often among the things which make the behavior most satisfactory to the child.

Sometimes when he is around four, you can plan that he will move into a bigger bed. Some children are at this time susceptible to a build-up to the effect that *they won't rock any more* after they have the big bed.

Sometimes a more prolonged going-to-bed hour which involves some activity or activities especially pleasing to the child will reduce tension and can send him off to sleep without rocking. Or you may find that your child can respond to some prearranged signal—such as your knocking on the wall—by stopping his rocking.

Your own ingenuity may, or may not, find some means of cutting down rocking which will work in your particular case. But whether you find such a means or not, at least try to appreciate the normality of this behavior and do not be unduly concerned.

HEAD BANGING

Somewhat similar to rocking but rather more frightening to parents, since it often causes actual bumps or welts on a child's forehead, is head banging. The child usually picks out the hardest surface he can find and then bangs his head against this surface. This is sometimes done in anger, sometimes not.

We have found that many, though of course not all, head bangers have the following personality characteristics:

1. They frequently are highly aware of sounds and sensitive to them.
2. Often they have musical ability and interest, like to listen to music and may sing on pitch early.
3. Many are ritualistic and patterned in their behavior.
4. They may be slow to approach a new activity or person, then slow to give it up.
5. They often are poor sleepers, waking up in the night and crying or singing to themselves.
6. Many have extreme temper tantrums. Desires are strong and ability to inhibit is poor.
7. They may be very cautious physically but have considerable energy.
8. Many are neat and show marked dislike of dirty hands or of anything spilled.

Knowing these characteristics of course will not prevent the head banging. But it can at least help you to realize that the behavior must be common enough if it is possible to describe head bangers as a group.

Best methods of dealing with this behavior are picking the child up and comforting him, but without talking about the head banging. Or distracting him with music or some other device. Or, best of all, if you can, try to prevent recurrence of the kinds of situations which led up to the banging. Scolding or punishing are as a rule completely ineffective.

It is very unusual for a head banger to do himself real damage (other than making black and blue spots) by his banging.

HEAD ROLLING

Another similar behavior is head rolling. This may go on till a child is five or six years of age or later. Spanking and scolding, urging and bribing, usually are of no avail in stopping this. Some mothers try appealing to the child's vanity (since the behavior tends to snarl the child's hair and make it look untidy, or it can produce a bald spot). This too is usually unsuccessful.

What usually does work is providing some form of substitute outlet. Since the behavior usually occurs when the child is fatigued—it is at those times that you will need to provide him or her with something to think about or something interesting to do.

Reading to him or playing music to him are two things which will be worth trying. (This behavior often occurs in the daytime as well as just prior to sleep.) Either may help. However, on the other hand, the child may roll or sway while he is listening. If he does, try having him color or play with clay. Or, instead of playing slow rhythmic music to which he may rock, try speeding up the music and getting him to dance to it.

You yourself may be able to think of other things which the child can do when he is tired and this urge to roll the head comes on. Whatever you do, it will be necessary to break into the behavior with some interesting, positive stimulus. It is seldom useful at the younger ages to attack the problem directly. If head rolling continues until the child is as old as eight years, he may be motivated toward some goal he wants to achieve, *e.g.* he can go for a visit to grandmother's as soon as his hair grows in.

HAIR PULLING

An extreme and often actually disfiguring tensional outlet is the pulling out of hair. Some children pull out only enough to make small bald spots. Others pull out enough that they make themselves completely bald.

As with all other similar behaviors, the parent can best attack this one in two ways, neither of them direct.

First of all, try to determine when and under what circumstances this behavior is most likely to occur. Then so far as possible, prevent the tension-arousing circumstances which cause the behavior or provide other more soothing and relaxing activities.

If the behavior is general and not localized to any special times or places, it will be necessary to try to find out ways of simplifying and improving the child's life so that he will have less need of tensional outlets. Specifically what you do will of course be different for each child.

At the same time it is possible to try to reduce the bad effects of hair pulling as well as the satisfaction which the child gets from tugging at his hair by providing a tight angora cap (provided that he— or she—will accept this; some who will not accept it in the daytime will accept wearing it at night). Such a cap allows the satisfaction of pulling at something, *i.e.* the fuzz on the cap, but protects the hair. It is less satisfactory than pulling at the hair itself (though less frustrating than physical restraint of the arms). Often by the time one cap is worn out, there will have come an end to the pulling.

WHINING

Whining can be a tensional outlet. It may occur in any child at any age, though it probably reaches its peak in many around three and a half years of age, at which time some children seem to their mothers to be whining all day long.

Many mothers threaten their whiners with, "If you don't stop that whining, I'll spank you (or send you to bed)!" And yet the best way to treat whining is actually to prevent it rather than to punish it.

No matter how much time you may be giving to your child, if he whines, he is giving you a clue that he needs more attention. He may need someone to play with him. He may simply need to be helped to play more creatively or more constructively or satisfactorily.

He may need to have his day planned a little differently. He may need more rest or more frequent snacks. Or he may need more interesting things to fill his life. A chance to attend nursery school, can, for example, often cut into whining.

Patience is what the whiner needs from those around him. Impatience is, unfortunately, what he most often attracts.

DIRT EATING

Some preschoolers worry their parents considerably by their habit of eating dirt, paint, wallpaper, soap—whatever comes to hand. Though such a diet can lead to lead poisoning (if it is paint with a lead base which is consumed), it is amazing how much foreign matter of this type can be taken in by the child without too bad effects.

However, this behavior is not to be encouraged, and most parents would like to know how to stop it. First of all, they should consider the possibility that this behavior indicates a lack of calcium in this child's diet and should check with their pediatrician to be certain that this is not the case.

Aside from this, the best approach is (a) to give the child more supervision and (b) to try to provide him with more satisfactory and interesting activities.

It is very difficult to teach a young child (especially if he is only 15 to 18 months of age) not to eat dirt, paint, wallpaper. If the hand to mouth reaction is still very strong, and if he does not discriminate what his hand puts to his mouth, about the best you can do is to keep him away from these materials as much as you can, watch him as much of the time as possible, and try to keep him occupied as much as you can with permissible activities. If you try all three of these tactics, what little foreign matter he does get into his mouth will probably be little enough to do him no harm.

TICS

Definitely one of the most worrisome of all the tensional outlets are those automatic, repetitive, purposeless movements known as "tics." Such movements may occur quite normally at certain ages in certain children, and usually disappear more quickly if ignored than if attention is focused upon them.

Thus ticlike nose sniffing at five, ticlike throat clearing around five and a half to six years of age, ticlike grimacing and head shaking at six, eye-blinking at six to seven, general bodily writhing at seven, various facial tics and grimacing at eight to nine—all may occur quite "normally" and briefly and may be a sign of no more than the normal tensions of the age.

Even when such behaviors are quite irritating or worrisome to parents, as a rule it is best neither to call attention to them nor to attack them directly. Usually they will be of short duration.

However, when they persist or become extremely exaggerated, it is generally wise to consult a child specialist. *Persistent* severe ticlike movements are generally considered to be a response to an environmental situation which is deeply disturbing to the child. They are usually considered to be signs of serious emotional strain.

In treating tics, with the aid of a specialist, first of all it is important to be sure to remove any and all possibly physical sources of irritation. Next, an attempt should be made to try to discover which parts of the child's life are causing him unhappiness or concern. Home and school conditions both will need to be carefully reviewed to find out how life can be made more satisfactory and less frustrating for the child.

Sometimes very simple changes in home or school can give the necessary relief, but in severe cases prolonged psychiatric treatment may be required. One reason why it can be useful to seek the guidance of a child specialist is that the mere fact that this particular child does respond to an adverse situation in this particular way is an indication that here is an unusually sensitive organism. One which is perhaps not too well co-ordinated. One which may, even after the immediate symptom is cleared up, be expected to respond to future difficult situations in a similarly extreme manner.

STUTTERING

Broken fluency (repetitions and prolongations of sounds, syllables and words) is a characteristic of normal speech development, and most young children manifest this behavior at some time or other. It comes and goes in waves during the preschool and early school years, and is more pronounced in some children than in others. We have found that such repetitive speech is most marked at the ages of two and a half, three and a half, and six years. Normally a child goes rather quickly through these periods, and his speech will again become relatively smooth.

On the average, the child from two to six years of age, who is still in the process of speech development, repeats forty to fifty times in every one thousand words. He may *re-re*-repeat a *s—s—*sound or syllable like this, a word *like like* this, or a phrase *like this like this.* He may have inappropriate pauses and prolongations.

Speech is a complicated process, and it is not surprising that the speech of the young child is unstable and subject to nonfluency. The young child is busy mastering sound production, new vocabulary words, syntax and all the other complexities of spoken language. Even normal adult speech is characterized by occasional breaks and repetitions.

Although stuttering can follow an emotional shock or crisis, the onset of developmental nonfluency is usually quite gradual and commonplace, and it is, in the majority of cases, first noticed in the routine situations of everyday life.

Parents are often overanxious and alarmed by this behavior and are apt to label normal nonfluency as "stuttering." However, this behavior differs from that of the chronic or adult stutterer. The young child is seldom conscious of his "difficulty" unless someone in the environment brings it to his attention. He bubbles along repeating in rather an effortless fashion. The older stutterer, on the other hand, is very aware of his speech hesitations and has many more complicated symptoms.

Parents who are alarmed by this behavior often wonder if "something is the matter with his tongue," or if he is "retarded" or "neurotic." However, repetitive speech occurs so commonly in children who are normal in every respect, with excellent home situations, good co-ordination, etc., that we do not necessarily think of it as a sign that anything is "wrong" with the child.

However, this normal nonfluency can be aggravated by adverse handling. The child who is forever interrupted when trying to talk, the child who is penalized for his repetitions, one who must compete for a chance to talk, or one who is harshly forced to confess to a misdeed, is certainly apt to show intensified nonfluency and a more pronounced tensional outlet through speech.

Speech therapy is not recommended for the ordinary repetitive speech of the preschool child. But there is much that the parents can do to help their child progress more easily to fluent speech. The best approach is preventive and indirect. Here are some of the important *do's* and *don't's* to serve as guideposts for parents:

Things to do:

1. Do give him the attention he deserves when he is speaking to you.
2. Do listen with patience and understanding as he tells you about something that has happened that is important to him.
3. Do let him finish what he is saying without interrupting him, no matter how much difficulty he appears to be having.
4. Eliminate as much as possible the causes of tension and frustration in his daily routine. Remove disturbing influences that seem to aggravate his nonfluency. For example, see that he has a chance to express himself at the table without too much competition from the older children.
5. Try to maintain as calm and restful an atmosphere as possible in the household. This can be done by slowing down your own pace and by handling routines in an easy and unhurried manner.
6. Try to speak more slowly, calmly and simply to him. If you are relaxed and unhurried, he is apt to feel more relaxed when speaking to you. Sometimes it is difficult for him to "keep up" with adult speech. If you speak in shorter, simpler sentences and at a slower tempo, it will be easier for him to achieve fluency.
7. See that he does not have too much stimulation and is not overtired.
8. Do all that you can to keep him in good physical condition.
9. Try to keep the demands made on him in regard to his training within his capacity to understand and carry them out.

Things to avoid:

1. Don't refer to his nonfluency as "stuttering." Once it is called stuttering (or by any other name) in front of him, he may begin to react to the label and become self-conscious of his speech, and his difficulty may increase.

2. Never discuss in his presence the "trouble" he is having with his speech.

3. Try to avoid becoming anxious about his speech. It will be easier for you to relax in your own attitude if you remember that most children do go through perfectly normal developmental nonfluency and most come through it with normally smooth speech. Anxiety can be transmitted to the child by the attitudes of those around him.

4. When he speaks to you, do not show in any way (by facial expression, impatience, etc.) that you notice his difficulty in speaking.

5. Do not ask the child to "speak more slowly," "stop and start over," "take a breath," or "think before you speak"—even if such suggestions seem to bring temporary relief. Such demands usually serve only to increase the child's difficulty.

6. Do not reward him for fluent periods or punish him for difficult periods of repetitive speech.

7. Never force him into upsetting verbal situations (such as reciting for company, apologizing, confessions, etc.).

Many of the above suggestions are aimed at preventing the child from becoming aware of his repetitive speech. This is our ideal, but it doesn't always work out that way. Perhaps a playmate or another adult might bring it to his attention. Should this happen, the wise parent will respond by reassuring his child. You might tell him that "everybody gets tangled up in speaking once in a while if they are excited or talking very fast."

If the child's stuttering persists and you do not feel that he is having longer periods of fluency, and especially if you feel that you do not fully understand his stuttering or feel capable of handling it, you should consult a speech specialist or speech clinic.*

* You may obtain a list of the qualified speech specialists and speech clinics nearest your home by writing to the Secretary of the American Speech and Hearing Association: George A. Kopp, Ph.D., Wayne University, Detroit, Michigan.

MASTURBATION

There are perhaps three main points of view about masturbation in babies and children. The position to the most extreme right is that this behavior is not only wicked but harmful, and that the child who masturbates should be punished and forcibly prevented from further indulgence in this activity. (However, it has been shown that masturbation causes no physical harm, and few people now hold the view that it is a sign of depravity in the young child.)

A second attitude is more middle of the road. It considers masturbation to be a common (though by no means universal) and relatively harmless activity; something in the same class with thumb sucking but a little less desirable. People in this group, in fact, deal with masturbation more or less as they do with thumb sucking. They do not attack the behavior directly, but rather attempt to improve the child's life in general ways so that he will be well adjusted and happier, or more interestingly occupied, and will feel less need of tensional release. They particularly try to note at what times and under what circumstances the behavior occurs. They then try as far as they can either to prevent the circumstances or to provide other outlets at the times when the behavior is most likely to occur.

In addition, some parents are helped if they realize that masturbation, like thumb sucking, follows a definite course in many children. Thus they do not make too many (even indirect) attempts to prevent it when it is at its height.

Often parents find that their own attitude toward the problem relaxes if they can ask themselves not "How can I stop him?" but rather, "Why does he do it?" Sometimes the "why" becomes quite apparent, and you can then prevent the circumstance or situation which brings it on. In other cases, you can't find out the exact "why," but at least your attitude may be softened by the search.

A third and more recent point of view is that masturbation not only does not do harm, but that excessive efforts on the part of parents to stop or prevent it actually may in themselves be harmful. We should like to quote Dr. Redlich of Yale on this subject. He gives, in his recent book *The Inside Story* * the following possible arguments for ignoring this activity when it does occur:

First, there is no danger that our child will suffer physical harm from a limited amount of masturbation. The old wives' tales about its causing blindness, insanity, bad complexion, and what not have been scientifically disproved. Secondly, there is some danger that an emotionally charged parental forbidding of the child's touching himself may result in such repression of the child's sexual urge that when grown up he may not be able to function normally in this respect. Thirdly, there is comparable danger that the child may develop terrible self-loathing and lack of confidence when he finds he cannot (when half-asleep) completely keep himself from doing what he has been so forcefully told is unnatural and vile. Fourthly, we may be sure that even though we never say a word about it our child will pick up the idea that this is an activity about which people he admires are not exactly enthusiastic. Fifthly, if we have never frightened our child about masturbation he may feel free to tell us when and if little school friends make physical advances (which little school friends sometimes do), thus enabling us to protect him by insisting on supervision when the children visit each other's houses, or even by cutting out the visits for a while.

The last argument—perhaps most controversial of all—is that through allowing our child to keep a few deep dark secrets from us we may be reinforcing his grasp on reality and diminishing his unconscious tendency to believe in symbols and magic and other forms of unreality. That is, it may lessen his feeling that we are omniscient, if we seemingly are not aware of everything that he does. Particularly since we are not sure of the wisdom of what we would say if we did say anything, and also since the child is likely to outgrow the behavior of his own accord.

Of these three attitudes we cannot say which one you will choose, but we hope that it will not be the first.

ILL HEALTH

Colds! Earaches! Sore throats! Stomach-aches! These may not seem to fall exactly under the heading of tensional outlets. Yet it is

* Fritz Redlich and June Bingham, *The Inside Story—Psychiatry and Everyday Life* (New York, Alfred A. Knopf, 1953), pp. 145ff.

true that many children when overtired and overtense do respond with physical illness.

Many children seem to have one special kind of illness with which they respond to any overdifficult situation. They *always* get a cold, or are sick to their stomachs, or become constipated.

In addition to these special individual ways of responding, there are also certain ages when children are likely to have certain sicknesses. Of course no disease is unique to any one age. And even when a sickness can be determined as being characteristic of a certain age, you still have to do something about it.

However, many parents worry less when they recognize a certain illness as one which is especially characteristic of a certain age period.

Here are a few of the sicknesses which in the early years seem to have an age tie-up. (You will of course consult your pediatrician when any serious illness occurs, but your anxiety may be lessened by this information.)

18 months: Convulsions may accompany illnesses, especially those with high temperature.

21 months: Elimination difficulties; frequency of both functions; diarrhea common.

2½ years: Elimination difficulties. Long retention span; constipation more common in girls.
Frequent colds with ear complications, especially in slow-speech children.
Gets a bloody nose if falls.

3 years: Expresses marked fatigue.

4 years: May have one cold right after another all winter.
Stomach-ache in social situations.
Needs to urinate in difficult situations or at mealtimes.
May have "accidents" in emotional situations.
Knocks out front teeth if falls.

5 years: Good or even excellent health characteristic. May have only one or two colds all winter.

Some increase in whooping cough, measles, chicken pox..

Occasional stomach-aches or vomiting in relation to disliked foods or just prior to elimination.

Constipation in girls.

5½ years: Complains that his feet "hurt" him.

Some have frequent colds. Headaches or earaches.

Stomach-aches with some nausea and vomiting connected with school or other demands.

Somatic symptoms may appear after a week or two of school.

Whooping cough, measles, chicken pox the most common communicable diseases.

Hypersensitivity of face, head, neck region to washing, hair combing, etc.

Child may endure large pains yet fuss about a splinter or nose drops.

6 years: More susceptible to diseases and sicker with illness than earlier.

Frequent sore throats, colds, with complications (lung and ear); increase in allergies.

Chicken pox, measles, whooping cough. Diphtheria and scarlet fever, German measles and mumps.

Stomach-aches and vomiting in connection with going to school.

Toilet "accidents" with overexcitement.

May break arm if falls.

Hypersensitivity of face, neck region if washed or touched.

Increased redness of genitals in girls.

7 years: Fewer illnesses than at six, but colds of longer duration.

German measles and mumps frequent. Chicken pox and measles may occur.

Complain of headaches with fatigue or excitement; complain of muscular pain, especially of legs or knees.

Minor accidents to eyes, but fewer gross accidents; eye rubbing.

Extreme fatigue—yawning, stretching.

8 years: Improving health. Fewer illnesses and of shorter duration. Less absence from school because of illness.

Increase in allergies.

Headaches, stomach-aches and need to urinate in connection with disagreeable tasks.

Accidents frequent: falls, drowning, and in relation to automobiles and bicycles.

May break leg if falls.

9 years: Improving health and few illnesses, but marked individual differences.

Some have a prolonged illness or show marked fatigue.

Many minor complaints related to the task at hand (eyes hurt when tested; hands hurt when writing). Or may say, "It makes me feel dizzy."

10 years: Health much better in most. Many report, retrospectively, that there was a period of bad health around six with earaches, sore throats, contagious diseases. A few worry about their own health.

CAR SICKNESS

Car sickness! When the writers were young, this was the name of a dread malady which attacked young children on street cars—usually when they and their families were dressed in their Sunday best and out for an excursion.

Nowadays it more commonly strikes the victim when he is out in the family automobile. It is probably most common in the first six years of life, though in some it persists till adulthood.

This problem can loom large indeed. In fact, it can not only cause much discomfort to the child who suffers from it, but if severe, may even seriously interfere with the social life and vacation and visiting habits of the whole family.

The scientific literature on this subject is extremely scant. And in many cases not only is an effective remedy not found, but even the cause is difficult to determine.

Some years ago the analysts introduced a theory that car sickness resulted from antagonism to or hatred of the sufferer's mother. We ourselves do not subscribe to this theory, though it may be true of some isolated cases.

It has been our observation that oftener than not, a visual factor seems to lie at the basis of car sickness. Children with too peripheral vision (that is, those who are overresponsive to things in the distance or in the margins of the field of vision) frequently have this difficulty. If you can get them to lie down in the back seat of the car or even to lean against your shoulder with their eyes closed as you sing the time away, frequently their symptoms are relieved. Or you may interest them in some activity on the floor of the car. Or sometimes dark glasses with fairly wide rims will cut down the too strong dose of visual stimulation which they are getting.

Especially avoid having such children use their eyes in reading or even in looking at road maps while the car is in motion. Sometimes a correct prescription of glasses may do the trick. Or your eye doctor may, in extreme cases, suggest the wearing of a patch over one eye.

In any event, if your child does suffer from car sickness, a thorough visual check-up from a skilled children's eye doctor may help out. And in the meantime, you may find that some specific medicine for motion sickness—given of course at your pediatricians' prescription—may turn out to be all that is needed.

8

Fears

DIFFERENT FEARS AT DIFFERENT AGES

THE children frightened Davey on Halloween night and he's been jumpy ever since. A baby-sitter threatened Joe with the "bogeyman" and he's suddenly refused to sleep without his light on. An unfamiliar dog bit Betsey, and now she's afraid of dogs.

Into any child's life can come frightening and unhappy incidents which set up special fears, and you as parents naturally do your best to protect your child from such specially frightening incidents.

But you cannot protect him from all fears. As the child grows up, he seems to need to go through a series of fears which come in and then later drop out. Each child differs somewhat, but, in general, each age seems to bring its own characteristic fears. A much abbreviated summary of some of the most outstanding fears which are likely to develop in almost any child, from age to age, is as follows:

2 years: Many fears, chiefly auditory, as trains, trucks, thunder, flushing of toilet, vacuum cleaner.
Visual fears: dark colors, large objects, trains, hats.
Spatial: toy or crib moved from usual place, moving to a new house, fear of going down the drain.
Personal: mother's departure, or separation from her at bedtime. Rain and wind.
Animals—especially wild animals.

2½ years: Many fears, especially spatial: fear of movement or of having objects moved.

Any different orientation, as someone entering house by a different door.
Large objects—as trucks—approaching.

3 years: Visual fears predominate: colored or wrinkled people, masks, "bogeymen."
The dark.
Animals.
Policemen, burglars.
Mother or father going out at night.

4 years: Auditory fears again, especially fire engines.
The dark.
Wild animals.
Mother leaving, especially going out at night.

5 years: Not a fearful age. More visual fears than others.
Less fear of animals, bad people, bogeymen.
Concrete, down-to-earth fears: bodily harm, falling, dogs.
The dark.
That mother will not return home.

6 years: Very fearful. Especially auditory fears: doorbell, telephone, static, ugly voice tones, flushing of toilet, insect and bird noises.
Fear of supernatural: ghosts, witches.
Fear that someone is hiding under the bed.
Spatial: fear of being lost, fear of the woods.
Fear of the elements: fire, water, thunder, lightning.
Fear of sleeping alone in a room or of being only one on a floor of the house.
Fear that mother will not be home when he arrives home, or that something will happen to her or that she may die.
Afraid others will hit him.
Brave about big hurts but fears splinters, little cuts, blood, nose drops.

7 years: Many fears, especially visual: the dark, attics, cellars.
Interprets shadows as ghosts and witches.

Fears war, spies, burglars, people hiding in closet or under bed.

Fears now stimulated by reading, radio, cinema.

Worries about things: not being liked, being late to school.

8 to 9 years: Fewer fears and less worrying. No longer fears the water; less fear of the dark. Good evaluation, and fears are reasonable: about personal inability and failure, especially school failure.

10 years: Many fears, though fewer than in the ages which immediately follow. Animals, especially snakes and wild animals, are the things most feared. The dark is feared by a few. Also high places, fires and criminals or "killers" or burglars.

A few are beginning spontaneously to mention things they are *not* afraid of: chiefly the dark, dogs and being left alone.

Our studies of thousands of normal children have shown us that as any child matures, he is likely from time to time to exhibit fears of things which often seem to his parents to be quite harmless. However—and this should be most reassuring to parents—these fears do not appear completely at random, nor are they different for every child.

On the contrary, we find that they appear, and soon disappear, in an ordered, patterned fashion which often shows great similarity from child to child. For example, as the preceding list suggests, 2-year-olds often fear any sudden loud sounds, like vacuum cleaners or locomotives. Two-and-a-half-year-olds are more likely to have spatial fears, or fears of moving objects. Threes may most often fear things seen.

Each age brings its characteristic fears.

Withdrawal from Feared Stimuli Is Natural Response

In a large downtown department store a determined-looking mother pushed her crying 3-year-old into one of the waiting elevators.

"It's very embarrassing," she explained to one of the other passengers. "But you see my little boy is terribly afraid of elevators and I know that the only way to get him over this fear is to make him ride on them until he gets used to them."

Actually, it is not the only way. It is not even a very good way in most cases. It is astonishing, and unfortunate, that this mother's notion is so widely prevalent.

Celia is afraid of heights. Take her up the highest hill! Joe is deathly afraid of cows. Take him out to the pasture! Even worse— Dave is afraid of water. Throw him in!

Too many parents for too many years have followed this unfeeling policy because, for some reason or other, they believe it is "the way" to cure fears in the child.

We do not say that it never works. In our years of clinical practice we have known the most unusual ways of dealing with children to work, on occasion. Child behavior tends as the child matures to proceed toward an optimum regardless of parental handling. But good handling certainly helps, and for the more sensitive souls it is essential.

The best handling of a child's fears is handling based on the realization that fear is not altogether a bad thing. In primitive or natural societies the person or organism fears that which may harm him and withdraws from it as rapidly as possible. Often he thereby saves his life.

It is not so different with us. The child withdraws from those things which are or seem dangerous or harmful to him. This period of withdrawal may be long or short, depending on the child and the situation. But, unless you have strong reasons to act to the contrary, *you should respect* the child's natural tendency to withdraw from the thing he fears.

In some situations this withdrawal may be short—only momentary. In others it may last for weeks or months. As a rule, even without your help, the child will get over his fear. As he grows older, things look different to him. He understands more about them. They seem less threatening.

If he does not of his own account get over his fear in what seems to you like a reasonable length of time, you can help him gradually to overcome it. If he is afraid of large, fierce dogs, let him play with a puppy of his own. If he fears the ocean with its noisy surf, give him a chance to bathe in a small, warm pool or lake.

But don't try to do the whole thing at once. Don't be too impatient if he doesn't get over his fears as quickly as you think he should. Most important, don't use shock methods! Don't force him to face the thing he fears.

Above all—respect his fears. As a rule they drop out much more quickly if they are treated with respect. In fact, in the ordinarily stable child most fears are relatively short-lived. Not only short-lived, but often they are followed by a brief period in which the child may seem almost compulsively attracted to the thing or situation which he has formerly feared.

Overwithdrawal, then Overapproach

"Most contrary child I ever heard of," complained Jake's father to Jake's mother.

"Why, what do you mean, dear?" replied Mother. "I think he's a pretty good little boy. I know you're disturbed about his setting that fire in the back yard. But he didn't realize it would spread over to your tool house."

"That's just it. This business of setting fires. Six months ago he was so terrified of fire that he wouldn't even go near the fireplace, and now he goes around setting fires every time he can lay his hands on a match. That's just what I'm trying to point out—it doesn't make sense. He's just contrary."

Contrary he may be—but if this is contrariness, make the most of it, because Jake's actions are perfectly "normal" according to what we know of human behavior. We can learn a lot from analyzing these actions.

To begin with, when Jake was about six years old he had a spell of being afraid of fire, a not unusual fear at this age. And, as most people do, he just naturally withdrew when he could from the thing he feared. This did not alarm his family unduly.

But now, six months later, he not only no longer fears fire, but seems to be almost compulsively attracted to it. He just loves fire and can never seem to get enough of it. So much so that if there are no fires at hand, he will often set one, sometimes with disastrous results.

This is within a predictable response for this child around the age of six. In the natural course of events a child will first withdraw too far from, and then later approach too closely, some feared object. Finally, in a third stage, he settles down to a more adaptive state. He is then in control of his fear. He can take the thing or leave it. With fire, for instance, he does not fear it unduly, nor is he unduly attracted to it. He will be in control of his reaction. If we were more understanding of this mechanism, we might even be able to help those who compulsively light fires.

Knowledge of these facts may help you to work out successfully your own handling of your child's fears. You will see that if a child's first reaction to a feared object is withdrawal, if you force him to face the thing before he is ready, you are going directly against his natural tendencies. Withdrawal from a feared object is natural and should be permitted.

The natural period of withdrawal may be long or short, depending on the personality of the child and on how frightened he is. If the withdrawal period is short, the time of the child's approaching too closely will also be short. If it is long, the time of too closely approaching may also be long.

In general, you will do best if you permit the period of withdrawal without scolding, shaming or forcing. Sometimes it is wisest to be on the sidelines, not making him more aware of his fear, but protecting him from experiencing it before he is ready. At other times and with other children, it may be wisest to discuss the fear. Tell him that there will be this period of withdrawal and that he can count on your protecting him during the period. This can relieve the tension so that he may be able to resolve his fear more quickly than when he is trying to resolve it alone. And then, when the child comes to the period of overapproach, find calm ways of dealing with this, too. Each situation, of course, varies in detail and each has its own individual solution.

However, there are a few generally applicable do's and don'ts (though remember always that each child is an individual and that each case has its own special aspects which make any generalized advice of only limited value).

What not to do when your child is afraid:

Don't ever make fun of his fears.

Don't shame him before others because of them.

Don't force him to "face" the thing he fears before he is ready unless you are very sure you are right to do so. (And you seldom will be.)

Don't become impatient and treat him as if he were babyish because he is afraid.

Don't assume that it is necessarily your fault, or his fault, that he is afraid.

Don't necessarily feel that it is bad or unnatural for the child to have some fears.

What to do when your child is afraid:

Respect his fears.

Realize that he will outgrow most of them.

Allow him at least a reasonable period of withdrawal from feared things before you attempt to help him adjust to them.

Give him a chance to become gradually used to fearful situations, a little at a time. If he fears great heights, accustom him first to small elevations; if he is afraid of dogs, let him first get acquainted with a puppy. (This gradual approach does not, however, work with all children. Some children need to take the plunge and get it over with.)

When and if he comes to the period of compulsively overapproaching a formerly feared object or situation—his natural method of tackling his fears—help him to have the experience he desires, but under your supervision. If he has first been afraid of fires, he may later have a strong desire to set fires and to play with fire. Let him light the fire in the fireplace or the candles for the table. Or let him help burn the trash, or help with a bonfire, of course under your most careful supervision.

Analyze his fears in relation to his personality. Does he characteristically fear strange sounds or sights? Does he fear movement? Try within reason to spare him situations which you know will cause him to be fearful.

Familiarize yourself with the kinds of fears which children naturally experience at different ages. You can take more lightly a fear which is common to the majority of children at some one age. It will usually not last long.

If your child seems to fear some large, general situation which he must nevertheless experience, as school, analyze the situation to find out what specific aspect of it has caused his fear.

But if your child's fear is excessive and troublesome and you cannot find out the cause, and time does not take care of it, you may wish to seek specialized help in aiding him to solve his problem.

FEAR OF THE DARK

One of the most common and most persistent of all the child's fears is fear of the dark. Starting in many around two and a half, it goes on in some, in one form or another, even up into the late teens. (Before one year of age many children seem completely fearless so far as the dark is concerned, though the 10-to-11-month-old child may shy away from a darkening room at twilight as he creeps about, or hurry past an open closet door where it is dark inside, making for the nearest window.) Around two years of age many can move about their own room in the dark with great deftness, especially if they are supposed to be in bed, as though their eyes were adapted to darkness and they could see in the dark.

Ways of dealing with this very common fear have been suggested on page 96, in our general discussion of fears related to sleeping.

FEAR OF DOGS

Some children never show any fear of dogs. In the majority of those who do exhibit this fear, it is fairly temporary.

Fear of dogs, when it is expressed, should like other fears be respected. It can usually best be overcome by allowing the child as much experience with dogs as he can accept.

Thus, small dogs or puppies can often be tolerated when large dogs cannot. Or dogs in the distance can be accepted even though he does not like to have them too close at first. Or the child himself can approach a dog when he is still afraid of one which approaches him. He may be able to pat a dog which his parents are holding. Or better still, if he himself is safely held by his parents, he may then be less fearful.

Some have to start in even more remotely—with a toy dog, or with stories or books about dogs. Some can accept a small kitten at a time when they are still afraid of puppies.

With many, having a small dog or puppy of their own, planned for in advance, is the best way to overcome fear of dogs. However, even after the dog has been introduced to the family circle, the young child should not be forced to approach it till he is fully ready.

Even children who are not excessively afraid of dogs may quite normally show some fear of them as late as six or seven years of age. And even as late as ten some will tell you spontaneously and proudly that they are *no longer* afraid of dogs.

FEAR OF AIRPLANES

An extremely up-to-date fear, shared by many, is fear of airplanes. This is not a fear of airplane travel (which is often remarkably well accepted by young children) so much as a fear of planes flying overhead.

Some children may be so extremely frightened by planes overhead that they may need to run into the house and to be held and comforted, at first, whenever a plane goes by.

Gradually they may be able to stay in the yard, still held in someone's arms, and watch the planes go by. Eventually most will need only a hand held; and finally not even that.

As with other fears, hearing stories and reading books about the feared object, or playing with toy planes, will help bring about a comfortable familiarity. That is, you start in by protecting the child from the feared object or situation and gradually build up in him a feeling of familiarity and acceptance.

Other children of today may become frightened if a truck or sometimes even an automobile approaches them, particularly if it approaches by backing up. It is probably in these cases the large menacing object moving toward him that is so frightening. You handle this fear about in the same way as the fear of airplanes. Often the child will not be afraid of the truck or car when it is stationary and may even be willing to sit or ride in it after he has been calmed down.

FEAR OF THE WATER

The most common and earliest fear of the water comes in in relation to being bathed. This may occur at any age, but is most frequent around eighteen to twenty-four months of age. The child suddenly refuses his bath and screams every time he is approached with a washcloth.

As a rule, when this kind of objection first comes in, it works out best to respect it. The more times you force a bath on a resisting, screaming child, the stronger may become his resistance to it.

Simply discontinue the routine bathing situation to which he is objecting, for a few days. Put him on the set tub in the kitchen, or beside the bowl in the bathroom, and, until the period of resistance seems to be over, merely give him a sponge bath. Always approach with the washcloth from behind and not from the front. Reduce even this necessary sponging to a minimum.

With most, some such simple tactics are all that you will need. With extreme resisters, someone other than Mother may need to take over the bathing situation for a while. Some will accept bathing from an outsider better than from Mother. Perhaps they recognize the fact that an outsider is not quite so soft-hearted and vulnerable to their objections, or at least they haven't set up the same patterns of response as with the mother. Some will accept the idea of sharing Father's bath, especially if they are held in his lap or on his knee as they are being bathed.

Fear of the water at the beach or lake is a different problem, less difficult, in a way, because for most children it is not absolutely essential that they get into the water.

The old-fashioned notions of "throw him in and he'll get over his fear," or "shame him into it" are no longer much in vogue. As a rule we find that it works best with most to give a little encouragement—by word or by example—but for the most part to avoid any real pressure. And know that interest in swimming and a real desire to tackle and overcome any fear of the water comes in many at seven years of age.

In the meantime, let the child play on the shore till he himself feels the wish and confidence to get into the water.

This problem, if not exaggerated by adult mishandling, is in all but the most timid of children a fairly temporary one. We know of one family who even went so far as to pay for their son's swimming lessons at a local pool with the understanding that he could watch and not swim for as long as he wanted to. After seven lessons of just watching, this boy got into the pool and soon swam as well as, or better than, the other pupils.

FEAR OF FIRES

Fear of fire is a common fear with young children, particularly when there has been an unpleasant experience with fire.

This fear, like others, should be respected. But at the same time the parent may try to overcome the fear by familiarizing the child with fire under agreeable circumstances.

Watching father burn the trash, having supper cooked outdoors on a campfire, or corn popped in the fireplace, or seeing the candles lit for dinner may help such a child to feel the friendly side of fire. Later on he may, under supervision, be able to light some of these fires himself.

Visiting the fire station may help such a child to feel the protection that the fire department gives.

Hearing stories about fire or reading children's books about fire can also help. Among the good books now available are *The Big Book of Real Fire Engines,* or *Hercules* by Hardie Gramatky, and *The First Book of Firemen* by Benjamin Brewster. Or beyond the fireman stage is *Fire, Friend and Foe* by Bertha Morris Parker.

The opposite difficulty, namely too great fascination with fire and even fire-setting, may be actually handled in somewhat the same way—by familiarizing the child with fire in its more positive aspects as suggested above. (Always under proper supervision, of course. Younger fire-setters can also be helped to restraint by keeping matches under lock and key. This is not always easy, but can be done.)

Fear of Reciting *

The school life of some children is made quite miserable by the fact that they are afraid to recite. Often it is the very slender child of ectomorphic physique who is actually quite good at his studies who has this difficulty.

Sometimes it is a special inability with some one subject which seems to cause this particular fear. In this case, special help with that subject, or lessened demands (if the requirements of that particular class are beyond the child's abilities) may help. Children like this want to absorb everything they have heard before they are ready to give their knowledge out again. They are the perfectionists who cannot tolerate failure.

With some, a little respite from reciting can work wonders. It is not always necessary to force the child to "face" the feared situation. Sometimes substituting written work for reciting, for a few weeks or till the child himself reports that he is ready to recite, will do the trick.

Other children find it possible to take part in classroom plays, or to recite things which they have memorized, even when they cannot get up and speak in their own words.

Fear of the Dentist

Most children, unless their temperament is extremely sturdy and their experience fortunate, have at least some slight fear of having dental work done.

In many, this is a minor and reasonable fear (or dislike) of a potentially painful, or at least uncomfortable, experience. It presents no practical problem since the child can control his fear enough to go to the dentist and allow the necessary work to be done.

* Fear of or objection to school in general will be discussed in Chapter 15, School.

Others do express some resistance, but this resistance can usually be overcome in simple, common-sense ways. With many children it is enough if parents simply take a firm stand—the work has to be done.

With others, a little preplanning, the offer of simple but meaningful rewards, sometimes having Father (if he will) rather than Mother accompany the child to the dentist's office, will be sufficient to overcome resistance.

With still others, a preliminary (and paid for) get-acquainted visit to the dentist's office will do the trick. The child is promised that no actual dental work will be done on this occasion, but that he will have an opportunity to find out just what is going to happen.

Some children, however, in spite of any technique the parent may use, still resist violently the idea of having any dental work done. In times past, parents nevertheless insisted and dentists often used force. We have even heard of a dentist who had a policeman bring reluctant patients to his office.

Most dentists today take a very different attitude. As one young dentist commented to us: "You should never force a child, against his will, to have dental work done. Actually it should seldom be necessary if you let them see that you like them. If you don't like them, you can't expect them to like you. And it's important that they do like you—because it makes the whole experience easier for them."

However, he had found that in spite of reasonable preplanning, promise of reward and efforts on the part of the dentist (by use of novocaine and such) to make the treatment reasonably painless, some children still resisted. In these cases he believed that some postponement of treatment was usually indicated, since he had found that a child who was bitterly and obstructively resistant in October might by January be more receptive.

There are a few cases where necessary dental work simply cannot be put off and when all reasonable common-sense efforts at overcoming the child's fears and resistance do not seem to be effective. Even in such cases the majority of modern dentists do not favor the use of force. Instead, many nowadays believe that the best method is to resort to the use of extensive anesthetic. Some dentists' offices are set up for this procedure. In other cases, the child can be admitted to the hospital for overnight, and the work done there.

Only in a minority of cases would one need to go so far. But today's dentists seem mostly to agree that even this rather extreme procedure is preferable to using physical force to overcome a child's fear and resistance.

FEAR OF HOSPITALIZATION

The problem of how to prepare a child for necessary hospitalization in such a way as to avoid arousing unnecessary fears is a problem for which there is no one "correct" solution.

Children vary tremendously in the way in which they accept hospitalization—depending partly on the length of the stay, the severity of the illness, their own familiarity or unfamiliarity with hospitals. More, however, probably depends on the child's own temperament and the skill with which parents have prepared him for the experience than on these other factors.

The child's own basic temperament—the ease with which he separates from his parents and accepts new and unfamiliar surroundings and experiences—is probably the thing which makes the most difference in how he will adapt to hospitalization. This is something that you cannot do much about.

But you can, taking his temperament into consideration, do your best to prepare him as adequately as possible for the experience.

Whether you plan with the child a long time in advance or a short time, whether you plan in detail or superficially, depends on your knowledge of his personality. Some do better with a great deal of advance preparation. Others become too apprehensive and do best if things are more or less "sprung" on them.

In any advance planning, you can talk to the child about what a hospital experience is like. You can let him play doctor or nurse with the very adequate toy doctor and nurse kits now available for children. Some parents even go so far as to have the child visit the hospital in advance of the operation.

Best of all, perhaps, there are now available several books which tell of children's experiences in hospitals. Three of the best are:

>*Johnny Goes to the Hospital* by Josephine D. Sever, (Public Relations Department of the Children's Medical Center, 300 Longwood Ave., Boston 15, Mass.);
>
>*No More Tonsils* by Ellen Paullin (Island Press Co-operative); and
>
>*Linda Goes to the Hospital* by Nancy Dudley (Coward-McCann).

You will also get some very good suggestions from Dr. Lester L. Coleman's book *Freedom from Fear* (Hawthorn Books) which devotes a chapter to the child's hospital experience and what you can do to help him accept it.

Actually, in most instances it is the unfamiliar aspect of the hospital rather than any specific thing that happens there which some children find it hard to accept. Thus anything done in advance which familiarizes the child with what is going to happen to him can be helpful.

Aside from this, the main thing to keep in mind is that you should always tell your child the truth, in this as in other situations. Don't promise him that it won't hurt. It may. Don't promise him that you won't leave him. You will probably have to. Don't promise him that he will have a wonderful time. He may not.

While he is in the hospital, if you cannot visit him often, keep in touch by mail or by sending packages (if allowed), or by leaving things which he can open up at certain times.

Also plan in advance for some nice thing which will happen after he gets home from the hospital. This will give him something to look forward to.

And it will not be all up to you. Hospitals themselves are becoming increasingly aware that it is not only the child's physical welfare which is important during his hospital stay. They will therefore be more than co-operative in trying to make your child's hospital experience an agreeable one. Many hospitals are now providing a place for the parent to stay with the child, either in his room or in an adjoining room.

Fear of Medicine

More common than fear of the hospital is fear of, and refusal to take, medicine. Here again, as with other fears, parents are often faced with the problem: Shall we use force if necessary to make a child accept necessary medication?

In general, the answer is, "No." Even with extremely resistant children, the increasing availability of "tasteless" or liquid forms of medicine makes the taking of medicine fairly easy. If the necessary medicine is available only in pill form, you can crush it and suspend it in a sirup such as Cocillana.

There are, of course, many other simple ruses for getting medicine into children: hiding small pills in bread, or disguising the taste with some strong and accepted flavor.

Trial and error will show you what method will be most useful with your own child. Long bouts of bargaining and too much bribing are both to be avoided. If the child puts up too much of a fuss, it may be better for the parent to retreat temporarily and then later to try some different ruse than to force the issue through at the moment. As a rule, if very little is said about the whole thing to begin with, the child may accept the medication just as a matter of course.

9

Intelligence and Retardation

IN SPITE of all our democratic conceptions, and misconceptions, about everybody being equal, there is scarcely a home in which parents and grandparents do not take a natural interest in the "smartness" of their particular baby or preschooler.

At times this interest can and does become excessive. In moderation it is both reasonable and practical.

Common-sense ways of judging growth have in recent years been supplemented by norms and standards of development, so that we can now tell you when, *on the average,* a child can be expected to walk, talk, dress himself, stay dry at night. This information as to when, on the average, various everyday behaviors may be expected is available in many different popular books on child behavior. (In the old days of large families, people knew most of these things from their own experience.)

Here are a few clues as to the ages when we have found that some of the common behaviors occur in the early years of life. These are, however, only clues. If you are worried about your child and really feel that he needs a developmental examination, you should of course have it done by a specialist.

16 weeks: Spontaneous social smile.
Laughs aloud.
Anticipates on sight of food.
Can sit propped ten to fifteen minutes.

28 weeks: Sits briefly, leaning forward on hands.
Held standing, takes large fraction of weight and bounces actively.
Grasps objects placed before him.

Transfers objects from one hand to the other.
Many vowel sounds.
Takes solids well.
Feet to mouth when lying on back.
Pats mirror image.

40 weeks: Creeps on hands and knees; cruises along, holding onto furniture.
Pokes at small objects with extended forefinger.
May be able to vocalize "mama," "dada," and one other "word."

12 months: Can walk with one hand held.
Has two words besides mama and dada.
Co-operates a little when being dressed.
Plays peek-a-boo.

15 months: Walks a few steps alone.
Can creep upstairs.
Helps turn pages of a book. Pats pages.
Has four to six words and uses jargon.
May inhibit grasp of dish on tray.
Says "ta-ta" or equivalent.
Shows or offers toy to mother, but wants it back again.

18 months: Walks well, seldom falls.
Can walk upstairs, one hand held.
Can seat self in a small chair or climb into adult chair.
Has ten words, including names.
Looks at pictures in a book.
Feeds self in part, spilling.
Toilet may be regulated in the daytime.
Pulls a pull-toy as walks backwards.

24 months: Walks up and down stairs alone.
Turns pages of a book singly.
Speaks in three-word sentences.
Inhibits turning of spoon when feeding self.
May be dry at night if taken up.
Verbalizes toilet needs, in daytime, fairly consistently.

Refers to self by name.

36 months: Alternates feet going upstairs.
Can ride a tricycle using pedals.
Uses plurals in speech.
Feeds self with little spilling and pours from a pitcher.
Can put on own shoes.
Knows a few rhymes.

48 months: Can count, with correct pointing, three objects.
Can skip on one foot.
Can wash and dry face and hands, brush teeth.
Can draw a man with two parts—head and legs.
Dresses and undresses if supervised.
Laces shoes.
Plays co-operatively with other children.
Can go on errand outside home (without crossing streets).

60 months: Skips using feet alternately.
Can count ten objects correctly.
Can tell how many fingers on each hand.
Can name a penny, nickel, dime.
Can name colors correctly.
Dresses and undresses without assistance.
Can print a few letters (sixty to sixty-six months).

Since individual differences in the rate of growth are quite normally tremendous, even fairly marked deviations from such standards should not necessarily be a cause for alarm (or for undue rejoicing). Many perfectly normal children are late walkers or late talkers, or are late in staying dry all night, or in learning to read or write. Furthermore, the fact that any of these standards are only averages means that in the first year of life a variation even of several months from this average—at four or five years of age a variation of even a year—can be quite within normal limits.

Particularly we would like to say a word of warning about "late talkers." In this field, even more than in the field of motor behavior, individual differences are very great. Some children are already speaking in short sentences by eighteen months of age. Others are saying very little at two and a half years or even later.

If your child seems to understand clearly what is said to him, and if in his other behaviors he seems to you to be about up to other children of his age, lack of spoken language should not be of too much concern to you before three or four years of age. After that age, you will probably be wise, if talking has not come in, to check with a child specialist.

In measuring child behavior we usually think of four fields of activity. These are: motor behavior (how the child uses his body); adaptive behavior (how he solves problems); language behavior (how he understands and uses words); and personal-social behavior (how he manages the tasks of everyday living and of getting on with others).

The fact that there are four fields of behavior to be considered will suggest to you, as is the case, that the human organism does not, as a rule, develop all of a piece. Most children are not uniformly advanced (or retarded) in all these fields.

Most are good in some things, less good in others. Thus one child may be above the average in language and personal-social behavior, below average in motor and adaptive. So long as in most things he is around average or above, actually it is his pattern of strong points and weaknesses which should perhaps interest you more than just exactly where he rates on any given test.

PREDICTING THE BABY'S FUTURE

A number of recent research studies from many branches of science are showing us that there is a surprising amount of predictability in the infant's early behavior. In his behavior during his very earliest months we can see hints and traces of what he will later be. (Many parents, of course, could have told us this all along, as they say of their own children, "He was like that from the very beginning.")

The infant shows signs of what his basic physical structure is, and is going to be. He shows glimmers of personality traits which we can find in him many years later. He gives, too, a general picture of his potential for development and whether his behavior will in all probability be near the average for his age group (or above or below the average) as he matures.

In a very general way, children's behavior develops in a reasonably consistent course from infancy to adulthood. On the average, infants who are "a little slow" during the first few years are most likely to be a little slow at six and at sixteen. Those who are above average early will very likely continue to be above average.

We have, in our research in this field, even started on the next step beyond the stage of saying, "He's average now; he'll probably always be average." We know that *some* children do pick up along the way; some slow down. From the quality of early behavior we can sometimes tell which ones will do which.

Predicting the infant's later *ability* from early performance is a task for the expert. (It is a difficult one, but a helpful one, substituting knowledge for guessing in many cases—as in the case of the slow child, the handicapped child, the child who is to be adopted.) But watching the growing infant as he unfolds the signs of his *individuality* is a task for parent and expert alike. You can in many instances recognize (and then accept and respect) this individuality very early. You do this not with an eye to *changing* it, but rather that you may help your child to express his inborn potentialities to their fullest.

"But What's His I.Q.?"

Everybody has inevitably heard a great deal about the Intelligence Quotient. You know that in general it is a figure (100 for average I.Q., above 100 for above average or below 100 for below average) which is supposed to indicate the child's intellectual endowment. You get it by dividing his "intellectual age" by his "chronological age."

Actually, we shouldn't talk about *the* I.Q. because there are many tests which give a total score in I.Q. terms. But they all tend to give similar results and have in general a similar composition. Mostly they deal with words—how you define them, how you compare them, how you understand them. Problems of fact and of arithmetic are included in most tests. Wooden puzzles and other performance tests of ability are included in some. Some tests give separate scores for each special kind of ability—verbal, numerical, perceptual, etc. —and all give an over-all total score which averages the abilities of the child. This is the I.Q.

Psychologists know quite a lot about the I.Q. They've been studying it for some fifty years. They know that it remains reasonably constant over a long period of years and under varying environmental conditions. They know that it is especially useful for "sorting out" groups of children, and for gearing the tasks we set to the child's ability to respond. It is, on the average, useful in predicting. excellence of school performance.

Certainly the child with a high I.Q. has a greater chance of succeeding academically (and sometimes in other fields) than does the child with a lower I.Q. A high intelligence (including that portion of intelligence which the I.Q. tests measure) is naturally useful to any individual, not only in school but in other life situations.

Useful it is, but not always enough. As we have suggested, the child does not develop all of a piece. He may have a high I.Q. and still be very poor in social behavior, in motor skills and athletics, or in everyday practical living. He may also have a high I.Q. but be extremely immature (that is, below the average ability for his age) in regard to such basic growth items as toilet training, establishing handedness, giving up an afternoon nap.

Thus, though we should not overlook the I.Q. as an important measure of one kind of ability, we should always remember that a high I.Q. alone does not guarantee all-round excellence of performance.

If we remember this, we will not make the too common error of saying, especially about schoolwork, "He could do better if he would. We know he could because he has a high I.Q." It takes more than a high I.Q. to make a satisfactory adjustment to school.

In fact, the situation in which a 6-year-old has a high I.Q. and may read and write with some facility, but is in other ways immature or young for his age, presents one of the trickiest problems of school placement. Intellectually the child is ready for first grade— developmentally (or so far as his general behavior is concerned) he is not ready. The practical solution of this problem is always difficult and often unsatisfactory. But here as always the total child in the total situation should be the primary consideration.

MENTAL RETARDATION

Assuming that your child's intelligence is average (that is, he has an I.Q. which is around 100 or above), or, more important, that in all other major ways of behaving he is more or less up to other children of his age, this whole problem of how "smart" he is need not concern you too greatly. Probably more important for you as a parent is that you be concerned with what kinds of things he is good at, rather than that you worry unduly about just *how* good he is.

However, there are unfortunately many children who do not come up to the average, but fall below. Not just a few months below, but far below. And not just in some one or two fields of behavior but in all fields.

It is not good to be overconcerned about the baby in his first months of life. Don't worry if he is just a little slower than average in some one kind of behavior. But if he seems to you to be seriously slow in comparison with others of his own age, or with what you have come to expect of a baby his age, you will do well to consult your doctor.

If he feels that you have grounds for real concern, he will probably advise you to consult a psychologist or psychological clinic. Here you should be able to obtain a thorough developmental examination, that is, an examination which can tell you just exactly how your child is developing in all the major fields of behavior.

If it turns out that he is really seriously slow—the terms most commonly used for this are "retarded" or "defective"—then it is important that you know it. The value of having a careful examination by a qualified child specialist is that such an examination can tell you just how far behind the average expectation your child's behavior falls; can tell you which are his strong points and which are his weak ones; and can give a general prediction of about how behavior will develop in the years to come.

This specialist can help you plan for the child's future. He can help you decide the vital question of whether it will be best for the child and the family to keep him at home, in case there is serious retardation, or to plan for institutional care. He can make practical suggestions as to how to make living with such a child easier, for you and for the child, if it is decided that he should continue living at home. And always any decision is a family one. Sometimes parents aren't ready emotionally to let the child go to an institution, even though such a decision would be better for the child. It may not be acceptable to the parents until it is evident that undue demands of adjustment are put on the other siblings of a retarded child and that the retarded child could live a happier life in a place where he could more easily grow at his own level of development.

A specialist can answer the many questions which you will have in your mind: Is your child's slowness a result of something that you yourself have done or failed to do? (The chances are that it is not.) Is there something that you can do now which will increase the child's intelligence? (The chances are most often that there is not, though you may be able to help him use the intelligence he has more effectively.)

The specialist can also help you plan for schooling and can tell you what facilities are available in your neighborhood.

Besides your pediatrician and child specialist, there is another excellent source of help which you will be wise to seek if you are faced with the problem of retardation. This is a most praiseworthy organization called the National Association for Retarded Children, Inc. This organization, made up of relatives of retarded children and of others interested in the problem, has branches in most large and in many small cities. If you do not know the address of your local group, you can get it from the national headquarters, whose address currently (1955) is 129 E. 52nd Street, New York, N.Y.

These groups have frequent meetings, discuss with local speakers practical problems of caring for retarded children, and plan for better local facilities for them. It is a wonderful example of people who are most directly concerned with a problem getting together in practical organization to solve that problem. Without waiting for help from outside—or above.

Thus, though there is not too much you can do to change a retarded child into a "normal" one, there is much that you can do to help him to live as enjoyably and effectively as possible.

10

Sex Behavior and Sex Interests

How to Tell Your Child about Sex

"How shall I tell my child about sex?" parents ask time and time again. They seldom ask, "How shall I tell him about war?"—though war, to our way of thinking, is much harder to explain than sex. Nor are most parents too stumped about how to explain the nature of the universe, though that, again, seems to us a more difficult task.

So our first suggestion might be to try to think of sex as an unembarrassing, natural subject about which you are really qualified to speak. Realize that here is a field in which the chances are that you, as parent, know the answer to any question your child may ask. Which is probably not true in the fields of relativity or atomic warfare, which do not, we suspect, worry you half as much as topics of discussion.

Feel, if you can, confident and unembarrassed. Believe in yourself. Not what you say but how you say it is what will really influence your child.

Second, let the child's own questions be your guide as to what you tell. There is probably no safer rule.

If you give only what information the child asks for, and for the most part give it only when he asks, you will avoid that greatest error of all—telling too much too soon. You will also be fairly sure of a receptive audience, since the child is not likely to ask unless he wants to hear the answer. His questions can be your guide as to how much he is ready to hear.

A third suggestion is not to read too much into the child's questions. Don't let your own more detailed knowledge of the subject lead you to believe that he wants to know all the details when often a very simple answer would suffice.

Lastly, do not make the mistake of thinking that you have given this kind of information once and for all. Perhaps here more than with any other topic, the child asks and asks again. And you will need to answer over and over again, with increased elaboration and detail as he matures. It may not be so much that he forgets what you say as that, as he grows older, the same questions (and the same answers) mean different things to him.

Information which may have gone over the head of the 4-year-old may make sense to the five. So just because you have given a piece of information once, don't check it off your list. You may need to tell the same thing half a dozen times with further elaborations.

GIVING SEX INFORMATION

"Why is it dark at night?"

"What makes the train go?"

"Where do babies come from?"

All these are among the questions your 4-year-old will ask you. And in all probability his questions about sex and babies are to him little different from his questions about other things. If we, as adults, could match the child's matter-of-fact, unembarrassed attitude about sex, we would find it easier to answer his questions and would probably do a better job of it.

Typical of the average child's matter-of-factness about sex is the answer one 5-year-old girl gave to a friend who asked her, "Are you old enough to have a baby?"

"Goodness, no," replied the little girl. "I can't even tell time yet."

It is important in giving sex information to avoid bewildering the child. Often in our embarrassment we find ourselves talking around the subject and confusing more than we clear up. When the 5-year-old asks, "Where do babies come from?" what he wants to know is that they grow "in Mommy's tummy." If we use such words as "seed" and "egg," we may make him think of gardens and chickens and may merely confuse him.

"What was your mummy telling you about just now?" a little boy asked his friend.

"Oh, some wild story about the birds and bees," the friend replied.

For most children, simple, direct answers to their direct questions are most effective. But there are some parents who find it hard to give direct answers, some children who find it hard to ask direct questions. If you find it too difficult to discuss matters of sex with your child, it may be best to provide him with books on the subject. *A Baby Is Born* by Milton Levine and Jean Seligmann, *Growing Up* by Karl De Schweinitz, *Human Growth* by Lester F. Beck, and *The Stork Didn't Bring You* by Lois Pemberton are among the many good books now available. (The last two books are for somewhat older children.)

Many authorities feel that you should give this kind of information yourself personally and not leave the child to read it from a book. Better, however, for him to read it clearly from a book than to hear a confused story from an embarrassed parent.

"And what if he does not ask?" you say. The chances are that if you have answered his questions about other things adequately, and have not adopted a hush-hush attitude about sex, he will ask. But, if you feel that your child is way past the age when he should be asking, check up. You will very likely discover that he already has found out what he wants to know elsewhere, especially from his friends. Then it is wise to check up on the correctness of his information. Many children harbor misconceptions when their "sources" are not adequately informed.

If he is not already informed, tell him what you want him to know, directly if possible, through books or other people if you cannot comfortably do it yourself.

When to Tell about Babies

How best can you tell your child about babies, their source and production? Obviously, in as straightforward and unembarrassed a manner as you can muster.

What to tell him? Well, you know the facts. And the child's own questionings will give you clues as to which bits of information he needs and desires.

But when to tell him may puzzle you a bit. We have found certain usual stages in the child's interest in and understanding about babies (as reported fully in our publication A. Gesell and F. Ilg, *The Child from Five to Ten*). A brief summary of these usual stages may help you with the timing of information.

3 years: Beginning of interest in babies. Child wants family to have one. Child asks, "What can the baby do when it comes?" "Where does it come from?"

Most do not understand mother when she says the baby grows inside of her. But they can understand the idea that baby comes from the hospital. Many spontaneously believe that you purchase a baby from the store the way you buy groceries.

4 years: Asks where babies come from. May believe mother's answer that baby grows inside her "tummy," but may also cling to notion that baby is purchased. Asks how baby gets out of mother's "tummy." May think the baby is born through the navel.

5 years: Interest in babies and in having a baby of his own; may act this out in play. Re-asks "Where do babies come from?" and most accept "mother's stomach" as an answer.

6 years: Strong interest or re-interest in origin of babies, pregnancy and birth. Vague idea that babies follow marriage. Interest in how baby comes out of mother and if it hurts. Some interest in knowing how baby started. Accepts idea that baby grows in mother's stomach and started from a seed.

7 years: Intense longing for a new baby in the family. Knows that having babies can be repeated and that older women do not have them.

Interested in mother's pregnancy. Excited about baby's growth. Wants to know how it is fed, how big it is, how much it costs.

Interested in books about babies, such as *The Story of a Baby*, by Marie Ets.

Associates size of pregnant women with presence of baby.

Satisfied to know that baby came from two seeds (or eggs), one from mother and one from father.

8 years: Understands slow process of growth of baby within mother.

Wants more exact information as to where baby is in mother's abdomen. Confused by use of word *stomach.*

Some girls may ask about father's part in reproduction. They prefer to receive their information from you rather than through books. Their questions can be very searching.

9 to 10 years: The majority, though not all, do know about menstruation.

There is, in some, mild interest in the father's part in reproduction. Especially interested in the "seed-planting" aspect. Such books as *A Baby Is Born* by Milton Levine and Jean Seligmann are very satisfying to children of this age. Their thoughts are often clarified by the written word.

Your child's ability to understand about babies may be a little ahead of or a little behind this "schedule," but this will give you an idea of about the rate at which his understanding will develop.

SEX PLAY

The child's interest in sex may be embarrassing, but it usually is not particularly devastating to you so long as it remains in the realm of pure theory. His questions about babies and about the relations of the two sexes to each other may embarrass, but they usually do not really disturb you.

When his interest takes the form of actual sex activity, however, your reaction may be less calm and much more emotional. There is probably nothing which disturbs the mother of a young child more than to discover him taking part, with other children, in sex play—or to hear of his activities along this line from other, indignant, mothers.

A knowledge of the customary stages of sex play which we have found to take place in perfectly normal, well-brought-up children during the first ten years of life may help you to meet neighborhood sex-play situations calmly and without too much horrified surprise:

2½ *years:* Child shows interest in different postures of boys and girls when urinating and is interested in physical differences between the sexes.

3 *years:* Verbally expresses interest in physical differences between sexes and in different postures of urinating. Girls attempt to urinate standing up.

4 *years:* Extremely conscious of the navel. Under social stress may grasp genitals and may need to urinate.

May play the game of "show." Also verbal play about eliminating.

Calling of names related to elimination.

Interest in other people's bathrooms; may demand privacy for self, but be extremely interested in bathroom activity of others.

5 *years:* Familiar with but not too much interested in physical differences between sexes.

Less sex play and game of "show." More modest and less exposing self.

Less bathroom play and less interest in unfamiliar bathrooms.

6 *years:* Marked awareness of and interest in differences between sexes in body structure. Questioning. Mutual investigation by both sexes reveals practical answers to questions about sex differences.

Mild sex play or exhibitionism in play or in school

toilets. Game of "show." May play hospital and take rectal temperatures.

Giggling, calling names or remarks involving words dealing with elimination functions.

Some children are subjected to sex play by older children. Or girls are bothered by older men.

7 years: Less interest in sex.

Some mutual exploration, experimentation and sex play, but less than earlier.

8 years: Interest in sex rather high, though sex exploration and play is less common than at six.

Interest in peeping, smutty jokes, provocative giggling; children whisper, write or spell "elimination" or "sex" words.

9 years: May talk about sex information with friends of same sex.

Interest in details of own organs and functions; seek out pictures in books.

Sex swearing, sex poems, beginning.

10 years: Considerable interest in "smutty" jokes.

It is very important to keep in mind that usually none of the children who take part at any of these ages in recurrent neighborhood sex play are to "blame." Sex play often just naturally occurs if several children are left together unsupervised, with nothing better to do. Giving them more supervision, or providing ideas for something better to do, will often prevent such behavior, or at least keep it within certain confines.

And, as you will note from the gradient, this interest in sex play tends to go in fits and starts. Ages when such interests are intense alternate with ages when there is relatively little such interest.

Individual Differences

Not only are there ages when sex interest is strong, but there are also children who are, by nature, much more interested than others in the whole subject of sex.

There are the highly sexed children who show an early and intense interest, not only in asking about sex, but in trying things out for themselves. There are others who show a very lukewarm interest in the whole topic and ask practically no question. There is the intellectual type of child who wants much information early. There is the more practical type who asks few questions but finds out for himself.

There are some children who prefer the direct approach in all things. Such children want and need clear, direct answers to their questions about sex. Others are not able to approach anything directly. They do best with a little information given late, and may be able to accept information about the sex activities of animals better than such information about people.

There are the aware and the unaware children, the observant and the unobservant. This is not just a matter of intelligence. Some extremely intelligent children are quite unobservant about sex. Other less intelligent, or younger, children are quite alert. The two Jones boys—Eddie aged six, Peter aged four, who had a baby sister Patty —had just been told about cats and kittens. Eddie was amazed, but Pete said matter of factly, "Always that way. Same thing with people too. Don't you remember that Mummy carried Patty in her stomach before Patty was born?" Pete, by nature, not by training, was interested in and observant about matters of sex. Eddie, though older, was not.

In regard to sex interest and sex behavior, as in regard to other things, children vary. You will do well to study your own child, find out what his response to sex is, and be governed accordingly.

Try to accept all the different stages through which the child passes as he learns about sex, and as he reacts to the opposite sex, with equal calm.

INTEREST IN THE OPPOSITE SEX

This does not mean that you need welcome the occasions when your child indulges in sex play. Most of you, in our culture, will prefer that your children avoid such activity. But at least attempt to regard this behavior as calmly as you do other undesirable behavior

—swearing at four, lying and cheating at six. Make no more and no less of it than you do of other lapses from the standards you choose to set up. Try to realize that it may be better for the child to show too much than too little interest in sex. Sex play at six is at least a sign that your child is developing normal sexual interests.

Similarly, when the child reaches the age of making smutty jokes, again you have the right to discourage such activity. But you should not be unduly shocked and distressed about it. Generation after generation, it appears to come in, and subsequently in most children to drop out, as regularly as do the usual childhood diseases. Eleven and twelve seem to be a high point for smutty joking. It may seem unfortunate to you that the child's first strong interest in the opposite sex sometimes takes this seemingly unattractive turn, but there it is.

Sex play and smutty jokes may seem to you to have little relation to your daughter's first long dress and her first formal party, or to your son's demand for the family car of nights. Actually, however, all of these things are part of a general growth gradient through which most children pass. First they are interested in the facts of sex and sex differences. Later they are interested in the opposite sex. But even here, in their interest in the opposite sex, they go through alternating periods of interest and indifference or repulsion. And even these latter are a cause for worry to some parents.

Most, however, are calmer about this matter of interest in the opposite sex than they are in the matter of actual sex behavior. They view quite calmly, or even with amusement and pride, the heterosexual activities of their 3-year-olds, some of whom even in the nursery school set up strong crushes. We remember one little boy who, at the age of three and a half, grew tired of his first "girl" and got another, and then didn't dare to turn up at nursery school for fear of what the jilted damsel would think.

Through six, seven and sometimes eight years of age, twosomes continue to be frequent. And then comes a long more subterranean period. (It is not the "latent" period of which you all hear so much.) Even here, interest in the opposite sex may be strong, but it is expressed in an interesting way. Girls and boys, beginning at nine years, draw away from each other and profess to hate the opposite sex. A little boy of nine told us the other day, "Your book is all wrong. It says here that boys of nine don't like girls, but that they will like them again when they are fourteen. Well, all the boys in my class say they will *never* like girls again, and we treat them just as bad as we can just to be sure they will never like us."

This period, in its intensity, is extremely amusing to observe. Amusing because as adults who have once gone through it, we realize that if all goes well, your boy and your girl will emerge from it and many of them will go to the opposite extreme. "All she thinks about is boys," say the parents of teen-age girls. "All we talk about at the table is boys," says another parent. "Sometimes, though, we change the subject and talk about a different boy."

And here again, calmness on the part of the parents, especially on the part of fathers, is necessary. Growth does not proceed evenly, and often it does not proceed gracefully. Too much at one age, too little at another. But the knowledge that other parents are also suffering from this too-much and too-little, and a knowledge that it is the common lot of mankind to develop mature sexual abilities and interests through a long, complex and sometimes difficult series of stages may help you to accept tolerantly what goes on. Accept and perhaps even to welcome. Accept so calmly that by your very calmness you can help your child through this difficult series of stages toward a well-adjusted maturity. Such an attitude can also bring enjoyment. Bringing up children shouldn't be all work and control.

Sex Education in the Teens

And how can we best give this needed help?

To very young children we give information about sex and babies in order that our children will have a basic fund of knowledge. We are interested in giving them facts. This is not, in most cases, too difficult.

But in the teens our problem becomes harder. Here we give instruction not so much to inform as to guide.

Shailer Lawton, M.D., in a recent authoritative but rather shocking publication *The Sexual Conduct of the Teen-Ager,* reports current findings as to the too-free sex behavior of many of today's teen-agers. He lays the blame for much of the undesirable sex activity which goes on at this age to lack of knowledge and education. He quotes J. Edgar Hoover, who urges parents "to pay more attention to the sex education of their children."

We then face the question: What kind of sex information or education can we give our teen-agers which will be most effective? Here we may take a lesson from our own behavior when the child was younger. When your child was a preschooler, you did not prevent sex play and experimentation by forbidding and objecting to it. You largely prevented it by providing other, more acceptable interests.

Similarly, in the late teens you do not prevent undesirable sex activity by scolding, discipline or constant supervision. You prevent it by recognizing the realness of the sex drive in the teen-ager and by providing a child with a view of himself and his life plan and life role which is not consistent with getting early sex expression and fulfillment. If this ideal is strong enough, it may help him to be willing to wait till his education is finished and until he is in a position to set up more mature sex relations.

It is helpful to many teen-agers if you can make them appreciate that sex relations involve a problem of responsibility as much as one of morality. And that in the teens most people are not ready to take on the responsibility which such relations bring.

And, lastly, you may ask yourself as parents, what is your ultimate goal in giving sex information? Is it just to inform? Probably not. Is it merely to help your child keep out of sex difficulties as he matures? No, it is more than that. Is it not to help your child to look at sex in such a way that he himself can one day grow up to lead a happy, successful and responsible sex life? If you keep this goal in mind, it will help you to know what to say to your child and how to say it.

11

Mother-Child Relationship

THE mother-child relationship! The first, and one of the most important and exciting that the human being ever experiences! If it goes well, it may lay the groundwork for a series of other good relationships with persons throughout life. If it goes badly, it can in some cases influence adversely other later relationships.

Nearly all mothers try hard to make their relationship with their children as perfect as possible. Some try too hard. For the relationship depends not just on the mother alone but on the child as well, and often failure in this relationship is due, not to the mother's ineptness, but to the kind of child she is dealing with.

We should like to suggest some of the characteristic ways in which children of different ages tend to behave, and how this affects the mother-child relationship.

The more a mother knows about the behaviors which commonly characterize each different age level, the better job she can do in dealing with her child. If she knows that despite her best efforts all will not be smooth sailing, she can be better prepared to meet and recognize the different problems she will inevitably face as the child grows older.

The mother-child relationship cannot, no matter how skillful and gifted and kindly a mother may be, always go smoothly. But fortunately the problems she will meet are not all unpredictable. Despite individual differences, there are many similarities in the development of different children. Thus the 5-year-old tends to be loving, docile and obedient in his relations with his mother. The 5½- to 6-year-old tends to thrust out against her and to resist her strongly in his efforts to be a big boy. And the 7-year-old may feel that she is mean and cruel.

Behavior changes, even in something as complex as the mother-child relationship, tend to be patterned and somewhat predictable. How you and your child get along depends not just on how well or skillfully you treat him. It depends a good deal on the changes which occur in him, the growing organism. Understanding these changes may help keep you from being too surprised or worried when certain undesirable but normal changes in behavior take place. It can also help you not to blame yourself or the child for unattractive but apparently necessary disturbances which do occur at some ages.

You will feel differently about certain resistances to you which the child may show if you know he shares these resistances with most other children of his same age.

INFANCY

"My baby is on a self-demand schedule and I think it's a wonderful idea. The only thing is that he cries for a feeding every hour and a half and it certainly ties me down," said a young mother to a chance acquaintance.

"Well, my baby is on self-demand, too," replied the other woman, "and it certainly ruins my schedule because he seems to have worked out a thirty-six-hour instead of a twenty-four-hour day for himself. But I guess there's nothing much I can do about it. I suppose that's the whole idea of self-demand, to let the baby make his own schedule and to let his natural demands determine when he will eat and sleep."

Actually that is not the whole idea, but only half of it. The policy of bringing up the baby in response to his own natural demands and rhythms is correctly called not just "self-demand," but "self-demand and self-adjustment." And that is where the mother has her constructive part to play. It is not enough for her simply to sit by passively and give in to the child's every demand. Some babies seem easily to fit into the idea of self-adjustment as well as of self-demand. Others merely function on the demand side, with no tendency at all toward self-adjustment. A good combination of these two is what we are seeking for—that is, self-regulation, which includes both inner and outer forces.

In some cases, the baby's demands may be many more and much greater than his mother can reasonably or conveniently meet. Some babies are so excessively demanding from the beginning that it is not practical or reasonable for their mothers to give in to their every whim. Mothers of such babies need to protect themselves from the baby's too excessive demands.

Adaption on both sides is ideal, but if the baby shows no ability to modify his demands, his mother will have to step in and arbitrarily refuse some of his requests. And this is true not only in babyhood, but often in the years that follow as well.

Or the opposite may be true. Some babies are so adjustable that they don't know when they are hungry. They may not cry to be fed more than twice a day. These babies readily accept a more definite schedule. They like things to be arranged for them.

Modern mothers in their wish to follow modern methods may stick too closely to the letter of the law in trying to satisfy the baby's every need. Remember that not only the baby is to be considered, but also the mother. Some mothers grow overly anxious with a fluctuating schedule. They feel more secure in a more definite schedule. If they know, however, that the most important time to allow for flexibility is during the night and on waking in the morning, they may be able to manage more comfortably. Those on a schedule should be aware of that late afternoon hunger when the infant often cannot wait comfortably until the established 6:00 P.M. feeding. Dinner at 5:00 would be just as good as dinner at 6:00.

Eighteen Months

"He's such a big boy now. He's been walking for ages and he really can talk very plainly. I think we'll have a lot of fun together from now on," a young mother commented to one of her friends. As she spoke, her 18-month-old Jackie bumbled across the living room and managed to push an ash tray to the floor, spilling the contents.

Eventually, we are sure, Jackie and his mother will have a lot of fun together, but the time may be a little further distant than she, in her optimism, anticipates.

An 18-monther, big as he looks, mobile as he may be, is still very much of a baby so far as his relations with his mother are concerned. For the present, and for some time to come, things will still be pretty much all take and very little give so far as he is concerned.

He has words, but he will use them mostly to make known his demands, and if he does not know the actual word for things he wants, he will be quick to make his wants known by pointing and vocalizing "eh-eh!"

He does not readily take "No" for an answer, but, as any parents of 18-monthers well know, "No" is probably his most frequently used word. And if he is seriously crossed, even a relatively gentle 18-monther may amplify his "No" with a temper tantrum or a sit-down strike.

The 18-monther, as he bumbles around, almost seems to think with his feet. And he tends to grab what falls within reach of his hands.

His sense of time has expanded very little beyond "Now"—and he definitely wants what he wants "Now!" He cannot wait, though with guile you may be able to divert him to a different objective.

But the 18-monther will grow past all these trying ways before too long, and Jackie's mother will, perhaps by the time he is two, be able to realize her hope of having a lot of fun with Jackie. Eighteen months is not a fair sample of what comes after.

TWENTY-ONE MONTHS

"What shall I do?" asks Jeffrey's mother of Jeffrey's father. "He just sits there in that high chair and howls, and he won't eat a thing. He's so terribly definite about what he wants and what he doesn't want. If he could only talk!"

"Well, we can't let him starve to death," replies her husband, "and I don't suppose we can force him to swallow food, even if we could get it into his mouth. So we'll just have to keep guessing."

So they patiently guess and guess—for 21-month-old Jeffrey is their first baby and they are determined, if possible, to do right by him. Spinach—peas—carrots. Each they offer and each in turn Jeffrey rejects.

In the slight struggle which results when the carrots are being offered, and refused, a spoonful of carrots lands on Jeffrey's new bib. His mother who, even after twenty-one months of motherhood, still likes to keep everything spick and span, quickly whips off the new bib and replaces it with an old one, just back from the wash.

Jeffrey's howls quiet down to mere sobs, and the sobs are followed by a quiet sigh as Jeffrey takes up his spoon and at long last starts to eat his supper.

"It was the bib!" exclaim his parents in chorus. "He wanted his old bib!"

Now, to the casual observer, one bib might be as good as another bib, one spoon as good as another, one cereal dish as good as another. But not so to the average 21-monther!

There is probably no age at which the child's needs are more definite or at which he is more insistent on having things just exactly the way he wants them.

But since the average child of this age has only an extremely limited vocabulary, he is often quite unable to tell what it is that he wants.

Parents of the child of this age need to be patient, and they have to be good guessers. But it is hard to be a good guesser unless you know all the details of his day. To do this you need either to be with him all the time yourself or to have good baby-sitters who can report to you in detail about what has happened when you are away.

Above all, you need to realize that the 21-monther is not just being bad when he makes all this trouble. His insistent demands— for a special bib, romper, doll, food—are real needs to him. Lucky the 21-monther whose parents are willing to realize the realness of his needs!

Two Years

"Jackie, come here, dear," calls Mother; and Jackie comes pattering over to where Mother is sitting and climbs cozily up onto her knee.

Jackie—who six months earlier, when he was eighteen months of age, would at a similar command either have run in the opposite direction or have shouted "No" and stood stock still, refusing to budge.

Has a miracle taken place? Has his parents' good discipline taught Jackie that he must mind immediately when he is spoken to? Probably neither. Our own interpretation, arrived at after watching hundreds of 18-monthers turn two (we were not always right there on the spot—sometimes we watched simply through the mother's eyes), is that the average 18-monther does not obey direct commands too easily—in fact, he is inclined to be a bit mulish. The average 2-year-old, on the other hand, often finds it easy and pleasant to obey.

And so, if you have been relatively calm at your 18-monther's resistance, and, knowing what seeming miracles age can bring about, have waited more or less patiently till he might be a bit older, and abler—you will have been rewarded. You will find that much of the time your 2-year-old will mind you nicely.

Jackie has just taught his mother an important lesson, if she but looks at it that way. He has shown her that readiness for many important behaviors—coming when called, and later being able to read the printed word or to write his name or being able to admit wrongdoing when faced with the evidence—develop in the human at their own pace.

If parents can know approximately what that pace will be, they can fit their demands to the child's capabilities. And can be successful.

This does not mean that you should make no demands. It does mean that it is most effective if you can make reasonable ones. Two can "come here, dear" when Mother calls.

Two and a Half Years

"Me do it myself," clamors Two-and-a-half as his mother, in the interests of speed and efficiency and of getting through her morning chores before lunchtime, tries to dress him. But if she should give in and leave him to dress himself, the demand would change to,

"Mummy do, Mummy do." If Mummy then comes to the rescue, but Daddy is still on the scene, we will soon hear a chorus of, "Mummy go way. Daddy do it."

The 2½-year-old lives in a world of opposite extremes: "I will— I won't . . . I can—I can't . . . Yes—No." He thrives by shuttling from one extreme to the other. His choices are all multiple choices; he wants both of any possible alternatives. And if alternatives are not offered, he sets them up himself.

No matter what his mother wants him to do, he wants to do the opposite. Opposite extremes are to the 2½-year-old like magnetic poles pulling him in two directions at once so that he may, if not prevented, shuttle endlessly from one to the other. "Don't want spinach." (Mother throws it out.) . . . "Want spinach." (Mother opens a fresh can.)

It is therefore the mother's problem to keep the child, so far as possible, on a one-way street. Streamline daily routines; don't give choices; take over the direction of activities; talk glibly of the next thing (the walk you're going to take) while you steer him rapidly through this thing (putting on his outdoor clothes).

And at all costs avoid direct questions which can be answered by "No," such as, "Do you want to go for a walk or not?"

Avoid choices to which, even if he makes them, he cannot stick: "Do you want to go for a walk or play in the yard?" "Do you want a brown cookie or a white one?" Recognize his opposite extremeness and try to give his behavior the one-way direction it lacks.

All of his activities, all of his demands and commands, are carried out with an imperiousness which would befit a Roman emperor. No wonder that some mothers, in mock despair, rechristen their children at this age "King John," "Queen Mary." Thus the wise mother may, instead of worrying about keeping the upper hand and making the child "mind," give in to him on unimportant matters— "Certainly, your majesty!" A little humor on Mother's part can do a great deal toward making things go more smoothly.

And remember, mothers, that Two-and-a-half is at his best and at his worst with you. He is most loving with you but also most demanding. His most remarkable new abilities he expresses in your presence (and often cannot repeat them when you later try to get him to show off for Father or friends). But also he is most contrary and demanding when you are with him. Therefore, if you find yourself becoming too exasperated with your child, take a few hours off on occasion, and you can return to him with renewed patience and enthusiasm.

Two and a Half to Three Years

From two and a half to three years many children go through an odd period of wanting to relive their babyhood. Emotionally they may relive their whole previous lives, with help from their mother. They demand that their mothers treat them as if they were little babies. When tired, they want to be carried, rocked, even fed from a bottle. The more verbal child talks about his feelings. "I'm a little baby. I can't talk. I have no teeth and I have no hair," one little boy told his mother.

Another, a bit more accurately, reported, "I'm a little baby. I have to have a bottle. I sleep out in a carriage. But I can talk!"

The wise mother, appreciating the child's need to thus relive his babyhood before he gives it up (once and for all?) to become a big boy (or girl), helps him to do so. She does not punish him for his babyish ways, or try to shame or laugh him out of them. Nor does she blame his behavior just on jealousy of the new baby (if there is one in the family). Nor does she worry that he is "regressing to an earlier phase."

Once he has had enough of this experience of reliving his babyhood, he will be ready to go forward, more independent and more grown up; to look forward rather than backward; to think of himself in relation to the future rather than the past.

Three Years

Three is an age period when the mother-child relationship is characteristically smooth and satisfactory to both of the people chiefly concerned.

It is for many children a "we" age, and for many, mother is the especially favored companion. From two and a half to three years the average child progresses through his concentration on "I" and "me" and personal needs, and on "you" and his demands from "you" (both of which were so strong at two and a half)—and arrives at a friendly and sharing "we."

And so, not only does he give considerable pleasure to his mother as a friendly companion, but he is easier to "manage"—daily routines go more quickly and with less friction than earlier.

The 3-year-old, for example, does not get lost between opposite extremes—trying to choose both at the same time. Rather, he can make a choice. If he is hesitating about coming into the house (when you want him to do so), you can say to him, "Do you want to come in the front or the back door?"—and he can usually choose one and stick to his choice.

Furthermore, you can often bargain with a 3-year-old—if you are not above using such tactics. The younger child had such a strong sense of "now" and of wanting what he wanted when he wanted it that bargaining was apt not to work. But the 3-year-old can often be persuaded to do something distasteful "now" if "later" he can look forward to some attractive reward.

The 3-year-old, as we have told you, is increasing tremendously his ability to use language effectively and to respond to verbal approaches. He not only will respond with gratifying pleasure to being allowed to share a "secret" or a "surprise," but he can often be persuaded to do what you want him to in return for a "surprise" reward.

And the 3-year-old will, on occasion, listen well when you try to reason with him. He may even sometimes do things he does not like to do if given a good reason why he should.

All in all, he is much less demanding of the adult than was his younger self, easier to get along with and more fun to be with.

Three and a Half Years

Dinner is for the moment taking care of itself on the stove and Jennifer's mother has sat down, just for a minute, in the living room, to talk over the day's happenings with her husband.

Father has had a good day. Mother is feeling relaxed. There is a fire in the fireplace and 3½-year-old Jennifer is looking very angelic as she sits in her little chair by the fire.

Mother, with part of her mind on the dinner and part on what her husband is telling her, still spares a thought for the total scene. What a nice family! What a pleasant picture!

And then, without warning, Jennifer spoils the picture with a most unexpected outburst. "Don't you talk," she shouts bossily at her parents. "Stop talking."

Jennifer's mother doesn't know what to make of this. But since the dinner is calling her anyway, she just skips the whole problem by going kitchenward. Her husband, also surprised at his daughter's outburst, picks up his evening paper and starts to read it.

"Don't read your paper, Daddy," whines Jennifer. "Play with me."

. . . After Jennifer is safely in bed for the night—looking once more her usual angelic self—her parents discuss her recent odd behavior.

"Do you suppose she is what they call insecure?" Mother asked Father. "She seems to feel so unsure of herself lately. She asks me a dozen times a day, 'Do you love me?' and she seems to want to have everybody's complete attention right on her. If I talk to anybody else while she is around and leave her out of it, she makes a terrible fuss, just as she did tonight. Do you think we have done something wrong to make her feel so uncertain?"

Jennifer's father said he didn't know. He, too, had read a lot about "insecurity," and like many parents was often worried that he might, without knowing it, be making his child feel insecure.

What could have helped both of Jennifer's parents, and relieved them of their worry that something they had done had caused her to act the way she did, would have been a little more knowledge about child development. The knowledge that many 3½-year-old children go briefly through a stage when not only are they uncertain and badly co-ordinated in motor ways—that is, they stutter and stumble—but they are uncertain and insecure in their emotions as well. They fear that people do not love them. They demand extra attention and reassurance. They are excessively demanding of their parents' love and attention.

This is a natural stage of growth and behavior. The parents have not caused it and they do not have to cure it. Growth itself will, in the normal course of events, do that.

Four Years

"My mommy says so!" The 4-year-old, with this statement, has quoted the highest authority. He has proved his point beyond all dispute. He has said the last word.

"My mommy says I have to have four cookies!" The nursery-school child gives the teacher what he genuinely believes to be a fool-proof reason for having four cookies.

He will go even further. "My mommy says you have to do so and so," he will tell his playmates. And they may even obey—unless they are quick enough to cite their own mothers in rebuttal.

But the 4-year-old is not an entirely consistent creature. If Mother is such a tremendous authority, you would almost expect that he would on all occasions mind what she had to say to him.

But not at all! The child of any age may have his moments of resistance, but the 4-year-old's vocabulary fairly bristles with, "No, I won't!" or even with, "Try and make me!"

At some ages the child resists because he does not want to do the thing in question. Four often seems to resist simply for the sake of resisting. Mommy (or Daddy) is the authority, but he can resist (or can at least attempt to resist) Mommy or Daddy.

Four has been described as an out-of-bounds age in which the child seems to feel a real drive to go against any established bounds. And one of the boundaries which he tries hardest to go beyond is that of parental authority. He will usually succumb (and obey) in the long run, but he will often put up quite a fight first.

This kind of behavior does not apparently occur just in "bad" children who have been "badly" brought up. We have seen it crop up too often, as batch after batch of children whom we have studied have turned four. It seems almost as inevitable as growing pains. It gives way at five to behavior that is contrastingly more docile and agreeable.

Four revolts and delights in the revolution. Five obeys and enjoys his obedience. The same child but a different age!

Deal with it as you personally choose, but do not take Four's resistance too seriously.

FIVE TO SIX YEARS

Five-year-olds are characteristically, in relation to their mothers, so docile, friendly, helpful, so willing and even anxious to obey and carry out instructions, that the mother may think of herself as, briefly, in paradise—in fact, many a mother has in our presence described her 5-year-old as "just like an angel." Mother seems to be the center of the child's world when he is five, and he frequently seems to put her welfare ahead of his own.

Not so at six. The 6-year-old is once again, as when he was younger, the center of the world himself, and he wants to be first, to be loved best, to have the most of everything. Why should Mummy have more money in her pocketbook than he has in his? Why should Mummy stay up later than he does?

He not only competes with his mother, but he is extremely resistant to her commands. He defies her with, "I won't. Try and make me."

He takes things out on her—she is to blame for everything. "Finish your dinner, Joanie dear," says Mother to Joan, who sits with arms folded, staring stonily at her plate.

"I can't. I have no fork," replies Joan coldly. What else can she do, she implies, but sit there and wait till her mother brings her a fork?

Six is an emotional age, and emotions are violent and often contradictory. Perhaps they are oftenest expressed toward and against the mother. "I love you, Mummy, most of anybody in the world," says the 6-year-old, giving his mother a crushing bear hug. Mother is delighted. "He really loves me," she thinks.

"I hate you, Mummy, I wish you were dead." Mother is in despair. "What have I done that he should feel this way about me?"

Actually, neither of these expressions represents a reasoned judgment. They both mean merely that Six is an emotional little creature and that he is, in his immature fashion, taking out his emotions on the person nearest at hand, and the person who means the most to him. If things go well with him, he loves her. If they go badly with him, he blames her.

His disobedience may mean that he is tired and things are going wrong with him. Or it may mean that he is trying his wings. What more natural than that he should try them by disobeying his mother, whose word was law a few short months ago. Disobeying Mother may be the most daring and grown-up thing he can think of to do.

We see this in the child who is sent back to the dining room till he has finished his milk. Mother, in the living room, hears loud gulping sounds, then a little figure comes in with sparkling eyes and milk-rimmed mouth. "I didn't finish it!"

"What! You didn't drink your milk!!" says Mother—but, of course, he did, and both are delighted with the joke. His delight in such a pretense shows us how daring disobedience seems to him, and yet how pleased he is to do things right.

Seven Years

Seven-year-old Cynthia was feeling very sorry for herself. Nobody liked her, she insisted. The other kids didn't like her. Her teacher was mean to her. And even her mother and her father weren't treating her right. Everybody was picking on her all the time.

Cynthia's complaints may seem to you unreasonable—and they actually did not fit the facts. But they are extremely typical of the 7-year-old child. Seven is very likely to feel that he is getting the bad end of things, that everyone is mistreating him.

In fact, some children of this age become so resentful and unhappy that they may complain, "I don't even want to be a member of this family!"

The 6-year-old tends to be an aggressive little miss—or mister. If he thinks people aren't treating him right—as he frequently does—he just fights back. With words or fists, or both.

But Seven's tendency is just the opposite. Six approaches trouble aggressively. Seven withdraws, complaining.

And his parents are among those of whom he complains most. They are mean to him. It is even possible—he figures—that they don't even like him.

Most stop there. But a few vigorously imaginative ones go even further and develop what has been called the adoption fantasy. The child figures first that his parents don't treat him right. He goes from there to the conclusion that they really aren't his parents at all. And from there he goes on to the fantasy that he really comes from some rich and powerful family and that his present mother and father just "got hold of him" somehow and are now mistreating him.

Marvel at the fertility of the 7-year-old imagination! Sympathize with his discouraged mood. Don't make fun of him. But on the other hand, don't take his complaints too seriously. The mood—we can practically guarantee it—will pass.

Eight Years

"Ever since her father died six months ago, that child has simply haunted me. She just doesn't let me out of her sight for a minute except, of course, when she's at school. She won't go to the movies with anybody but me and won't even go out and play with her friends very much. She just hangs around the house and talks to me."

This was Mary's mother's complaint, and she went on to say that she was afraid that Mary was getting some sort of an attachment or fixation on her, and it seemed unhealthy. She wondered if it would not be wise to take Mary to a psychiatrist to get her over this attachment.

"How old is your Mary? About eight?" we hazarded a guess.

"Why, yes, she is, but how could you know?" replied Mary's mother, quite surprised.

We were not too much surprised at the success of our guess because it had not been at random. Mary's mother had given a brief but accurate description of what we have come to know as typical 8-year-old behavior.

A typical 8-year-old child may literally haunt his or her mother. The child's need for a real relationship at this time is deep and demanding. And it is not only the mother's actions which are important to the 8-year-old, but her very thoughts as well. The death of Mary's father may well have accentuated this behavior, but it still would have occurred in any event.

The 6-year-old wants his mother to do what he wants her to, but the 8-year-old wants her even to think in a way that pleases him. And he is so sensitive to her approval and disapproval that he is quick to notice the slightest change in her facial expression.

In fact, his wish for closeness is so great that it often leads to his being "embroiled with" his mother. It seems to many mothers that their 8-year-olds prefer even fighting with them to being left out of a relationship.

If this excessive demand for attention, affection and response from the mother should go through the years unabated, it might well be considered a danger signal. But we do not consider it a danger signal when it occurs only around eight years of age, as it appears to in many children, in the normal course of growth.

And though this excessive demand on the part of the child may be somewhat of a drain on a busy mother's time and spirit while it lasts, a mother who can and does respond to it will be amply rewarded. For this is, in many children, the first demand for a deep, close relationship with another person, and if it is fulfilled, it may well pave the way for other successful personal relationships in the future.

NINE YEARS

"Jack! You come straight home from the movies, now mind. They get out at five o'clock, remember, and I'll expect you home promptly at five-thirty. And be sure you wear your rubbers. It looks like rain. And you'd better take your cap along. I don't want you going bare-headed in the rain. And don't forget your gloves."

"Aw, Ma, fer gosh sakes, let me alone. I'll be all right. I don't mind a little rain," mutters Jack.

Even Jack's father is moved to chime in. "Dear, let the boy alone. He can look out for himself."

This scene, quite typically, takes place in many homes on a Saturday afternoon, but it perhaps takes place most often in the homes of 9-year-olds, judging from our experience. And the frank reporting of many of the mothers who come to see us has taught us that it is often preceded by another, also typical, scene:

It is almost movietime and the 9-year-old son comes out to the kitchen and comments casually—almost too casually—to his mother, "I'm going to the movies now, Ma."

"Oh, fine. Just a minute, dear, and I'll get my things on."

Her son shuffles his feet, ducks his head, looks embarrassed and mumbles, "Well, the thing is, I'm going with Bill."

"You mean you don't want your own mother to go along with you?"

This is one of the hardest lessons that many mothers have to learn. The 8-year-old child is as a rule "all mixed up with" his mother. He wants her attention and he loves her company. She is often his favored and chosen companion for the movies, for playing games, just for company. Some mothers find this a little exhausting. But at least it is flattering. It shows that your child likes you and appreciates your company.

And then, often quite suddenly, when he is nine or so, the child comes to a point where his friend is more important to him, at least as a companion, than his mother. This is actually a sign that he is developing normally—he cannot stay dependent on his mother all his life.

But it often comes as a shock to a mother who, without realizing it, has come to count on her starring role in her child's life.

Most mothers do not come right out and say, like the mother just described, "Don't you want your own mother?" What they do is say, "All right. Run along. But—wear your rubbers. Come home early." Etc., Etc.

What they are saying, though they may not realize it, is, "I may not be the most important thing to you any more, but I can still boss you around." Much of the trouble that mothers have with their 9-

year-olds comes from this giving of too many directions, this over-insistence on complete conformity.

If you are giving your 9-year-old too many orders and he is rebelling, just check to be sure whether all the commands you give are really essential—or whether you may be just trying to convince yourself, and your child, that you still have the upper hand.

TEN YEARS

"When Mummy and I are shopping, if she likes a dress and I like it, we get it. But if she likes it and really wants me to have it and I don't like it, she gets it for me. And if I like it and she doesn't, we don't get it," explains 10-year-old Betty calmly. There is no tone of complaint in her voice. That is just the way things are—"If she likes it, she gets it for me."

"Do you pick out your own movies or does your family decide?" we asked a 10-year-old boy.

"Oh, my family decides! Some movies aren't suitable, Mummy says."

"Mummy usually can argue me out of things because she argues best," reports another 10-year-old.

Others say, "I don't have a chemical set yet. Mummy thinks they are too expensive"; "I'd like to have a gear-shift bike, but Mummy doesn't want me to have one yet"; "I just started taking music lessons this year. My mother says I'm as good as I should be, but not too good. I usually do scales four or ten times, depending on what my mother tells me."

All of these comments reflect the gratifying docility of the 10-year-old which makes him, in many families, a thing of joy (more or less) in the household. He is still accepting Mummy (or Daddy) and their directives as ruling forces which he just naturally lives by. In little ways he may disobey—he does not always mind the minute he is spoken to; he may on occasion argue and tease. But basically he accepts, and cheerfully, the idea that mother's commands are reasonable and are to be obeyed.

Ten marks a happy period in the mother-child relation, somewhat reminiscent of Five. The child obeys his mother cheerfully and seemingly with the feeling that it is right and reasonable for him to do so. Ten is docile, and it might seem at first glance desirable that he should remain so. But it would not really be desirable. We would not really want our adolescents to be guided entirely by their mothers' decisions.

The adolescent, if he is to grow up into a mature capable adult, must learn to think for himself; must grow beyond the places where he is completely guided by what "Mummy says."

12

Father-Child Relationship

Nowadays fathers are coming into their own. They are not only being discovered by science, but they are also discovering themselves. Many are still a bit bewildered by their new role, especially because it is so different from the old role of authoritarianism.

The last few decades have indeed been a period of "bringing up Father," or, better yet, "Father bringing himself up." At times he has been so helpful that he has been exploited. Too often he has been thrust into the middle of household turmoil, making things worse instead of better. Too often he has been expected to play the role of second mother instead of his own special role.

Furthermore, in recent years many households have disregarded father's personal needs in order to make him a better father. Might it not be preferable, for instance, for him to have a little relaxation at the end of a busy day at work, a time to read his paper and to relax a little before he joins the family group and meets its demands upon him?

We've already described for you the changing mother-child relationship. In this chapter we'll tell you a little bit about what happens to Father from year to year as his child grows up.

Of course, what happens depends a great deal on the child. But it also depends on the father. Fathers differ, we find, as do mothers and children.

Some, from the moment the new baby arrives, seem almost as adapted to the demands of baby and child rearing as the mothers. We have seen new fathers of today (unlike the authoritarian Life-with-Father fathers of an earlier generation) who are almost as handy with a bottle or diaper pin or burp cloth as are mothers. We congratulate the families of such fathers.

Others, equally enthusiastic about the whole thing, just don't have the knack of handling young babies. Or as Gail Little comments in her extremely amusing book *Design for Motherhood* (The Ronald Press):

> Father is supposed to be a Vital Factor in the baby's development. Mothers read this. Fathers do not. There seems to be no effective way of impressing on the male parent his important status. His enthusiasm for his infant offspring is overpowering. For himself as a Vital Factor, nil. . . . He is proud as punch of the baby and loves to misquote vital statistics on weight gained, nourishment consumed, and sleep slept; but after a few days he is perfectly frank to say that he doesn't specially want to hold it. He will remark dubiously, when graciously offered the privilege, that he doesn't seem to have much luck with the bottle, and shortly comes right out flatfooted with his loathing for a messy diaper.

So fathers vary, just as do children, in their personalities. And the father-child relationship varies from age to age.

EARLY YEARS

Most new fathers take to fatherhood, we find, about as easily as new mothers take to motherhood. But, as we have suggested, each in his own way and according to the dictates of his own personality.

Each, we would say, to his own type of participation in the family scene. Some fathers, for instance, take very naturally to the currently popular participation in natural childbirth (Father is right on the scene) and enjoy the classes for father preparation which precede it. The interest of others does not become really wholehearted until the baby is an accomplished fact and safely home from the hospital. (And others become enthusiastic at varying ages much, much later.)

In our opinion, it is a mistake (and not very effective anyway) to try to fit all fathers into one mold.

Our purpose here is certainly not to mold, but merely to mention one of the minor hazards of the early father-child relationship. A hazard which less often occurs between mother and child.

This is the fact that babies and preschoolers often go through periods when they are "strange" or unfriendly to people who are ordinarily their friends and in good favor.

Often around 20 weeks of age, again around 32 weeks, and once again around 44 weeks of age, many babies go through periods of not responding to the approaches of father or of former friends. They may even cry when father comes near. (Mother is too familiar a figure to elicit such a response, but nearly anyone else may.) It is important not to take such a rebuff personally.

Again, at two and a half, we run into somewhat the same kind of thing. Father, home from work, generously offers to take over the feeding or the putting to bed routine. Son or daughter will have none of this. Tears and demands of "Mummy do" meet his offer.

This can be very disconcerting to Father. But, again, it is important for him (whether he insists on rendering these services or gives in to the demand of "Mummy do") to remember that this does not represent a real breakdown in the father-child relation. It is just the way of the 2½-year-old. He treats Mummy and any other member of the family the same way. Whichever one it is who tries to "do" for him, it is somebody else he wants.

A third hazard of this same type is the middle-of-the-night demand for Mother which many preschoolers—no matter how much they may like Daddy in the daytime—are likely to make. For many, in the middle of the night, nobody will do but Mummy.

Fathers should not—though many are—be surprised or deflated by these temporary "rejections."

FATHER VERSUS MOTHER

But once the hazards of these earliest years are over, the father-child relationship may settle down pretty well. As a rule this relationship seems to be less variable, and less vulnerable to the passing whims of the child's own age changes than does the relationship with Mother.

It is true that the preschooler tends to worship Father as he does

Mother. Later, from six to ten, he tries himself out against Father in little ways, though he still thinks Father is pretty wonderful. From eleven to sixteen he tries himself out in bigger ways and sometimes doesn't think Father is as wonderful as he used to be.

But the little year-to-year variations do not seem to affect the child's behavior toward his father as much as they do his behavior toward his mother. (Unless, of course, by some trick of fate the father has had to assume a mother's role and is the one to supervise the daily routines and chores.)

This is perhaps because the mother-child relationship seems to be more sensitive, delicate, intense, but more easily upset than the relationship with the father. Three-and-a-half whines most with Mother. Four boasts and defies Mother more. Five clings hardest to Mother. Six battles against her authority more vigorously. Mother attracts the child's best behavior too, but she certainly does attract his worst.

His feelings about Father are not as intense, not as mixed up, not as variable. Father tends to represent stability, firmness. He is the one to whom Mother reports extra-bad behavior. He is the court of last appeal. He is the person who gives out important rewards as well as important punishments. He is the prized companion on those welcome occasions when he can spend time alone with son or daughter.

Thus fathers should not under ordinary circumstances expect to attract from their children the same kinds of responses which mothers attract. Father's role in bringing up the children is perhaps, as in their production, an essential but a supplementary one.

Above all, it should ideally be Father's role, as disciplinarian, to back up Mother's policies. If he disagrees with her methods of handling the children, he should *always* express that disagreement in private—not where the children can hear or observe.

We don't mean that Mother will always be right and that Father should just agreeably go along with her decisions. We mean simply that if there are differences of opinion about child raising and disciplining, they should not be discussed in front of the children. Even a very young child can learn to play one parent against the other if he senses disagreement. In such instances, discipline really flies out of the window.

Of course each family differs in its own way—in some, parents agree completely, in others it is Mother who is firm and Father who is soft-hearted. The most common situation, however, appears to be that in which Mother pleads for tolerance—"He's just a baby," "It's just a stage he's going through." Father is most commonly the firm one: "You and your stages! He's just got to learn to mind. It's time that he found out that he can't get away with that sort of thing!"

Now Father may be quite right. Especially if when he says, "It's time that," he is sure that he knows that children of his child's age and temperament quite normally are able to do the good thing (or to refrain from doing the bad thing) in question. Most often, however, he simply means that he's tired of waiting for the good behavior to appear. Yet, alas, his child's inability, or inadequacy, or naughtiness, may be quite "normal" and reasonable for that child at that time.

Mother's "just a stage" is not as a rule simply spinelessness on Mother's part or a weak giving in to the child. It most often represents an objective realization that this child at this time can't seem to do any better and that this stage, like others which have preceded it, will probably be short-lived. Mother's hopes and wishes as to the way her child should act have been, more often than not, cut down to size by the actual daily living reality of the child himself. Father, being away from home more, clings to his illusions.

However, all of this doesn't mean that Father should be afraid of clamping down when necessary. Mother's gentleness and understanding, Father's firmness but also, we hope, understanding, are both essential ingredients for a stable family life.

THREE TO FIVE YEARS

We've discussed briefly some of the high (and low) points in the father-child relationship in the very early years. Here are a few of the changes which will take place between the ages of three and five.

Three is an easy age for most children in all respects, the father-child relationship included. The 3-year-old is less rigid and demanding than he was at two and a half and now, though Mother tends to be the favored parent, Father can often take over in many situations. In fact, he can often take over most effectively. If snags have crept into the going to bed, or other routines, things often go much more smoothly for Father than for Mother.

At three and a half in many, there is a change from favoring Mother to showing a great favoritism for Father. Girls may even go so far as to propose to their fathers, who may at this time be their idea of utter perfection.

And at four—that exuberant, out-of-bounds, rebellious age—many "No I won'ts" can be turned to relatively docile obedience by a word from Father. Not only is he respected in the home, but he is often quoted outside. "My father" is for many the ultimate authority. And even the boldest, most bossy and boastful 4-year-old can be quite a gentle creature when Father turns an eye on him.

Excursions and times alone with Father are greatly prized, and his word is often law even when Mother's has temporarily ceased to be. Name-calling 4-year-olds seldom call their fathers names, no matter what they may call their mothers.

Five is, as a rule, fond and proud of his father and may obey him more promptly than he does Mother. But most Fives are at heart mothers' boys (or girls), so that though relationships with Father are usually smooth, pleasant and undisturbed, Five is usually more casual with Father than with Mother. It is Mother, not Father, who is the center of the 5-year-old's world.

FATHER-CHILD AT SIX YEARS

"Sometimes I think I'm the cause of all his difficulties," mothers of 6-year-olds often admit to us. "He's certainly at his worst with me."

They are, unfortunately—at least more often than not—correct. For the 6-year-old (who was so much of a mother's boy at five) is now fighting to be free of his mother. Mother is the center of the world for many 5-year-olds. Most children are—or would like to be

—the center of their own world at six. The shift is not always accomplished without bloodshed.

So the 6-year-old is traditionally defiant and violent. He defies his mother. He will not mind. He shouts, "I hate you, Mummy!"

And what is father's role here?

Most commonly, we're afraid, he steps into the fray and makes things worse, either by (1) bringing vigorous physical punishment to bear on the erring 6-year-old, or (2) explaining to Mother what a poor disciplinarian she is to have allowed things to come to such a pass.

Other fathers, happily, follow a more constructive program. We would like to recommend their policy to all.

Two general, very simple principles are involved. The first is that at those ages when the child is at his very worst with his mother, he is, fortunately, often at his best with his father.

This means, in actual practice, that the worst trouble areas in a 6-year-old's day—dressing, eating, going to bed—can often be gotten through with relative speed and a minimum of confusion by a patient and even moderately inventive father. A visit to the doctor's or dentist's office is far more successful with Father than with Mother. Needles will be accepted with less emotion. Teeth can be filled without too much fuss or fear of pain.

This is partly because the child of this age doesn't seem to be having such a struggle for power with his father as he does with his mother. It's partly because most Sixes have more respect for Father's authority than for Mother's, and don't dare to be as bad with him as they are with her. In fact, Six organizes under the firmer rein of the father. Fathers may well realize this and profit by it.

So any father of a 6-year-old who will, even on occasion, be willing to take over some of the child's routines, just temporarily, can contribute a very great deal to the harmony of his household.

The second general principle which the father of any 6-year-old might usefully keep in mind is this: It is far more effective to step in and prevent trouble before it occurs than to try to pick up the pieces afterward.

Don't wait till mother and child are completely embroiled to lend a hand. Step in before that tantrum occurs! It will save wear and tear on everybody.

SEVEN TO TEN YEARS

There is in most families great need for father to step in and stabilize things when the child is six. When he is seven, this need becomes much less intense. Worrying Seven may be quite unhappy within himself—you would be too if you figured as he often does that everybody hates you! But he isn't as a rule too hard to manage. Mother can usually provide what discipline is needed. Seven, with his tendency (stronger at eight) to go to extremes, may now "worship" his father, but for many children the father-child relationship is not intense at seven.

At eight, the intense demanding emotional relationship of the child with his mother often quite overshadows any other personal relationship. Father may feel a trifle left out at this point, but he is actually fortunate. Eight may love him less intensively, but is also usually less demanding of him. Father can make a mistake and get away with it. But not Mother. She has to do and say and even think just the way that her 8-year-old son or daughter wants her to. And trouble comes when Eight is too aware of the mother-father relationship. Some parents of 8-year-olds have to be careful of exposing either their affection for each other or their disagreements before a jealous son or daughter.

On the whole, however, Father can go his own way. And what is more, Eight—increasingly bold with Mother—usually will mind, and quickly, when Father speaks. Father's role at this point, as so often, is in many ways easier than Mother's.

At nine, many children are less interested in and less demanding of either Mother or Father than they were earlier. Friends are the big thing and what Bill or even Bill's mother or father says may be much more important than anything said at home.

However, many boys do at this time come into a new relationship with their fathers. Children are now quite old enough to be interesting to those fathers who may not have enjoyed them too much earlier. And they are old enough, themselves, to respect Father's technical knowledge and abilities. Children now share real interests with their fathers; and boys and their fathers may group together against feminine interference.

The relationship may be largely in the things they *do* together—but many boys are extremely sensitive to any criticism from Father and think highly of his good regard. Some, especially at this age, may feel great superiority and pride in relation to Father's occupation.

Ten is one of the happiest ages from the point of view of the father-child relationship. You don't even have to be an exceptionally superior or expert father for things to succeed now.

For at this age most boys and girls just naturally think that their fathers are wonderful. Mothers tell us, "He thinks his father is the end answer to everything"; "He idolizes his father"; "Thinks his daddy is wonderful"; or, "To her he is the shining light."

Ten-year-olds themselves make approximately the same report: "I think he's just about right," they tell us. Or, "I think he's just about the best father in the whole world." Or, "He's just right. He's strict, of course, but he has to be. You can't be too patient with your children."

We suggest that you make the most of this golden age. In the years that follow you may not feel that you are changing very much. But unless yours is the very exceptional child, his whole-hearted approbation and adoration will very probably diminish. Because, as we have commented before and as most of you realize, one of the biggest tasks of adolescence is getting free of the parent. And to do this, most children seem to have to go through at least a stage of running you down.

Most 10-year-olds, however, still in the admiring stage, love to spend time alone with their father. It doesn't matter too much what you do, so long as you are together. Ball games, movies, walks, playing games, reading, wrestling—Ten is ready for most anything.

"Companionable" is the word which mothers often use in describing the father-child relationship. And children themselves use this same word about their father—"He's very companionable; we get on very nicely."

So even though, like many fathers, you're pretty busy and don't have much spare time—we still suggest that it is a good idea to enjoy your 10-year-old's company and to let him enjoy yours. Don't make the mistake of waiting until he is a little older (and more interesting, you may think). By the time you get around to it, if you do wait, you may find that now he himself does not have time for you.

13

Brothers and Sisters

FIGHTING—THEY TAKE IT FOR GRANTED

"IT's nice I was born without any brothers and sisters, isn't it?" a 6-year-old friend of ours commented to her grandmother.

"Why is that, dear?" asked her grandmother. "Don't you think it would be nice to have brothers and sisters?"

"Well, it might be nice, but you see I would probably be fighting all the time," was the reply.

And she probably would be at that. Let's look in on almost any home scene.

"Mummy, he keeps poking me!" whines 7-year-old Betsy.

"Well, she tried to trip me up," counters her 9-year-old brother Joe.

Crash! goes the living-room lamp as Betsy tries again, and this time cleverly succeeds in tripping up her brother, who is too big for her to tackle head on.

"Can't you make those children behave for a minute?" thunders the children's father, who barely escaped the falling lamp.

And so the whole family is involved. What started out as a teasing poke is now ruining the dispositions of four people.

And tomorrow will bring another poke and more chaos. Because Joe, like a great many other children, just can't seem to keep his hands to himself when his sister is near by. He cannot and does not resist the temptation to take sly little digs and pokes at her. And she, though not his equal in size and strength, has her own ways of getting back at him.

Each child seems to know just what things will bother the other most, and to delight in doing just those things.

Betsy is old enough to know that Joe treasures his collections and the things in his room more than anything else in the world. And she seems to delight in interfering with or even harming his most prized possessions. "Mama, make Betsy stay out of my things," Joe yells a dozen times a day.

Joe, on the other hand, knows how Betsy hates any one to take her "place"—her place at the table, her place in the car, her place in front of the radio. And he delights in teasing her and in pretending that he is going to take that place.

What can you do about all this?

Perhaps most important is to give up any Utopian ideal that you may have of a houseful of children all getting along nicely with each other without fighting. "They think we should get on better together than we do," is the report of almost every child we interview. If you can cut down your expectations to meet reality, you will worry less about your children's quarrels.

It may be a comfort—even though a cold comfort—to know that if your 6- or 7- or 8- or even 10-year-old seems constantly to be bickering with brothers and sisters and not to be improving as you had assumed he must, he is not out of the ordinary.

The thing that will interest most of you as parents, however, is probably not so much whether or not this is the case, as what you can do about it. We suspect and fear that there is less you can do about it than you would hope. Trying to get a rise out of siblings, teasing them, bickering with them, squabbling and wrestling with them, are probably some of the many things that increased age alone finally cures for sure.

Furthermore, each family situation differs in so many ways from every other that it is most difficult to give any general advice. (Nor is the literature on child behavior too helpful in this respect. We recommend *Brothers and Sisters* by Edith Neisser [Harper & Brothers] as one of the most useful books we know of on the subject. An excellent pamphlet on the subject is *Getting Along with Brothers and Sisters,* Science Research Associates, Wabash Avenue, Chicago, Illinois.)

We can, however, make a few general suggestions. The best way we know of to keep brothers and sisters from quarreling is to keep them apart as much as is necessary. Find out the customary limits of their ability to be together peacefully, and then try to separate them before those limits are reached.

In fact, the best time to step in in your children's quarrels is before they happen. Plan in advance that they will not be together unsupervised at their most tired times. This may take a lot of planning, but it will be worth it. Plan for Father to be with them—if he will. Plan for them to be engaged in separate activities. Plan if necessary for one or the other to be out of the house. Even plan for separate mealtimes if need be. In extreme cases some parents we know of have even resorted to having one child spend a season in the home of some willing relative.

Time and space can both be manipulated in this way. Have them do things at different times; or, if you possibly can, arrange that each has some space of his own which the others cannot invade.

Try to help each one build up interests of his own—even nursery school for the very young will help. With older children friends, clubs, any sort of outside activities, will refocus their interest and make teasing their siblings a less important and vital activity.

If one child is consistently and unreasonably bothering another, you can take steps to prevent it, as when a younger child consistently disturbs an older one's "things." Such steps should involve some practical long-range planning and should not be taken merely as each incident occurs.

With a few, if things are excessively bad without intermission, you can arrange that they plan with some outside person (other than Mother or Father), *as a surprise to Mother,* that they will try to do better. This person may help them draw up certain rules, for instance. This will not work like magic, but it may help, at least temporarily.

Most of all, though, separate them as much as possible. Recognize the normality of a great deal of bickering. And be willing to wait till they outgrow this long, long stage when fighting is a favorite activity.

STAYING OUT OF THE CHILDREN'S QUARRELS

"How does Mike get on nowadays with his sister?" we asked Mike's mother, who had brought her son to the Institute for a general check-up.

"Get on? Well, I don't think you could call it getting on," she replied. "The truth is that they fight all the time. I used to try to stop it, but I don't any more. It would be like cutting off their breathing if I stopped their fighting."

"Though, to tell you the truth," she went on, "I do think the time may come when they may get along better. Already, now that Mike is ten, they fight more with words and less with their fists. I look forward to the day when they may not have to fight at all."

Mike's mother is a very wise woman. She recognizes the value, and even the necessity, for her own peace of mind, of letting the children, at least to some extent, work things out for themselves (providing they are not too unevenly matched). When children realize that they are going to have to solve their own problems, they often drop the attention-getting mechanism of running to their parents with constant complaints about their brothers and sisters. Children are often capable of making extremely practical solutions when thus left to their own devices.

Also, instead of throwing up her hands and deciding that the whole situation is hopeless, Mike's mother observes objectively that the type of fighting is changing and decreasing with age, and she looks forward to its further quieting down. She believes that the time will come, even though it may still be some years away, when her children will get along better with each other than they do now. We can make the statement—based not on wishful thinking or sheer optimism—but on comments of our teen-agers themselves, that brothers and sisters do get on better as they get older.

FAIRNESS

"I have a problem which I wish you could help me with" [a young mother wrote to us recently]. "I have a boy and a girl. The boy is just seven and the girl five and a half. They continually argue. It gets on my nerves so that I put them to bed at night right after supper so that I can get some quiet in the house.

"They never seem to be satisfied with anything I buy for them or give to them. If I give them each a piece of jam and bread one will complain that I gave the other a bigger piece or that I put more jam on one than the other. They will argue until they come to blows. Then the girl being the smallest always gets the worst of it. If I break it up, the boy says I am always sticking up for the girl.

"I have tried very hard to be fair and give them both equal as much as I can, but nothing seems to solve it. I have tried to explain to them that both can't have exactly the same, but they either don't understand or don't want to understand. I don't know what to do. Can you help me?"

There is a trying, but oh so common problem! Certain children at certain ages would try the patience and ingenuity of Solomon with their constant demand that everything be exactly even, exactly "fair."

There are several possible methods of coping with such a situation. One is to ignore their demands for fairness, and just go about things in your own preferred manner. Make your own decisions uninfluenced by their demands for perfect fairness.

A second, and by far the most usual method, is the following: that is, do your very best to see that things are fair and equal, while at the same time explaining to the child that life is not always fair and that things cannot always be equal.

A third method is to go out of your way to see that everything is scrupulously and utterly fair. Be humorous about it, to show them how silly you think they are, but see to it that everything is divided perfectly evenly. Measure the pieces of cake with a ruler—weigh out the jam. Go to extremes. Most children get very tired of this before long, and they may see the humor of it.

A fourth method is the following. Allow one of any two children to divide whatever object or objects are under dispute (assuming that they can be divided). Then allow the *other one* to have first choice. Mothers tell us that it works like a charm.

GETTING EVEN

Thirteen-year-old Marcia is practicing her piano lesson. She is a conscientious girl and also definitely talented as far as music goes. The pleasant sounds of her practicing fill the house. Her mother, getting dinner in the kitchen, smiles to herself. It is really a pleaşure to hear the child play.

Suddenly comes a loud, blatant tootling, interrupting the smooth flow of the music. Marcia's younger brother, Nicky, has gotten out his trumpet and is making a really terrible racket. Marcia in tears comes running to her mother to make him stop.

After peace has been restored and Marcia has gotten on with her practicing, Nicky's mother asks him, "Nicky, why do you do such mean things? Why do you bother your sister like that when she is practicing?"

"Because," replies Nicky, "she's so bossy. She always tries to raise me and make me do everything better, and this is the best way I know of to get even with her."

Getting even with her (or him)! How many hours of childhood are spent in getting even with brothers and sisters! It may not be very nice, but it certainly is very natural.

Some of our nicest children not only do it, but shamelessly admit to doing it. Ten-year-old Jarvis tells us, "My sister's so funny. She's so afraid she's going to get poisoned. (A common fear at 7 years.) If she is eating one of the best things and you say it might be poison, she won't eat it. Like I might say, 'These cherries taste funny,' and she would think they were poison and she wouldn't eat them for a million dollars. That's one of my best ways of getting back at her."

And 11-year-old Teena says, "Well, what I do with my brother and sister, I try to get every bit of evidence I can against them so that when they do anything mean to me, I can get even with them and end up by being the right person." That is, the situations may not even have arisen yet, but she plans to be ready if they do.

What you as a parent decide to do about getting even is up to you, but we suspect, if you have more than one child in the family, that it is a phenomenon with which you are quite familiar.

Getting even is certainly an immature way of dealing with a situation in which another person offends or harms us. Gradually, as your child matures, you will find that you are able to help him find more effective ways of dealing with situations in which his brothers or sisters do things to him which he doesn't like. But it will take a certain degree of maturity on his part and skill on yours.

DIFFERENT KINDS OF BROTHER-SISTER RELATIONSHIPS

Personalities differ, and some personality types clash, on sight and forever after. Unfortunately brothers and sisters often are of clashing rather than matching personalities. Clashing personalities can, of course, learn to modify their behavior, but some are never, even after they are grown up, really sympathetic to each other or happy to be together.

We should recognize this, and though a certain amount of getting along is necessary if a family is to live together, we should, regretfully, recognize and respect the situation if it turns out that we have in the family two children who are just too different (or sometimes too much alike) to get along well.

Besides the children who like each other very much, and the ones who dislike each other very much, there is a third type of brother-sister relationship, and it is perhaps the saddest one there is. This is the situation where one child, usually the younger, just adores the other—but where this liking is not returned. "Ben just worships the ground Peter walks on," says their mother, "but Peter has absolutely no patience with Ben."

Peter himself confirms this one-sided state of affairs. "My main problem," he tells us, "is my little brother. He's a pest! I get so mad at him. Sometimes I beat him up. In fact, very often. Then he cries and tells my parents."

Each family, when personalities conflict, will solve the problems which arise in its own way. The important thing for all parents to remember is that, even with the most skillful handling on your part, some brothers and sisters will not get much fun out of each other's company; and that, regardless of how they are "brought up," others will, from the beginning, enjoy each other immensely.

AGE CHANGES IN BROTHER-SISTER RELATIONSHIPS

Each family of course differs in the way brothers and sisters get on with each other. But in our experience, it is generally not till the mid-teens that the relationships are as harmonious as most parents would like to see them. So most of you have to wait a lot longer than you would like to before things go entirely smoothly between your children.

However, even within the first ten years there are small variations from year to year. We'll tell you about them very briefly. This information may help you to keep down your expectations, which in the case of most parents are much too high.

18 months: Any adapting will have to be done by other members of the family.

2 years: The child now gets on better with siblings but is not too much interested in them. For the most part he takes them for granted. He allows older brothers and sisters to play with him and may give and accept affectionate advances.

2½ years: The child of this age has difficulty with siblings as with everybody else. He cannot share, wait his turn, or do things anybody else's "way." He is overrigid in his demands and has tantrums if anything goes wrong. May be extremely jealous and demanding.

3 years: Relations are better at this age, though not consistently so, since the 3-year-old may tease older siblings, break and spoil their things, then cry if they retaliate. Attitude and behavior toward younger children is variable.

4 years: Things are not very good now since the boy or girl of four is out of bounds in relation to siblings as to everyone else. He can be a real nuisance to older siblings and is selfish, rough and impatient with those younger. There is a great deal of quarreling and even physical fighting.

5 years: Five is a gentler age. Children of this age are usually protective and kind and even responsible toward younger brothers and sisters, particularly if someone else is present. They often play well with older ones, and will even willingly accept the "baby" role in domestic play.

6 years: Things usually take a turn for the worse in sibling relationships as in other things. Children not only "boss," hurt and fight with younger siblings, but tattle on them, "egg them on," insist that they are cheating, seem to like to see them punished or scolded. They quarrel a good deal with older siblings, get into their things, pester them, refuse to mind them.

7 years: Again a quieter age brings slightly improved sibling relationships. The 7-year-old may like to play a big-brother role to the younger children in the family. However, he "bickers with his sister though he thinks she's cute," or "protects his sister but teases her." Considerable jealousy and feeling that brothers and sisters are given more privileges than he is.

8 years: Many 8-year-olds are consistently bad with siblings— they tease and are selfish and quarrelsome about possessions and privileges. Others are variable— good part of the time, very bad at other times.

9 years: Again some improvement. Nines may be at times thoughtful and protective of younger siblings, proud and imitative of older ones. However, will resent efforts of older ones to "boss" them and are embarrassed in front of contemporaries by actions of younger ones.

10 years: The majority fight with siblings at least part of the time. This involves name calling and some real physical fighting. Mostly younger child pesters 10-year-old; Ten retaliates; younger calls for help. Get on best with siblings under five and with those older than themselves, but know that older ones may consider them a nuisance or a tattletale.

THE NEW BABY

It's an exciting time for your family! You're home from the hospital with your second baby—a happy, healthy baby who looks "just like his father" and is, to everyone's satisfaction, of the opposite sex from the child who is waiting for him at home.

And there, alas, lies the snag in the whole thing. That preschool brother or sister, waiting at home for you and the baby!

For in spite of all the careful build-up you may have given him, the chances are better than even that he will, sooner or later, both feel and express jealousy of the new member of the family.

He may show this jealousy directly or indirectly. He may merely say, "Naughty baby!" or, "Don't want baby." He may attack him physically. He may, on the other hand, express too much concern and affection for the baby. Thus he may warn you, over and over, "Don't drop him," "Don't stick the pin into him," "Carefoo, carefoo!"

Or he may express his jealousy and anxiety and unhappiness at this addition to the family even more indirectly by not sleeping, not eating, or by lapsing in his control of toilet functions. Or by always getting into trouble at the time when his mother is tending the baby.

Any or all of these signs of jealousy may come early or late. Some parents are extremely pleased if the first few months go by without there being any overt signs of jealousy. Others prefer to have the almost inevitable jealousy which will occur expressed early and plainly.

Some jealousy does seem to be felt by the majority (not all) when a new member is added to the family. If it is felt and expressed early, most parents are somewhat on their guard against it and more or less prepared to be tolerant and helpful about it. If it is not expressed early, parents lower their guard, more or less forget about it, and are apt to be both distressed and unsympathetic when it turns up later, when the 9-month-old infant is creeping and "talking" and showing off with bye-bye and pat-a-cake.

Then parents and friends tend to make even more of a fuss over him than earlier. Then the poor left-out preschooler's nose is really out of joint. He himself is all too likely to be around two and a half, that demanding age, or, even worse, around three and a half, that whiny, uncertain, insecure age. Nobody is cooing over him or praising him. Quite the contrary! And the contrast may be much too much to bear. Parents can be much less than sympathetic when a "big bad" 2½- or 3-year-old is careless, rough or even worse with the "poor little baby."

WHAT TO DO BEFOREHAND

What to do beforehand to prevent jealousy of the new baby?

Your own common sense and your knowledge of your child's personality will provide the best answers. If you want some word of "authority," almost any current book on child behavior will have at least a chapter on this subject. We can recommend, for example, the suggestions given in Edith Neisser's *Brothers and Sisters* (Harper & Brothers).

The two main principles which both your common sense and the child-behavior literature emphasize are preparing him beforehand and not making too much fuss about the baby—to the exclusion of your preschooler—afterward.

Preparation beforehand is certainly important, but it can sometimes be overdone. A preschooler has a very limited notion of time. Something that is going to happen in six months' time is too much for him to keep in mind. A month's warning, two at the most, should suffice. The amount of pre-preparation should vary, too, depending on whether yours is a child who likes to look forward to things or one who gets too excited if told about things beforehand.

It is important, also, to present the new arrival to the preschooler from his, not from our own, point of view. Much as the new baby may mean to us, it is in all probability not going to be too much fun for him. So be moderate in your descriptions of how wonderful the whole experience is going to be.

Helping to get things ready for the new baby is usually enjoyed by the preschooler. Particularly if any shopping trip includes some purchases for him. (Whether he goes along on the trip himself, or more likely you just show him what you have bought.)

Showing him a picture book about babies, or taking him visiting to a house where there is a baby can help to prevent fantasies in which the new arrival will be someone more or less his own age and size—a practical playmate.

Any tendency to set his heart too definitely on a brother or sister should be avoided, if possible, by pointing out the unpredictability of sex and the advantages in either case.

Even before the baby's arrival, parents should make every effort to see that the older child's life is not too much upset in any way which he will connect directly with his mother's pregnancy or the coming of the new baby. If the mother's time is more limited than usual or her temper shorter, she should make every effort for someone else, someone with whom the preschooler is fully familiar, to spend time with him.

WHILE MOTHER IS IN THE HOSPITAL

Of great importance in determining the child's adjustment to the new baby is the week or so while Mother is in the hospital. If your preschooler feels lonely, bewildered, left out while Mother is away, his demands may be excessive when she returns and his reception of the newcomer may be less than friendly.

Where "Mummy" is, is at all times important to the preschooler. It is especially important that he feel fully oriented while she is away. It will help if he can go to see the hospital. Then it becomes a part of his world—something which has a tangible reality for him.

A daily visit with Daddy to wave to Mummy as he sees her in her hospital window (if the location of her room makes this feasible) may be all that the preschooler needs to make him feel that his mother hasn't deserted him. And/or a daily phone call, if he is one who is good on the phone, can do a good deal toward reassuring him that he hasn't lost his mother. A daily postcard in the mail will also help.

However, a word of warning! There are some "all or none" children who seem to do best if they can be either right with Mother or completely separated from her. A visit to the hospital during which the child merely sees Mother from a window may be far worse than no visit at all. A postcard or a phone call may remind him all too poignantly that she is away from home. He might do better with no reminders at all.

Another thing that must be decided is where the other child or children will stay while Mother is in the hospital. For most children, the most satisfactory solution is to have them remain in their own home, usually with Father and some competent caretaker with whom they are entirely familiar. The child's familiarity with and acceptance of the person who will take care of him during the crucial period is the key thing here. Ideally there will be available some close relative or trusted baby-sitter. If not, plans should be made well in advance, so that the child will have plenty of time to get used to whatever person is going to be on hand.

Some children, however, seem to find it less disturbing to be at someone else's house entirely than to be at home without Mother. In that case, similarly, the child should ideally not be going to a new place for the first time. If there is no convenient grandmother to visit, he should have at least a preliminary get-acquainted weekend visit to the new home.

Particularly, if possible, is it important to avoid any air of mystery, secretiveness, furtiveness about Mother's departure for the hospital —especially if it happens at night. With all the things there are to think about, it is sometimes hard to keep in mind the effect on a susceptible preschooler of mysterious comings and goings, especially in the darkness. Have him where he can't see or hear at all, or else see to it that he understands fully that this is the time that everybody has been preparing for.

What to Do When the Baby Comes Home

Most very young children do not visit the hospital and thus they get their first glimpse of the new baby after he has been brought home.

Whether he should be right there at the door at the fatal moment of arrival, or might feel less threatened and more welcoming simply to see the baby for the first time when it is lying quietly in its crib, you can judge best for yourself.

His initial response can be a clue to you as to how much time he will enjoy spending in the baby's presence. The child whose first comment about his new baby is "Bad boy!" might do better if for a time he isn't expected to take part in the bath or watch the feeding and dressing.

Presents can help. We know of a father who cleverly brought back presents for his preschooler from the hospital, saying that the baby had sent them. This baby, the generous fellow, was welcomed warmly when he arrived at home. Presents for the preschooler should also definitely accompany the baby's arrival.

The feeling of displacement which even a reasonably secure young child must feel when a new baby comes into the household, taking up space, time and attention which formerly belonged to him, should not be underestimated. There are doubtless some children who do not feel this displacement, but we believe that the majority do.

Thus it is important for the family and for visitors and friends of the family to be careful not to "make" a good deal of the baby in the older child's presence. Or if they do make a fuss over him, make at least some fuss over the older child as well. Bring *him* presents, even though inexpensive ones. Comment about how much *he* has grown.

Father especially, when he gets home at night, can do a real kindness by not inquiring first about, not rushing right in to see, the baby. Some fathers very thoughtfully, after some preliminary play with the older child, will then ask, "How about showing me the baby?"

Mothers, too, may find that it works much better if in the first few weeks they allow the person helping them to take much of the care of the baby while they themselves spend as much time as possible with the older child.

And lastly, though many preschoolers do enjoy watching the baby in his bath, many find it too emotionally upsetting to watch his feeding, particularly if he is breast fed. It is thus probably wise to make every possible effort to have the preschooler occupied elsewhere during the baby's feeding times.

How the Preschooler Treats the Baby

Parents often ask what can be done with a 2- or 3-year-old who plays too roughly with the baby, or actually hits and pushes him— in play or in undisguised attack. What they can do, and what they will have to do, is to give up any notion of how an older child ought to treat a baby. And accept the fact that he is not mature enough to be left alone with the baby.

Not only should he not be left alone with the baby, but the baby must not be left where the older child can get at him. Baby must be protected from brother or sister by locks and other adequate physical barriers. Until such a time as he becomes more reliable and trustworthy.

The other extreme is the helpful "little mother" type of 5- or 6-year-old who is "so good with the baby." Accept her offers of help, certainly, without any sinister doubts as to her subconscious motives. But do not give her more responsibility than her age warrants. She can watch the baby, or help feed and dress him if you are right near by. She should not be left all alone with responsibility. Fatalities have resulted from giving a willing preschooler too much responsibility with a baby.

Jealousy

Jealousy of a new baby is common, more or less expected, and though considered by some to be unfortunate, it is not usually viewed with particular alarm. But, when the child is no longer a preschooler, and when the brother or sister is no longer new—what then?

Jealousy among brothers and sisters is usually discussed as though it were entirely a negative and undesirable response. One to be avoided, discouraged, even punished. Yet we sometimes wonder if jealousy may not, within reason, play as positive a role in the child's life as does the somewhat similar emotion of fear. Excessive fear can indeed be an unfortunate and crippling emotion. A reasonable amount of fear in a truly dangerous situation may result in actual saving of life. Objective investigation of the jealousy response might show that jealousy, too, if not neurotic or excessive, may also conceivably serve a real, positive purpose.

Selfless children do exist who seldom if ever express any jealousy of their brothers and sisters. Equally, or even more often, however, we do find real and very obvious jealousy between siblings.

In the preschool years how common such comments as, "That's not the way to do it!" Or, "She can't even ride a pony. She's too little!" Or, "*She* can't even read." Or, in situation after situation, "I can do it better than that. Watch me!"

When referring to the behavior of younger children in the family, such remarks, even though uncharitable, have at least the virtue of accuracy. When they are made by younger and less capable children about older ones, they are usually less accurate.

Accurate or not, they seem to mean, and not too unreasonably, that younger or older than their brothers and sisters, most children quite naturally want to be best, to come first with and to be loved most by their all-important parents. Such a reaction seems not too unnatural, not too unreasonable.

Jealousy expresses itself in many different signs and in many different degrees. In extra demands for Mother's attention. In naughty behavior when too much attention is focused on a brother or sister. In refusal to go to school and leave Mother alone with the baby. In demands for a toy just like the one that Brother has. Much of the fighting that goes on between siblings is undoubtedly motivated (as much as it is motivated by anything—some of it seems more or less instinctive) by jealousy.

Certainly jealousy can be considered to be at the basis of much of the excessive demand for fairness which burdens so many households. Much of this demand, obviously, is not so much a demand for fairness as such, as a demand that somebody else doesn't get more than they have. In fact, ideally, that somebody else doesn't get as much as they have.

There are many things that can be done about jealousy.

First of all, check things over to be sure that you are not unwittingly adding fuel to the fire. It is all too easy to praise excessively a favorite child, or a more helpful or more docile child. If Jane is a really good scholar, or is especially co-operative about practicing her music lessons or about helping with the housework, and Jimmy isn't —it is difficult not to verbalize such comparisons.

Sometimes this praising of one child at the expense of another is done unintentionally. It just slips out. Unfortunately, some parents actually use this technique on purpose. They say, "Teddy, you ought to be ashamed of that rank card. Why look at the grades your sister gets! You don't want her to do better than you do, do you?"

This approach very seldom works. (And even when it does, it still isn't a good one.) As one little girl commented to us, "Parents think they get you to do better by telling you how well some other child does. All that really happens is that you get to hate that other child."

Secondly, though of course things cannot always be perfectly equal, try hard not to give a favorite, or "easier," or more appealing child more privileges and favors than a perhaps less easy-going, less attractive child.

Try not to praise one child excessively (even though he may be much more praiseworthy); or at least don't praise him too often in the presence of other, less admirable children. (A schoolteacher once commented, very wisely, that what the child *deserves* is so often not what he *needs*. Often the least praiseworthy child in your family may be the one who craves and actually needs the most praise.)

More constructively, the most important thing that you can do when one of your children seems to be bothered by jealousy of the others is to help him find more satisfactions of his own in life. Not only is it important to try to spend more time alone with him and to make him feel convinced that you love and appreciate him—but you need to build up his satisfactions with himself as well.

Help him to find friends if he lacks them. Help him to find recreations which he will enjoy and can carry out successfully. Or it may be that lack of success at school is behind some of his feeling of inadequacy. If so, see what can be done about this.

Ordinarily, if a child is functioning adequately and securely in his own private world, he will be much less prey to feelings of jealousy. Dr. Edward Podolsky, in his recent book *The Jealous Child* (Philosophical Library), comments that jealous children are usually convinced that nobody likes them or will ever like them. Helping them involves a long process of demonstrating that they are and can be liked. Dr. Podolsky states, "Jealousy is of instinctive origin. Its suppression would only drive it under cover and poison the child's mind. It should be brought into the open and managed with frankness and honesty."

TWINS

A special kind of sibling relationship, on which published literature for parents is virtually nonexistent, is the matter of twinship. Scientific writings on this subject abound. A practical commonsense manual for mothers which will tell what to do with the second infant twin while you are feeding the first, or how to keep one asleep while the other is crying, is much needed and yet to be written.

The problem of twins getting on with each other, or quarreling with each other, is not too different from that of any other two siblings getting on, particularly if the twins are merely fraternal.

As a rule, twins work out a relationship with each other which is reasonably satisfactory to both. Parents often worry about the effect a dominant twin may be having on a seemingly more passive twin. They sometimes discover, from close observation, that the seemingly passive twin may in his or her quiet manner actually be getting his way quite as much as does the more assertive one of the pair.

However, if the relationship seems to be consistently unfair to one twin or the other, parents should of course step in to improve matters.

Usually, as we say, twins do work out a relationship with each other which seems to be satisfactory to both. Parents as a rule worry more about how *they* should treat the twins than about how the twins should treat each other.

There has been a tendency in the past to treat twins exactly alike: same clothes, same toys, same privileges and punishments, same room in school.

Then people began to feel that this was being overdone, and many went to the opposite extreme—dressing them dissimilarly and separating them in school, regardless of their own inclinations.

Gradually we are settling down to a more conservative middle road. Many wise parents follow a policy of respecting the fact that twins are individuals. If they seem to thrive best on a rather steady diet of each other's company, even in school, that may be the best answer for them. If, given the freedom to do so, they prefer to live their lives more separately, that again may be the best answer for them.

Some will prefer to dress pretty much alike, to share the same friends. They should be allowed to do so. Others will prefer just the opposite.

Their parents' ultimate goal for them will probably be that they should grow up independent enough so that when the fortunes of adult life finally separate them, as they probably will, they should be able to stand on their own feet. For the rest, their own inclinations as to being treated alike or differently should probably be respected.

We have noticed that in general there is a difference between identical and fraternal twins. There is often a unison or near unison of action in identical twins, though at one time one twin leads, at another time the other leads. Illnesses are often identical. Temperature charts during an illness may be identical. In adult life it has often been reported that identical twins, though widely separated in space, may develop the same illness with a similar course, may give birth to a baby at approximately the same time or may commit a similar crime at relatively the same time.

We need to respect this identity and to know that in the early years togetherness may be the basis of the twins' security. As each shows differences, these should be fostered so that later they may more readily lead separate lives. But to separate identical twins too soon may produce unnecessary hardship and even illness.

Separation of identical twins in first or second grade often produces wilting in the very twin who appeared the stronger. Third grade, when they are eight and ready for a new expansion, is a far better time for separation. But, as always, the child's readiness must be considered. The more superior the twins are, the more different they are likely to be in the midst of their identity, and the earlier they are ready to be separated. Less well-endowed identical twins who are more dependent on each other may not be ready to be separated in school before their teens. However, there are all sorts of other ways that they can be separated, apart from school.

The situation with fraternal twins, however, can be quite different, especially when one is a boy and the other a girl. Sibling rivalry may be rampant from an early age. A demanding, more rapidly developing girl may make the life of her twin brother quite miserable. We knew of one who took her brother's bottle away, drank his supply of milk, and returned his bottle to him empty without his parents being the wiser. (It was not until these twins were mature with families of their own that they were able to build up a friendly relationship.) In situations of rivalry, it is best to separate the twins as much as possible. So far as schooling goes, even separate schools may be better than separate classrooms in the same school. Then they can begin to enjoy each other as separate individuals and not as twins.

CAN'T PLAY PEACEABLY WITH OTHER CHILDREN

Many parents complain that their preschoolers (for this difficulty is usually outgrown by school age) cannot play with other children (friends or siblings) for any appreciable length of time without hitting, biting, destroying playthings, crying.

As a rule this kind of behavior is a clear indication that the child in question simply is not ready for unsupervised play with contemporaries. (Often even the worst ones can get along with much younger children whom they can "boss," or with older ones who "boss" them.)

When a child cannot play peaceably with the other children, the not very interesting but most effective solution is to cut down the length of time during which he is allowed to play with others, cut down the number of children with whom he is allowed to play unsupervised, and to provide more supervision.

If the child's social abilities are so limited that he can play peaceably unsupervised with only one child and for only five minutes at a time, that is where you will need to start.

"Talking" to them and telling them that they must play "nicely" won't, in most cases, do too much good. Nor will punishing them for doing badly.

However, even by the time some children are two and a half, you can help them to develop techniques for getting along with friends. You can tell Joey, "Talk to Jimmy, don't hit him," if Joey is a hitter. Or, "What can Danny have instead?" if you are addressing a grabber. Or, "Let Mary have a turn now," or, "You can have it after Betty is finished."

Nursery-school techniques can be effective and nursery-school attendance can be even more so. Helping children to learn to get on with their contemporaries is one of the most important things that a child "learns" in nursery school.

But more supervision is probably the easiest and most effective remedy for undue quarreling among preschoolers. Neighborhood mothers can sometimes arrange to take turns. A mother in the offing —or even more actively engaged if necessary—can work wonders in cutting down preschool battling.

First of all, though, you will want to check to determine at what time of day, in what special situations, with what if any special children, and after how long a period of unsupervised play the trouble is most likely to occur.

In general, our remedy for all this preschool quarreling among playmates is to try to simplify the social situation till the child can meet a complex one, while at the same time providing play situations which are not too quarrel-inducing, techniques which will help the young child to get on with others—and adult supervision as much as can be managed.

14

Comics, Television and Movies

COMIC books—nuisance or menace? In our opinion—except for
the most lurid and unnecessary of the crime comics which we,
like others, would be glad to see abolished—the comic book situation is one which can generally be kept under control in the average
home.

Not so much by outright opposition and prohibition on the part
of parents, as by reasonable supervision and regulation. However,
we believe that parents can be helped to take a calm attitude toward
the problem during those months when the tide of comic books in
the home rises to its peak if they have a preview of the course which
comic book addiction will probably follow in any given child.

Like paper-doll collecting, or stamp collecting, or a passion for
electric trains, interest in comic books increases slowly but steadily
over a period of months or years, reaches a climax in which it may
virtually blot out all other forms of recreation, and then, shortly
after it has reached this intolerable peak, dies out. In most cases,
almost completely. Dies out and in the reasonably stable child
leaves, in most instances, few scars.

WHO READS COMICS?

At any rate, we think it may be interesting and perhaps helpful to
you for us to give you a brief survey of the course of comic-book
addiction as we find it in the boys and girls whom we have studied
in New Haven.

In many, some mild interest in the daily and Sunday comics is
evidenced as early as four or five years of age. Some puzzle out the

pictures for themselves. Others like to be read to. Interest in "funny books" is in most instances very slight.

But 6-year-olds, thanks to their schooling, are often able to do simple reading for themselves. Nearly half of our 6-year-old group either spelled out the comics for themselves or asked to have them read to them. Interest at this age is, in most, fairly general. But a few already have their favorites. For the most part, we're happy to say, of the gentler varieties. By seven many are already struck with the funny book craze.

Within his limited financial and reading abilities, the comic-book-reading 7-year-old often goes as far as he can in buying, reading, collecting and bartering comics. The daily adventures of ordinary people or the adventures of supermen are usually his favorites. But with the typical 7-year-old passion for blood and violence, some 7-year-olds are already showing a preference for the more violent type of comics. This preference, however, can at this age usually be pretty much controlled by parents through financial if not through other restrictions.

By eight, in most (boys especially, but also in a good many girls), interest has increased. The 8-year-old, like seven, buys, collects, barters, borrows, hoards and, needless to say, *reads* comic books. He now definitely enjoys adventure and blood and thunder as well as the simpler daily life or animal comics.

Nine, in many, marks the peak of this comic book passion. It takes a long time to drop out entirely, but many mothers tell us that it is never again quite as bad as it was when the child was nine. Nine is the age when many children seem to live only for comic books. They exist surrounded by as high piles of them as parents permit. They not only buy, read, barter and borrow, but they arrange and classify their comic books. And woe to Mother if one is missing.

Strong parental supervision is needed at this age to keep this funny-book passion from engulfing all other interests. Some mothers complain that their children act as if drugged, looking up glassy-eyed if spoken to, from the comic book in hand. It is not too attractive to see the hope of the family so occupied, so immersed. We trust that your child, like many others, may have reached the peak of his addiction by nine years of age.

By ten, many children have temporarily passed this peak. Even though many children of ten will tell you that oh, yes, they have about two hundred funny books, they will add—"Not as many lately, though, as I used to have."

Or they will say, "I have old ones and new ones and I keep them pretty well stored so that I know just where they all are. Sometimes Mother throws a few out when they're old. I don't mind too much if they're old."

Well, a year ago he would have minded. Progress is really being made when Mother is allowed to throw out even a few of the old ones.

Though nearly 90 per cent of our New Haven group of 10-year-olds do admit to reading comic books, actually only one-quarter are still said to be "avid" readers and collectors. "Avid," we fear, does tell the story. This interest is still a real passion with some. Their mothers say: "He devours them. No letting up." But—this group is now in the minority.

By eleven, though some perhaps slightly immature boys and girls are at it as strongly as ever, the decline in interest continues. Thus there are some, like the boy who tells us, "I have around five hundred comics at home. Drawers of the bureau and two piles in boxes. Hasn't fallen off any yet. I like books more now but I don't like comics any less." But of our group at this age, only about 15 per cent are still avid readers, and an equal number are said to be definitely losing interest.

By twelve years of age, though two-thirds of the boys and girls whom we studied still do read comic books on occasion, only 10 per cent continued to be avid readers. By thirteen, only half our group read comics at all.

. . . Just a word as to the type of comics most favored by our New Haven subjects. Though some as early as seven years of age show an interest in crime and gore, it is amazing to notice that even as late as ten, the books most frequently purchased and read are of the benign Little Lulu, Superman, Bugs Bunny, Orphan Annie category. Not till eleven or after, when in many the whole comic book fad is beginning to die out anyway, comes a prevailing interest in tales of crime and passion.

WHAT TO DO ABOUT COMICS

As to just what to do about the reading of comic books—that of course is largely up to each individual parent. However, it has been our finding—and the finding of countless parents—that a complete home ban on funny books merely drives these books to the garage, the barn, the attic or some neighbor's playroom. "My mother doesn't allow me to have them but I secretly keep a pile down cellar." "My mother makes such a fuss about them that I hide them in the garage," children tell us.

Most of the parents whom we know find that they get best results by reasonable regulation rather than by complete prohibition. Many children will accept without too much controversy regulation of the amount of money they spend, the (approximate) number and kind of comic books which they may buy, the amount of time which may be spent in reading such books. And the amount of space in the house which can be filled with them.

All of this takes a good deal of regulating. True. But as a rule it is more effective than a complete and utter ban. In fact, we ourselves are not fully convinced that a complete and utter ban on comic books is necessary even if it could be effective. For it has been our experience that in the case of reasonably stable children, from reasonably good homes and neighborhoods, comic-book reading is no more likely than is any other entertainment medium to produce delinquency or emotional upset.

MOVIES

Movie going is not in most cases much of a problem in the first ten years of life. By five, some children have attended an occasional child's movie. A few before that have watched the projection of home movies. (Some have been taken to regular movies before five, but this is usually only if parents are forced into it by lack of baby-sitters.)

By six years of age some are quite enthusiastic about home movies, but many if taken to the theater become restless, close their eyes and won't look. Or they cry.

However, by seven, a certain number of children actually do attend the movies weekly—usually on Saturday or Sunday afternoons, and most often taken by some adult. Most who do go prefer musicals, dancing, singing and animal pictures, or cartoons. Some like adventure stories, while others are disturbed by them and later have bad dreams. Nearly all dislike love stories.

It is at eight years, when the child is expanding and adjusting outwards in all sorts of ways, including the visual, that a definite interest in the cinema is developing. Many 8-year-olds attend weekly movies, usually on Saturday afternoons. Boys now like action pictures—westerns, baseball, war. Girls prefer musicals. Both like animal and adventure stories and stories about children. All still very much dislike love stories.

By this age, many know which movies or which parts of movies are too much for them, and they very sensibly protect themselves by closing their eyes, hiding their heads or going to the back of the theater or to the rest room until the "bad" parts are over.

Enthusiasm for movies is more varied at nine. Some may like to attend weekly, still mostly on Saturday afternoons. Others attend much less often. Some are so enthusiastic about certain pictures that they want to see them several times. Most are much hardier than at eight about the "bad" parts. Most behave reasonably well in the theater so far as their stamina permits and if they do not become tired or restless because they do not happen to enjoy the picture. Taste in kind of movies liked, and disliked, remains about the same as at eight.

Ten is becoming a *little* more discriminating. There is some emphasis on wanting to see a "good" movie. Most go with some one friend of their same sex, though a few still go with parents. Attendance is a little less frequent than earlier. Some go weekly, but the majority report that they attend only "occasionally." Kinds of movies preferred are westerns, comedies, cartoons, horse movies, historical movies. Many like to see a favored movie more than once.

Some "don't look if it is too bad," though most are now quite hardy. Some complain that the movies give them headaches and bad dreams. Most will accept parents' refusal to let them attend certain movies or to attend too often.

RADIO AND TELEVISION

"He doesn't read a book a month since we got television," a mother complained to us not long ago.

"How much did he read before that?" we asked.

The mother looked thoughtful. "About a book a month," she admitted.

Remember this when you find yourself blaming radio and television for the fact that your child doesn't do his homework, doesn't help around the house, doesn't do anything constructive. Don't simply blame radio or TV until you figure out how well your child would be doing these other things without such entertainment.

Radio and television are probably here in our culture to stay. It will get us further, if we are not satisfied with the kind of programs now available and with their effect on our children, to try to see to it that better programs are presented, than simply to complain and talk about how much better life was before we had television.

Intensive radio listening does not begin with many children till they are around six years of age. From then on, radio is an increasing favorite. By seven it is part of the daily diet of many, who have definite favorite programs which they do not like to miss.

Between eight and ten, most have a regular schedule of programs which they listen to, and in some, radio (or television) takes up as many hours as parents permit.

Television watching starts usually even earlier than radio listening. And is even more of a full-time pastime with many.

Many parents have found that television has certainly as many good points as bad. In addition to its real educational value, it has an entertainment value that can scarcely be equaled. Many mothers admit that it is the best baby-sitter in the world—especially on a rainy day when there is company, or in that dangerous hour just before dinnertime.

Brothers and sisters whose every look at each other may be the prelude to a quarrel can often spend peaceable minutes together before the television set (unless they are fighting to see their favorite program).

If television watching seems to be cutting too deeply into free time and taking the place of outdoor play or more creative activity, remember that you still have the upper hand. (We hope!) You *can* make rules: only so much time to be spent in watching; or only certain programs allowed. (We hope that parents will take the time to check on the programs their children are seeing and really choose with them.) Or even, no television at all unless certain minimum home requirements are carried out. If television is banned, it should be banned for the entire household, parents included. Far better to have the set disconnected for a week which involves the entire family until the air is cleared. Then planning for the future will be more readily accepted and tempers will be under control.

Also, the very worst programs, like the worst comic books and movies, *can* be forbidden. If your child seems to be using television (or radio) unwisely, we suggest that you step in with a little regulation, rather than throwing up your hands and damning television entirely.

Effect of Comics, Movies, Television

Just what are the deeper effects of the customarily heavy diet of comic books, movies, radio and television on the growing child? We're afraid that our answer has to be: No one *really* knows. For all the allegations, dire predictions, and warnings that have flown around of late, no one has produced satisfactory evidence that comic-book reading or television watching has or has not produced in children serious problems where none before existed. (Several careful studies have shown that they have no apparent effect on schoolwork. And as someone recently remarked, "Juvenile delinquency has been with us a long, long time. Television is very recent.")

The best we can do here is to give you our own opinions, based on our studies both of normal children and children with developmental and personality problems. First of all, we do not view most children, as many seem to, as highly fragile objects, supersensitive to every aspect of the environment and likely to be permanently scarred by any and every event in life. Children for the most part are tougher than this. Time and time again they show a capacity to bounce back after a difficult real-life situation, let alone after reading a comic book. Bad dreams after a gory comic or scary movie are frequent—but not ultimately damaging. The "self-repair" capacity of the child is outstanding.

Children are active—not just passive and receptive—in taking in life. They *select* out of the environment what it is that they will respond to. Thus a comic that is to the adult horrible or blood-thirsty or sex-laden may be seen quite differently by the child. Many of the adult's reactions—complex and based on a wealth of past experiences and learnings—may be quite absent in the child's simpler response. So it is through the child's eyes that a comic or movie must be viewed before we can measure its effect.

All this is not so much a defense of comics and television as a defense of the parents who—though sometimes feeling guilty about it—give in and let their children read or watch or listen to these "dangerous" devices. There is admittedly a negative side to them, too. All of these entertainment media—the comics especially—do, sometimes or often, overdo themes of violence, gore and sex. If nothing worse, they often show bad taste. Efforts to improve them are certainly to be encouraged, and social legislation concerning the worst comics, it seems to us, can be made workable.

Not all children are fully able to resist the impact of these media without help. These children are vulnerable, not only to comics, but to many other forces in life, and will need support and help all along the way.

Actually, more effective than any amount of regulating or pro-hibiting is the substitution of more desirable and interesting activity —especially of more appealing reading matter. The Teen Age Book Club, conducted by *Scholastic Magazine,* represents one such effort. *Picture Progress* is another. We hope to see still others.

There is one especially dangerous thing about comics and television which we feel has been too rarely mentioned. This is that they make handy scapegoats on which to blame any difficulties a child may be having. And blaming is quite a different matter from understanding and helping: The understanding parent or teacher will realize that his children's world is bigger than comics or television and that their responses to this world are far too individual and far too complex simply to be blamed on comics, movies, radio or television.

15

School

THIS present volume deals primarily with home behavior rather than with school behavior.* However, we shall mention briefly a few of the most common questions and problems related to school.

NURSERY SCHOOL

The first school experience of many children nowadays occurs rather early. Many now start nursery school as early as two or three years of age. This early schooling serves many purposes, and for most children can be an extremely valuable experience.

The most obvious value, for the child, of a well-run nursery school is that it gives him an opportunity to play with other children of his own age in a setting where not only toys and equipment, but also the routines of activities are arranged to suit children of his age. Also, such a school is staffed with teachers who understand how to help children of different ages play more effectively with their contemporaries. Such teachers appreciate both the normal developmental immaturities and the possibilities for improving behavior of preschool children.

This is the most obvious advantage of attending nursery school. However, there can be many additional advantages. Surprising as it may seem, many early childhood problems such as poor eating, poor sleeping, poor relations with brothers and sisters, can be lessened or even solved by nursery school attendance. It is not, of course, that the teachers attack these problems directly. It seems to be rather that this satisfactory and interesting outside experience in a situation which is geared directly to the child (as even the most

* A forthcoming volume from the Gesell Institute will discuss school behavior in detail.

satisfactory home situation may not be) seems to be meaningful enough to many children to lessen the tensions, anxieties, frustrations which may have led to the original "problem" behavior.

Once he starts school, home is no longer the sole focus of the child's interests. He has, in a way, a life of his own. Thus, with the young child who has "his" school, even as with the older person with diversified interests, things that may go wrong at home are of less paramount importance.

Thus, if the nursery school is well run and the child's adjustment favorable, not only will he have a good time at school, but it can be for him a definitely maturing experience. It can help him to adapt to his home life with increased effectiveness.

For the mother, not only can it be a brief time of relief from the constant twenty-four-hour care of a preschooler (which can be extremely energy-consuming, to say the least), but it can provide for her an opportunity to talk over daily problems which may arise, or things about her child's personality which puzzle her, with trained and sympathetic teachers.

Some parents feel that nursery-school attendance is not necessary or desirable for all children. They are quite correct. There are a few children who in spite of the best "techniques" used by teacher and parent, cannot "adjust" to nursery school within a reasonable length of time. If this is the case, the idea of school attendance should be given up for the time being and postponed to some later date.

Other children seem to adapt well to school and to enjoy it, but at home their increased irritability, fatigue, repeated illnesses, as well as other adverse signs may show that school attendance is too much for them.

There is also the parent who says, "He doesn't need to go to nursery school. There are plenty of children around home for him to play with." Actually, it would be a most unusual neighborhood group which could provide the kind of satisfactory play opportunity for the child which a well-run nursery school provides. However, there are undoubtedly some hardy, sociable children who can fight their own battles and make their adaptations without help from adults and without unduly harming their contemporaries, and whose social needs may indeed be satisfied by an unusually favorable neighborhood play situation.

Thus we do not maintain that *all* preschoolers should go to nursery school. But in our opinion the majority not only can adapt, but do definitely benefit from a nursery-school experience.

KINDERGARTEN

Kindergarten is now, fortunately, an accepted part of most public-school systems. Thus most children around the age of five, whether they have had nursery-school experience or not, do start kindergarten.

Since five is, in many children, an age of reasonably good equilibrium and easy adjustment, and since most kindergartens are run more or less on nursery-school lines and do not as a rule make excessive demands of their students, kindergarten adjustment usually presents few problems.

Well-run kindergartens tend to do a surprisingly good job of fitting their demands to the child's abilities. Particularly do they take pains to provide the gross motor and play activity so necessary for children of this age. First grades might do well to provide a little more of this opportunity to move about the room more freely which very young children so definitely need.

The main problem which seems to arise in relation to kindergarten occurs when a child is entered before he is ready. When a kindergarten student is unable to meet even the flexible and minimal demands of that grade, he will show it in approximately the same way that a first-grader shows his unreadiness (as described in the following section). And the treatment for such difficulties is approximately the same as for troubled first-graders. First, seriously consider the advisability of waiting another year for kindergarten, and if that is not practical, cut down the weekly amount of time which the child spends in school. Most children are not ready to start kindergarten till they are fully five years of age.

First-Grade Difficulty

Your 6-year-old has finished his first month in the first grade. And, as one mother expressed it recently, the first grade has finished him, the teacher and herself.

The first-grade beginner's symptoms may be many, and may present unmistakable evidence that something is drastically wrong. To begin with, never a cry-baby, he now cries a good deal of the time, especially on school mornings. He dawdles over his dressing and over breakfast, and he often is sick to his stomach.

He plainly says that he doesn't want to go to school. In fact, he begs to stay at home.

In school his behavior is most unacceptable. He certainly could do the work if he would only try, the teacher says, because his I.Q. is high enough. But he can't seem to keep his mind on his work. He fools and whispers and he won't stay in his seat or pay attention to his lessons. He doesn't finish what she gives him to do. He bothers all the other children.

Worst of all, he seems so tired all the time at home. And his usually sunny disposition is seldom in evidence. Much of the time he is cross and cranky and seems definitely unhappy.

This may seem like an exaggerated picture. Unfortunately, almost word for word it is the story many mothers tell us each fall after school has been under way for a few weeks.

Certainly such a collection of symptoms should leave no question in anybody's mind that something is seriously wrong. Yet many parents actually do very little about such a situation beyond scolding the child, punishing him for being "bad," and attempting to motivate him to try harder and pay better attention in school.

What, actually, does all this disturbance of behavior indicate, and what can the parent do if his child acts in this way?

First of all, such responses should make parents seriously question the child's readiness for first grade. In our experience, the average girl needs to be fully six, the average boy does better if he is closer to seven before starting first grade. (Much harm is done by entering a child in first grade too soon just because he is "so smart," or "just a month under the required age.")

Since, however, a good many children do start first grade before these ages, it is perhaps not surprising that so many do exhibit the first-grade difficulties just described.

If your child is responding adversely to his first-grade experience, the first thing you should probably do is to check with the teacher and/or with a skilled child psychologist to be sure that your child is fully ready to be in first grade.

This doesn't simply mean that he should have an I.Q. that is average or above average, or that he seems ready for beginning reading and writing. It also means that his total behavior age should be up to his chronological age. Thus he needs to be behaving like a first-grader in all ways and not simply in his ability to read and write.

If a conference with his teacher or a psychological examination confirms your suspicion that he simply is not ready for first grade, you will be well advised to let him return to kindergarten without delay.

However, if careful review of the situation indicates that first-grade attendance is not entirely out of the question, less severe measures may remedy the difficulty.

Many children who are otherwise ready for first grade simply cannot hold up to all-day school attendance every day. They become altogether too fatigued and their excessive fatigue accounts for much of their adverse behavior.

The simplest solution in these cases is usually to cut down on the amount of school attendance. Actually, for most first-graders, a half-day schedule is much better than a full day.

Some, sturdier but not yet sturdy enough for a full five-day-a-week schedule, may be able to manage if they have merely every Wednesday or every Wednesday afternoon off.

Many schools nowadays actually plan for only half-day sessions for first-graders. Others will permit part-time attendance for those who can't stand more. If the mother's request or psychologist's suggestion is not enough, a pediatrician's note will nearly always enlist the school's co-operation in a cut-down attendance policy for any individual child.

However, there are cases where a child is developmentally ready for first grade, able to do the "work," and emotionally and physically sturdy enough to stand all-day attendance, yet he still has trouble in adjusting to school, and exhibits some or all of the symptoms just described.

What then? Then it's harder to advise, because the answers can be as myriad as the children who have difficulty.

One of the most common likelihoods is that there is some one aspect of the total situation which is making the trouble. Sometimes it is just some one tiny thing that has happened at school, or on the way to school, that is frightening, worrying or confusing the child.

Some bigger child may be bothering him on the way to or from school. Teacher may be expecting him to count as he passes things, and he may not be able to. Toileting may present an unsolvable problem. He may be required to clean up his plate at the school lunch, which is often difficult for Six.

Usually you can, by careful checking with the teacher and patient questioning of the child, find out what the difficulty is and take practical steps to make him feel happier and more secure.

In instances where his resistance to school cannot be overcome, or in cases where the teacher finds the child unmanageable in school, if putting him back, reducing the amount of school attendance or resorting to the usual practical measures does not do the trick—a child specialist should be consulted.

Problems of dislike of and resistance to school nearly always can be solved, but in some instances a solution does require expert help. It is seldom simply a matter of the child's "paying better attention" or "minding better"; and mere punishment and admonition by parents are seldom all that is needed.

Associated Difficulties

First-graders have other difficulties, many of which occur in the morning before they ever get to school. For instance, they often dawdle about dressing, they dawdle about breakfast, they just can't seem to get ready for the school bus. They may even be unable to eat their breakfasts, or may eat them and then be sick to their stomachs.

All of these things may be just some of the signs that either the child is not ready for first grade or that all-day, everyday attendance is too much. These possibilities should always be considered.

However, some who really are ready for all-day, everyday first-grade attendance, and able to manage school once they get there, simply have trouble in getting there.

Mornings can be difficult and trying for both mother and child. There are some things that you can do about this. First, every effort should be made to simplify and streamline routines. Give more help with dressing if need be. Perhaps take turns—you dress the child every other day; he dresses himself on alternate days.

If breakfast makes trouble, cut down the amount of food which the child is expected to eat to an absolute minimum. (If necessary, or preferably, school should provide a midmorning snack.)

Some children really need to have Mother accompany them to school the first few days—or weeks. Most of these, however, do not want her to go into the schoolhouse or beyond the threshold of their classroom. Others do better if accompanied to school by some older, responsible child.

Promotion to Second Grade

"Bryan entered first grade last year when he was five and a half, but he didn't do very well with it. So now they want to keep him back. But he's six and a half, and he's a big boy, and all his friends will be in second grade. Don't you think it would be better if he just goes along with the class and takes a chance that he will catch up later?"

This question, in one variation or another, is asked of us dozens of times every year. And our answer, just off hand, is usually, "No."

However, each case, of course, should be judged on its own merits —generalizations about school placement, as about anything else, tend to be hazardous.

So let's look a little more closely at the case of Bryan. Because there are many Bryans. You may even have one yourself.

Bryan's mother and father brought him to us with the above-described problem about school placement. He had not done well in first grade, it was true. But they felt it was partly because he was their first child and they hadn't "done very well" with him. Now they were getting to be better parents, and they felt that their improvement might be reflected in improved work on the part of their son. Also they felt that when he was a little more "used to" school, he might just naturally "catch up."

Both of these hopes turned out, when we examined Bryan, to be quite unfounded. Because Bryan just wasn't as ready for first grade as his parents had hoped he was.

Examination showed that even though he was six and a half years of age, much of his behavior was like that of a 4- to 5-year-old. In describing the picture of a man, for example, he pointed out the head, and the arms, and the legs, as a 4-year-old often does, but could not tell that it was a man. In copying simple geometric figures his performance was again more like that of a 4-year-old than that of a boy of his actual age.

And so on, with most of the other tests. Our notations on his behavior were that it was extremely restricted, extremely immature. Whereas he need not be classified as strictly "retarded," his potentials were below what we think of as average.

In fact, this little boy would do better if he could even wait a further year before being in first grade. Ideally—six and a half though he may be—Bryan *should* spend this next year in an enriched kindergarten situation. His family will probably not want to have him do that; but at least he should repeat first grade. Certainly he should not go on to second.

There are many little boys like Bryan.

Billy's case was different, though the practical solution was the same. Billy, unlike Bryan, did fine in first grade. In fact, his enthusiastic teacher commented at the end of the year, "If there ever was a boy ready for second grade, it's Billy."

What a surprise and disappointment for Billy's parents, then, when in second grade he brought home his first report card—failing in every subject. His teacher's comment was that Billy would be better off in first grade.

His parents just couldn't understand this. It must be the teacher's fault, they figured; she obviously didn't understand and appreciate Billy. Especially since, though she claimed that he couldn't do the work that the rest of the class did, he could do this work easily when he tried it at home.

So Billy came to see us, and we found that Billy, like so many other boys who enter first grade too young (before they are fully seven) was seriously overplaced in school.

His own real enthusiasm for school, his good intelligence, his willingness to try very hard and an extremely sympathetic and friendly first-grade teacher had been enough to get him through the relatively easy work of first grade.

Faced with the harder tasks of the second grade, for which he was not really ready, his basic unreadiness and immaturity made themselves apparent.

The fact that a boy or girl can get by in kindergarten or first grade is not always a guarantee that he is ready to do the work of the succeeding grade. His true potential can, however, be uncovered by a developmental examination. May the day come when we shall use developmental tools to determine where the child should properly be placed in school. He should be saved the disruption, embarrassment or disappointment of having to repeat a grade when he wasn't ready to advance in the first place.

BEING KEPT BACK

"But the other children will all make fun of him if he's kept back!" protested Bobby's mother when we suggested to her that her son would actually do much better, and would be much happier, if he could be put back to first grade. "It would be so embarrassing for him. He could never stand it, being put back with the younger children," she objected.

Was she correct? Was it true that Bobby couldn't stand being put back—or was it that his mother couldn't stand it?

Let's talk about Bobby's mother first. It is certainly true that in this country, at least, parents seem strongly motivated to get their children into school, and then through school, as early as possible. Most parents hate to have their children further behind in school than other children of the same age. A "smart" child who is ahead of others of his age seems to many parents one vindication of their success at parenthood.

And so it is hard for them to have their children held back in school.

As to her statement that Bobby himself "couldn't stand" being held back, the chances are that she is incorrect. He will, if kept back, not only in all probability stand it, but he will probably thrive on it.

It will almost certainly be hard for him at first (and even harder for older children in the same situation than for a second-grader). No matter in how favorable a light his parents and/or his teacher present the situation, he is going to feel that he has failed and will probably be unhappy for a while.

More than that, unless he is exceptionally lucky, there may be unfavorable or even jeering comments from his friends at school. Here the school should try to step in and help the other children to understand. (Sensitivity will be greater, but also understanding will be greater with increasing age of the child.)

But common sense tells us—and our own long-time experience with the many children we have known who have been kept back in school confirms it—that a little unhappiness or real emotional suffering is well worth it if it earns the child many succeeding years of being correctly and comfortably placed in school.

We are certain that both Bobby and his mother will consider themselves well repaid for any temporary unhappiness by the many improvements in all aspects of his behavior which we predict will follow when arrangements are made for him to be with the grade for which his present state of maturity fits him. Not only in the immediate situation, but in all the school years to follow.

SECOND-GRADE TROUBLE

"I certainly spoke too soon," admitted a second-grade mother at a fall P.T.A. meeting. "Last year I used to boast about how crazy

Nicky was about school, and I'm afraid I even said that ours was one family that wasn't going to have any 'don't like school' difficulties.

"But now that he's in second grade, the whole thing seems to have gone to pieces. He's a different child. He gets so cranky and tired. He complains that he doesn't feel well enough to go to school. He says everyone at school is mean to him. He just seems to have turned against the whole school situation. Has this sort of thing happened to any of the rest of you?"

It had indeed! Nicky's mother discovered that she was not the only one whose child had breezed through the first grade and then bogged down in the second. There can be many reasons for such a change for the worse, but one of the main explanations lies in the very nature of the 7-year-old child.

Seven is not the outgoing, aggressive, brash little organism that Six was. Six characteristically meets obstacles by coming up against them, head on. Seven meets them by withdrawing as far as possible. Six is adventurous. Seven is worried.

And so, many Sixes sail happily through first grade, and then, to everyone's surprise, fail to adjust to second. Second grade demands more of them, and also being seven demands more of them.

Their troubles often start in the summer between first and second grades. Many have trouble in leaving the first grade and their first-grade teacher. They are used to her just as they are used to their mother, and they don't want to change. One little boy asked his mother, "Why do the children go and the teacher stay?" A little girl of our acquaintance cried for days because she didn't want to leave her first-grade teacher.

Other 7-year-olds spend the summer in unhappy worrying about the unknown. Before first grade they did not have the maturity to wonder—but now they are filled with all sorts of shapeless fears of the terrible unknown adventure ahead of them. Many just think that the second grade will be *too hard*.

And once school has started, many are haunted by an excessive fear that they will be late for school. The requirement that they get to school on time causes panic and consternation in the hearts of many worrying 7-year-olds.

Then there are those children already mentioned who were really not ready for first grade but who managed to coast along, whose basic immaturity shows up all too clearly when they are faced with the harder tasks of second grade.

Also, many 7-year-olds tend to be much more dependent on the teacher as a person than they were at six, in fact, teacher is probably the most important thing about school to the 7-year-old. To the 6-year-old, school is a great, big, often wonderful experience. But by the time children are seven, it has, for many, narrowed down to the personal relationship between them and the teacher.

The personal relationship is all-important, and for this reason it is important for the second-grade teacher to be a person who really *likes* children. This is an age of strong emotional responses to the teacher. The second-grader, boys especially, likes to stand beside his teacher, likes to have her notice him, likes to bring her presents.

"Shall I start now?" "Am I supposed to begin on the top line?" "How far do we go?" Half a dozen little hands pop up. It is not so much that Seven needs the information he requests as that he needs the personal support of asking and of having the teacher tell him that Yes, it is time to start, Yes, he should begin on the top line. Even as late as five years of age he needed the same moral support from his mother in simple home situations, as when he would announce, "I'm going to the bathroom," even after he had become quite able to take care of his own needs.

At all ages the teacher's personal appearance is important to children, but especially at seven is the child responsive to pretty clothes —and to an attractive, smiling teacher. Many boys fall in love with their second-grade teachers. Many girls are antagonistic and might get on far better with a man teacher.

The extremely personal nature of the child's response to his (or her) teacher at this age often leads the child to act in a silly, embarrassed manner toward her. An experienced teacher of 7-year-olds understands the reason for such behavior.

And most troublesome of all, to everyone concerned, is the characteristic 7-year-old complaint that his teacher is being mean and unfair to him. It is not teacher alone who is thus blamed. Sevens often tend to get into a melancholy mood during which they think that everyone—parents, teacher, friends, brothers and sisters, are picking on them. It is the wise mother who does not rush down to school to find out why Egbert's teacher is picking on him. The unfair treatment may very likely exist only in Egbert's imagination.

The 7-year-old is characteristically tense, worrisome and aware (often overaware) of his own inadequacies. When these inadequacies cause him trouble, he feels unhappy and frustrated. For example, it is hard for Seven to finish anything. For this reason, he either goes into things too hard and "overfinishes," or he may give up before he even begins. His teacher needs to help out in these situations. She needs to help the child who can't begin, to start; to help the child who can't finish, to stop. This kind of help will give him a sunnier outlook toward his teacher and toward the whole school situation.

What to do about all this? There is no over-all answer. Each child will have to be considered in his own special situation and with regard to his own special personality. But if parents and teachers can appreciate a little more fully the personality of the 7-year-old which makes him so dependent on his teacher and so much a prey to fears and apprehensions, they will be more successful in helping him to work through these difficulties.

GETTING TO SCHOOL ON TIME IN THE SECOND GRADE

There are thus numerous danger points in relation to schooling in the second grade, but one of the most complicating can be the problem of getting the child off to school in the morning.

As in first grade, any excessive dawdling, fussing, crying, objecting which occurs consistently in the mornings as a child is being gotten ready for school should always be considered as a possible indication that something is really wrong. Either that the child is not properly placed in school or that some aspect of school life is difficult, confusing or unpleasant for him.

However, if a careful check reveals that everything seems to be all right, you may suspect that you are simply up against a juvenile form of filibuster. In such a case, many specialists now feel that even a 7-year-old is not too young for a slightly "hard-boiled" attitude on the part of parents.

They suggest that instead of taking all the responsibility and worrying and fretting and struggling to get the child to hurry so that he won't be late, you simply make all the proper provisions, give all reasonable help, and leave the rest up to him. Thus you call him in time, give him reasonable warnings and time signals, provide breakfast in plenty of time, and then leave things up to him. He is the one who is going to miss the bus and/or be late to school, not you, if he dawdles excessively.

Even very young children can quite quickly make the distinction as to whether the responsibility is theirs or Mother's. Most can respond accordingly, given a reasonable amount of help. The Seven who is ready to accept the challenge will dawdle as usual up to the last three or so minutes before he has to go. Then he produces a "blitz," dresses like a flash, downs his breakfast, and is gone like a streak. Fortunately he is learning to tell time, and the clock tells him unmistakably when he has no time left in which to dawdle.

Exactly the opposite problem is presented by the 7-year-old who worries excessively that he will be late for school. Such a child, if allowed to, would get up as early as six in the morning and from then on keep the entire family in a turmoil, not because of his dawdling and delay, but because of his anxiety that he will not get to school on time.

Up early, he rushes through dressing and breakfast. As the time goes by and his parents will not let him start off for school, he becomes more and more anxious and may, in his nervousness, have to go to the bathroom every few minutes. As soon as his parents will allow, he rushes out of the house and tears off to school, worrying all the way.

But the minute he crosses the threshold of the schoolroom, all this anxiety vanishes, and often the teacher has no idea of what the child (and his parents) have gone through since waking.

This kind of extreme anxiety is difficult to dispel. About the best that parents can do is to cut it down and control it a little (till increased maturity finally causes it to disappear). First, control the hour of getting up by telling the child that he cannot get out of bed till the alarm clock rings or the hands of the clock are at a certain place. (You can set the time at some hour halfway between the time when he *wants* to get up and the time when he *needs* to do so.)

Let him watch from the window till the first other children go by. Then he can be allowed to start out. (If he takes the school bus, the hour of starting out is, of course, somewhat controlled.)

The last impatient minutes can be filled by letting him read some book on which he will report to his teacher when he gets to school. This fills up the time and also makes something of a tie between home and school, which usually helps. By such a plan, it is almost as if he starts school before he gets there.

Best of all, however, would be if he were lucky enough to attend a school which had no set time for the first class to begin, but rather had a free, flexible period first. Such an arrangement, for the first few grades, can help prevent some children's fairly common anxiety about whether or not they are going to be late. They can then be thinking more about what they are going to do in the initial free period. The problem such a school has is rather that everyone wants to come early.

Eight to Ten

The 8-year-old as a rule, especially if he has not started school at too young an age and thus is correctly placed, usually has much less difficulty than the 7-year-old. He characteristically enjoys school and doesn't like to miss any. Fortunately, his lessened fatigue and his usually improved health often make it possible for him to attend very regularly.

Those who still have difficulty in getting to school on time can sometimes be motivated by having special tasks at school which they are asked to and desire to perform before class starts.

Eight's vigor, enthusiasm, interest in his fellows and love of variety all can be satisfied by a positive school experience. Lucky the 8-year-old whose teacher recognizes his need to communicate, at times, with his neighbor, and who also recognizes his need for a good deal of praise.

Eight as a rule tends to report more about school than formerly, so that his mother is now better informed about what goes on.

Nine, too, ordinarily enjoys school and is better than earlier about getting there on time, though he may still need to be reminded about anything which needs to be taken to school with him.

Many teachers report that the fourth grade is a difficult one to teach because the child at this age is such an individualist and has such marked likes and dislikes. Also, Nine tends to be more of a worrier than was Eight. He wants to get good marks, worries that he may fail, and is upset by failure and low grades. He may be particularly disturbed now if he has to be kept back, and that is one reason why any error in grade placement should ideally be adjusted before the fourth grade. Unfortunately, some children do manage to get through the first three grades, and their overplacement does not become fully apparent until fourth grade. (On the other hand, another group of children, especially boys, who may not have been doing too well in the early grades, or were too busy expressing their own individuality, will rise to the top in fourth grade. They pick up speed in fourth grade and enjoy the intellectual demands that perfecting skills and delving into thought processes make.)

Nine-year-olds often need more individual attention when they are having difficulty in school than do younger children. However, many at this age do have a better critical evaluation of their own abilities and weaknesses. Nine usually has a much better idea about his own intellectual processes than he did when younger, and thus it may be easier to help him straighten out his errors.

The Show-off

"He's such a show-off in school," wrote Jim's mother. "He drives the teacher crazy. And though the other children all laugh at his antics, I don't think they really admire him. He's always clowning around and drawing attention to himself—he'll do anything to get a laugh. And no amount of scolding him or talking to him seems to make things any better."

This is a familiar story, to parents, to teachers and to us. And so often, though not always, the little "clown" resembles Jim—small, bespectacled, below average in looks and muscle.

Particularly in the lower grades does this behavior occur. Jim, for instance, was in the third grade.

People sometimes think that it is the bold child who is "too full of himself," who is the class show-off. Actually, most often it is just the opposite. In our experience it is often the shy, diffident child, ineffective and not very sure of himself, who tries to find himself and to bolster up his own ego by calling attention to himself in any way he can.

If this is the case, then what is the solution?

There is, of course, no one over-all answer that holds for everyone. But in general, as in most child behavior problems, it usually proves more effective to try to find out why the child behaves as he does rather than simply punishing him for the disapproved behavior. Then try to remove his need to act this way or provide more acceptable outlets.

In Jim's case the need seems to be to build up his apparently weak sense of self by attracting attention to himself. So, as many good teachers have been doing since schools began, we would recommend that Jim's teacher give him legitimate opportunities to be the center of attention. Particularly, since he is such a clown and dramatist, to take part in or even to lead short dramatic skits. Then he won't need to clown so much because he will have a special part to play.

Jim is a naturalist too, we found out from his mother. Here too is something which the teacher can use to good advantage. Let Jim bring some of his flower or rock collections to class and talk to the other children about them. Some of his live collections too—barring rattlesnakes, which he says he has! Similarly, contests in which the children bring in as many "specimens" as possible could allow Jim a chance to excel and to give valuable information not only about his own specimens, but about those of the other children.

A show-off does not become a docile, amenable member of the class overnight—but a little help of this sort, rather than punishment, can often bring about a remarkable improvement.

Child Who Is "Unmanageable" in School

Extremely unruly behavior in school, continued over any period of time, calls ideally for a check by the school psychologist or guidance teacher to find out what is wrong and why the child needs to behave in such a way. Each case is in its own way unique and deserves individual attention.

If such a check is not possible, the best general suggestion which we can make is that this behavior may indicate, in the early grades at least, that the child is, if not actually overplaced in school, at least getting a larger dose of school than he is ready for.

Improvement is frequently brought about by cutting down the number of days a week on which the child is allowed to attend school. Have him do his schoolwork at home and let him know that he can attend school full time only when he has earned the right to do so by his good behavior.

On the days when he does go to school, one parent or the other needs to give him a pep talk about how he is going to behave. This talk needs to be given every school morning. A single omission may result in his lapsing back into unruly behavior. And always this type of child needs the kind of play outlets that he most desires. When given a choice, it is startling to see how often this type of child gravitates to water, sand or play with clay. He also likes the loose freedom that finger paint will give him. In short, he still prefers the play materials of the preschool child.

Remedial Reading

Seven years old, but he's failing second-grade reading!

Eight years old, but he still makes reading errors even on quite simple words.

These cases abound, as all too many teachers and parents know, much to their sorrow.

And what is the best solution? Any solution to the problem, of course, depends upon a point of view. From the developmental point of view, a child seven or eight years of age who is not reading is not simply a reading problem. Rather we feel that his inability to read is only one symptom of a complex developmental problem. Reading, which may seem utterly simple to the adult, is in reality a complex performance involving all the senses: vision, touch, hearing, speech, even taste and smell. Reading is the re-creation of experiences by an appropriate arrangement of jagged, circular and straight lines known as the alphabet.

The child of seven or eight who is not yet ready to read is often one who is developmentally immature. This does not necessarily mean that he is progressing at a slow intellectual rate—for he may have average or even superior intelligence. What it does mean is that the manner in which he thinks, the way in which he solves his problems, the way he behaves and his likes and interests are all typical of a child of a younger age.

Such a child may be one, two or even more years immature in his behavior. When he was six years of age, he may have acted more like a 5-year-old. As a 7-year-old he may be acting like a 6-year-old. These immaturities do not just suddenly appear when the child goes to school, nor do they appear because of something the school has done to him. Rather, the demands of school merely highlight and magnify the child's inabilities.

The preschool history of such a child often reveals that he was slow in learning to talk and slow to combine words into sentences or phrases. There was only fleeting or slight interest in books, and he would rarely sit and listen to a whole story unless possibly it was a factual story about trains, cars, trucks, etc. There was no interest in making letters of the alphabet or the letters in his own name. He never asked about the labels on cereal boxes or what road signs said, or the printing on the side of a delivery truck. A 6-year-old is not ready to read unless he has gone through these and/or similar steps in reading development. If he seems to be about a year behind in much of his behavior, the obvious thing to do is to delay the starting of school by one year. The popular trend of keeping the child with his chronological age group for "social" reasons is both illogical and inconsistent with the facts of development.

What can parents do? They can help their children by giving their own time and by providing materials to the child at the level where he is ready to learn. Those 5-year-olds who learn to read easily have such interests as the following: They like to print certain letters in the alphabet that appeal to them either because of their shape or meaning. They like to spell their own name, as well as a brother's or sister's. They like to put simple letters together to spell such words as *cat* or *dog* and will recognize them in print, especially in a story that they already know. They like to be read to. They like to draw numbers and letters and are becoming proficient at drawing such simple geometric shapes as a circle, square and triangle. Coloring books are popular with these Fives, as well as cutting out pictures and working with scissors. They ask about the names on cereal box tops and recognize a product seen on television when they visit the grocery store. These interests are the things to encourage. Without them the more formal aspects of learning to read are not likely to take hold. These may be the very interests which do not yet have meaning for the developmentally immature child who is not yet ready to read.

There are other kinds of reading problems. There is the emotionally disturbed child who needs a great deal of emotional help before he is ready to read. And there is the self-absorbed boy who can listen to stories by the hour and who can read a bit, but who doesn't come into good reading until he is nine years of age. Then it is almost as though the flood gates opened, and soon he may be reading better than all the girls who read early and well.

Special remedial techniques, whether they be by the visual or auditory method or a combination of both, are valuable when it can be demonstrated that they are the avenues of approach to a reading problem child. Without a proper appraisal of growth, however, we feel that much unnecessary remedial work in reading is done at the wrong time. That is why knowledge of the expected sequence of individual development is so important and why a developmental examination which can be related to the child's earlier history often gives us specific answers and guides as to what needs to be done.

"He Could Do Better If He Would"

"He could do better if he would!" What teacher doesn't say this about at least one of her pupils during the course of the school year!

"He could do better if he would only try. He has a perfectly adequate I.Q., but he just doesn't seem to care."

"He could do better if only he'd stop fooling around and pay attention."

"He could do better if he would only concentrate."

"He could do better if only he wouldn't daydream."

The teachers (and the parents) who make these statements all speak as if the pupil in question *could* pay attention and stop fooling around and stop daydreaming if only he *would*. As if it were just a matter of the student's exerting will power and disciplining himself into more effective behavior.

Yet our experiences with the many children who are brought to our Institute because of poor adjustment in school have led us to reverse the key statement. We say not, "He could do better if he would," but rather, "He would do better if he could."

These behaviors about which parents and teachers complain—the inattention, the fooling around, the lack of concentrating, the daydreaming, the poor reading performance—all in our opinion are not signs of weakness or badness which must simply be overcome. Rather they are danger signals which tell us that something (or often many a thing) is wrong with the school situation for this particular child at this time.

Careful psychological examination often shows that the child in question is doing remarkably well considering the equipment (*i.e.,* his basic personality structure) with which he is trying to meet the situation. Adequate as his I.Q. may be (and it is not always as adequate as people have said), he is usually working under many handicaps. His level of emotional development may be way below his chronological age; his manner of using his eyes may be grossly inadequate; his mathematical or reading process, as well as perform-ance, may be several grades below his class in school.

These and dozens of other inadequacies can be revealed by a thorough developmental examination. Once revealed, they can be taken into consideration and the child can be given visual help, special help with certain studies or (as so often is needed) can be reassigned to the grade for which his total behavior (and not just his age or I.Q.) suits him.

Too many parents and teachers, faced with a child's inadequate school performance, simply make one of the conventional comments —"He could do it all right if he would only concentrate"—as if they had solved the problem of the child's poor performance. They have assured themselves that he is quite capable of doing the work if he only will—and the rest is up to him.

We would urge that any parent or teacher faced with a child's poor performance in school consider the customary danger signals for what they are and give him the help he needs—often, to start with, a thorough examination by a trained child specialist—rather than just admonishing him to pull himself together and try harder.

The child's not paying attention, or whatever else he is doing that people object to, may be his desperate and perfectly reasonable effort to escape from a situation which is just way over his head or beyond his present stage of organization. Or he may be emotionally upset and thus unable to concentrate and do his best work.

Seldom do we find, when there is difficulty, that all aspects of the situation are just right and that the child is simply *not trying*.

More often than not, when a child is brought to us for clinical examination because of poor performance in school, we marvel that, given his inadequate equipment for the work of the grade in ques-tion, he is doing as well as he does. Most children, it turns out, are trying very hard indeed.

Vision

One special aspect of the child's behavior which should always be carefully checked when there is trouble in school is his vision. We should always ask, Is this 5-year-old visually mature enough for kindergarten? Is this 6-year-old visually ready for first grade? Does this 7-year-old have the visual sustaining power demanded of him in second grade? And so on right up through the various grades. Our clinical experience indicates that many children are not ready visually for the demands of the grade in which they are placed.

One reason for overlooking the child's vision problems has been a lack of understanding by some educators and even by some eye specialists as to what constitutes a *visual* problem, and how it may differ from an *eye* problem. Many children have a visual problem, but not an eye problem. That is to say, the interior and exterior parts of their eyes are healthy, they have the ability to see small letters clearly at twenty feet (20/20 vision), and there are no obvious errors in the optical systems of either eye. Therefore the diagnosis is healthy eyes and no eye problem.

In a proper visual examination, more than that is involved. In a visual examination we should be concerned with the child's visual *abilities:* whether or not he can focus and point his eyes together as as team; his speed of perception; his accuracy in looking from one object to another. We must find out whether he can keep his eyes on an object moving toward him, in a circular direction, from side to side, up and down, and at an angle. We must check on his power of sustaining focus at the reading distance; on how he uses his eyes and hands together; and on many other visual skills that are necessary within his school environment. When a child lacks some of these essential visual skills, he may find himself classed as a reading problem, a behavior problem, or more often just as a lazy child who could do the work if he would only try. When we speak of vision, we must be concerned with the child's ability to get meaning and understanding from what he sees by the skillful and efficient use of both eyes.

Parents and teachers will want to know what can be done for the child who is visually immature and/or lacking in some of the necessary visual skills mentioned above. If it seems to be a question of over-all immaturity, then the question of correcting grade placement as mentioned earlier should be seriously considered as a first step. For many children, visual therapy—that is, being taught how to move, focus and fixate the two eyes so that they co-ordinate properly —is essential for efficient visual development.

One 7-year-old boy was brought to us because he was failing in second grade and was unhappy in school. The boy had complained to his mother for several months that he kept getting the words wrong that the teacher wrote on the chalkboard. A routine eye examination indicated that there was no eye problem. However, our visual examination showed that he had very poor ability in moving his eyes from one point in space to another and in keeping his eyes on a moving target. After this boy had been taught, through visual training, how to use his eyes efficiently, he began to improve in his school work, took real interest in school for the first time and was no longer unhappy in school.

Sometimes when visual therapy is not available, it is possible to rearrange the school environment to get around the problem. For example, one very intelligent 8-year-old girl was forever disturbing the class with her childlike antics, which necessitated her being sent home from school, until it was discovered that she couldn't copy her daily assignments from the blackboard. When she couldn't succeed, she just blew off steam. The problem was solved in her case by having her copy the assignments at her desk rather than from the board —something that was within her visual ability.

Sometimes glasses that allow the child to focus his eyes more easily while he reads or works at his desk are used as an aid to visual development and to prevent certain types of eye problems. Many visually immature children in first and second grade have not developed their focusing ability at near to a degree where they can read or do deskwork for any length of time. This kind of glasses makes it easier for them to work without fatigue. Without such glasses, some of these children avoid reading and other near work as much as possible. Others, particularly 7-year-olds, may force themselves to achieve perfection and to finish their work to such a point that they lose their ability to focus their eyes at distance. The result is the development of myopia (nearsightedness). (Such a child has a visual problem and an eye problem, too!)

One way of avoiding or lessening the chances of a visual school behavior problem or an eye problem developing is to have your child given a thorough visual examination not later than the kindergarten year, to learn how his visual development compares with that of others of his own age. By insuring good visual development early in life, you can avoid many difficulties that often occur later on.

Conclusion

Thus, in conclusion, it is important to remember that much school difficulty can be prevented entirely by not starting the child in too soon in school. Proper grade placement might eliminate as much as 50 per cent of the difficulties which children do experience in school.

Second, do not be too quick to condemn a poor student by saying that "He could do better if he would." A good many school "failures" are, nevertheless, doing the best that they can in a situation which is, in one respect or another, too difficult for them. Remember that a high I.Q. alone is not enough to guarantee good school performance.

And lastly, if your child is experiencing school difficulty which simpler efforts cannot clear up, a careful psychological examination, including a visual examination if possible, can often reveal the source of his difficulty.

Music Lessons

A word about music lessons, which involve as they do both lessons and practice, and are not too removed from the general topic of schooling.

Many parents today, though they wish to give their children all possible cultural advantages, seriously question whether or not it is worth while to insist that a child continue his music lessons in the face of daily battles about practicing.

Our own feeling about the matter is that there should perhaps be at least some balance between the amount of actual ability a child has, the amount of progress he seems to be making with his lessons and the amount of difficulty his parents have in getting him to practice.

A good deal of ability and progress and only a small or "normal" amount of rebellion against practicing might certainly warrant continuing with lessons. Very little talent or progress and vigorous daily resistance (even amounting to pitched battles between mother and child) would make us at least question the value of continuing practice.

Many parents nowadays are deciding that it is *not* "worth it" to add daily battles about practicing to the other daily problems which are involved in bringing up a teen-ager or pre-teen-ager.

Certainly the fact that so many teen-agers do finally give up entirely after having "taken" reluctantly and under compulsion for several years, might make anyone hesitate before forcing a child, year after year, to practice.

Also, it should be kept in mind that many children make a strong demand for lessons when they are seven or eight years of age, and later show little interest and ability for going on once the initial excitement has worn off.

However, many good or at least adequate musicians have certainly benefited by being urged (if not forced) by their parents when their own spontaneous interest flagged. So, as one mother comments, "The struggle to get the practicing done is so constant that I sometimes wonder whether it is worth it. On the other hand, how does a parent know whether everyone concerned will regret it if she allows her child to stop?"

Of course you don't know. But if you have reason to believe that your child has a reasonable amount of ability and at least some enthusiasm for lessons (even though not for practicing), then you will naturally want the music instruction to go on if possible.

As a rule we find that if you allow children to have a "vacation" from lessons at such a time as their objections and rebellions become the worst—with the understanding that later *when they are ready,* they can start in again—they do come around to it later *if* there is real musical interest and ability there to begin with. We have known of a number of probably quite talented children who have benefited from such a vacation.

Or some parents find that cutting down the amount of practicing required or freedom from practicing over the weekends will do the trick. Some feel that a child benefits more by twenty or thirty min-utes of daily willing and serious practicing than by being forced to sit at the piano for an hour each day.

Or even, in extreme cases and at periods when practicing difficul-ties are the greatest, some teachers will allow the weekly lessons, which many children will accept, without any practicing at all. This latter is especially true of the 7-year-old who has such a craving for music lessons. Later it is different. When the child demands lessons at eleven or twelve years of age, he should not be allowed to take them unless he promises ahead of time that he will accept the de-mands of practicing.

Also, it is important to keep in mind the fact that many good modern teachers of music consider that it is, within reason, up to them to try to keep the interest of their music students. There is cur-rently a definite trend in the direction of assigning more interesting and enjoyable "pieces" and avoiding too much emphasis on the less pleasurable scales and exercises.

16

The Ethical Sense

THE young child may not appear to be born with an ethical sense, but he does show an awareness of the response of others to his acts, without necessarily being told verbally how they are responding. How he moves from this initial spontaneous response is, however, largely determined by the culture. The 6-year-old is often very aware of whether he is good or bad. His parents often wonder why he is so conscious of this. They also notice that when he has been particularly bad he almost invariably asks if he has been good. Some tenuous roots of the ethical sense are sprouting within him even at this early age.

But what the child does with these roots, how he develops from them, is more often than not determined by the culture. And each culture has its own notions of what is good and what is bad. We, in our society, believe that people should tell the truth, but there are societies in which it pays to lie. We believe in honesty and kindness. There are societies which do not.

So each society has to teach its children what it approves of and what it disapproves of. And for this teaching to be effective, the child needs to have reached at least a certain stage of maturity before he can learn what we try to teach him.

TRUTHFULNESS

Consider the matter of telling the truth. The average 4-year-old tells very tall tales, and often makes very little distinction between fact and fiction. Enjoy his imaginings. Don't be too concerned about the lion which nearly ate him up.

At five, the average child still exaggerates and tells fanciful stories,

276

but he begins to distinguish real from make-believe and to know when he is "fooling." Help him by identifying his wilder imaginings as "pretend," his truthful statements as "real."

Even by six, many children are far from truthful. They will deny having misbehaved if they are questioned directly, even though the evidence is before their very eyes, and will often tell falsehoods to get out of difficulty. Some are honest verbally but will cheat at games, especially if they are losing.

There is usually less lying at seven than at six, and much concern with the wrongness of lying and cheating, especially in friends.

By eight years of age many children are truthful on matters which they consider important, but the natural expansiveness of Eight leads to some telling of tall tales and some boasting. However, Eight usually distinguishes fact from fancy and will often size up the adult to see if he believes what is being told. You can help him here by saying, "That's a good story, Jim. Now, what really happened?"

Many 9-year-olds are essentially truthful and, though they may say they have washed their hands when they haven't or may support a brother or sister in a lie, they mostly tell the truth.

As parents we can give the best teaching possible and set the best example possible, but we should always remember that the child's ability to accept and profit by teaching about right and wrong develops slowly and that he has much to learn. We should not be too much discouraged if in the early years he makes many mistakes in this department.

In a few children, however, truth-telling comes in very early. This occurs mostly in those children who seem by nature to be exceptionally ethical. Even from a very early age they easily behave in the ways which we adults approve and prefer.

Such children simply seem to pick up ethical ways of behaving. Given the benefit of teachings about truthfulness, honesty and such, they absorb these teachings almost immediately and put them into practice at once. Some almost seem too one-sided, too rigid, about their ethical sense. It is as though it has been pasted on and may not have gone through an inner growth force that tests out both ways of doing a thing and then makes a choice.

The important thing to remember is that apparently it is a basic temperament for accepting the teachings of others which brings about this super-ethical behavior. (Such children are likely to be strong on manners, too. They like formal social situations and are often unhappy if they have to eat in the kitchen rather than at a nicely set dining table.)

At the opposite extreme from these very factual, ethical children we find the extremely creative, imaginative children who in their early years find it so difficult to distinguish between fact and fiction, and who rapidly shift from one to the other according to their fancy or the way the wind is blowing. They are the ones who are caught in the pattern of playing life both ways and who find it difficult to make a choice of direction.

It is sometimes hard for parents of such children to distinguish between creative imagination which should be encouraged and deliberate falsifying which should be discouraged. And sometimes the two are so jumbled and mixed up that the individual can reach the extreme point of deceiving himself. This is a sad state of affairs which needs to be laboriously unraveled so that the child can come to distinguish the two—fact or fancy.

Imaginary Companions

One evidence of creative imagination which most parents, and rightly, accept without undue concern is the phenomenon of imaginary playmates. Many children around the age of three and a half spend a good deal of their play time with imaginary playmates of their own creation. These playmates may be simply imaginary children, they may be animals, they may be mythical creatures. They often have extremely fanciful names such as Bisslebamboo or Yuke-a-Tuke. They may be good or bad.

Many children take these companions so seriously that a place must be saved for them at table, a seat reserved in the family car.

Children from large families enjoy such playmates as often as do only children. They do not seem to appear merely because a child may be lonely. Nearly one-third of a group of well-endowed children whom we studied did, at one time or another during the preschool years, have such playmates. Most often it is the well-endowed child, of good intelligence and adequate social adjustment as well as imagination, who has imaginary companions.

BOASTING

AT FOUR:

"I'm bigger than you. I'm bigger. I can keep you out of my house because I'm bigger than you," chants the 4-year-old to his friend in the nursery school. Actually, the child speaking may be the smallest one in the room, but the statement is always the same. The 4-year-old just naturally claims to be the biggest, the best, the smartest, the strongest of anybody.

And it is not only to the other children that the child of this age boasts. He tells us when he builds with the nursery school blocks: "I can make anything. I got much bigger blocks than this at home. You have to have awfully big blocks for me. My blocks at home are better than these. I got more than any other children have. They're ever so big. *You* couldn't pick 'em up, but I can. I'm awfully strong. I can even box."

And if his mother's friends are visiting the house, they may be disturbed to hear him boasting in front of his little sister, "I'm bigger than she is and I'm smarter too. She can't do anything; she's so little."

"Never boast," our parents and our schoolteachers, and especially our Sunday-school teachers, taught us. We may remember these teachings and feel disturbed when we run into these boastful 4-year-olds. Surely their parents are bringing them up wrong. Surely they will grow up to be horribly conceited and obnoxious adults unless somebody takes them in hand and stops all this awful boasting.

We have forgotten, or perhaps never realized, that we ourselves when we were 4-year-olds very likely boasted too. For that is the nature of the 4-year-old. The child of this age is just naturally "bursting out all over," and hardly anything else in the world is as wonderful to him as his own accomplishments.

AT SIX:

"That's easy! Easy for me!" Six-year-old George had been brought by his parents to the Gesell Institute for a developmental examination. He was showing the examiner how well he could write his name, and boasting of his ability.

He could do some of his numbers, too, he said. "Easy! Easy for me 'cause I'm smart!"

"Tricked you, didn't I?" he asked a minute later as, in writing his numbers, he skipped one and wrote eight instead of seven. "I'm too smart for you, I guess," he chortled.

And so it went throughout the whole examination. George did a good job on most of the tests, and he certainly enjoyed himself immensely. However, modesty was obviously at this point not one of his virtues. Nearly every achievement, no matter how minor, was accompanied by his own self-congratulation. George was, to hear him tell it, practically the smartest little boy ever seen at our Institute.

What shall we think of all this boasting (in a society which rates a certain degree of modesty to be highly desirable)?

Different people, of course, reacted to George differently.

His parents, who were watching the examination from behind a one-way screen (which allowed them to see George, but did not allow George to see them), considered it to be highly amusing. They laughed and laughed at each new sally.

His teacher, who had also come in to watch the examination— since George was having quite a bit of difficulty in school—looked jaded, as if to say, "That's George for you. Always showing off!"

Some child specialists (not present on this particular occasion) consider—and perhaps correctly—that excessive boasting is in many cases a sign that a child is poorly adjusted, feels insecure and needs to be helped toward a more adequate evaluation of himself in relation to the outside world.

A fourth point of view—our own (and *you* of course are entitled to *your* own)—lies somewhat between the other three. We did not find George's behavior so engaging as did his parents or as exasperating as did his teacher. Nor did we believe it to be a sign that anything was "wrong" with George—at least nothing that time would not take care of. On the contrary, we considered his boasts of "That's easy," "I'm smart," and his delight in thinking he had tricked us as some of the most convincing signs of his basic normality.

Interestingly enough, it was especially when he was having trouble that this boasting occurred. Whenever he said it was easy, you could be pretty sure that it was hard for him. His bragging seemed—at least to him—to turn his failures into successes.

At any rate, this is the way that the 6-year-old in our culture quite characteristically behaves, for Six, like Four, is a boaster. Six is, to himself, the center of the universe. If he can't win out by actually being right, he will at least tell you how right he is!

In the years which follow six, boasting does, in most happy, reasonably well-adjusted boys and girls, diminish considerably. If as the child grows older he still finds it necessary to boast unduly, you can try to make him realize how unattractive such behavior is. Though always you yourself should keep in mind that the boasting child (or adult) often boasts because he feels basically inadequate and insecure, or that he is going through a new phase of development of growth which makes him feel insecure.

So, actually, your best accomplishment with a boaster would be to help him to such achievement and success that he will begin to feel sure of himself and will not need to boast. This will be more effective in the long run, even though it will require more skill, patience and insight than simply using strong-arm methods to prevent his boasting.

ADMITTING WRONGDOING

Jimmy's mother had just come home from the store. She had left Jimmy at home alone for the few minutes that she was gone. After all, he was six years old and old enough, she figured, to take care of himself and not get into too much trouble.

But Jimmy's mother was wrong. Just as she entered the house, she heard a loud crash. Jimmy had climbed up onto the pantry shelf and had managed to knock over and break one of her best vases.

"Jimmy, you naughty boy, what have you done?" she scolded him. "Did you break that vase?"

"No, Mummy, no. I didn't," denied Jimmy vigorously, very much frightened. He hadn't meant to knock over the vase, and certainly he hadn't expected his mother to be back so soon.

"Now, Jimmy, I've always told you to tell me the truth. Admit that you broke the vase."

"But Mummy, I didn't, I didn't," protested Jimmy.

So off to bed went Jimmy while his mother cleaned up the pieces. . . . "It wasn't so much just his breaking the vase, though that was bad enough," she told Jimmy's father when he came home. "But it was his lying about it that I minded so much. So I did the only thing I could have done. I sent him to bed. He's just got to learn to tell the truth, and he's old enough to take the blame when he has done wrong."

We don't blame Jimmy's mother for being upset at broken bric-a-brac, but she was wrong here on at least two counts (aside from her questionable move in leaving him alone and unsupervised while she was out).

The average child of this age just does not have the maturity to admit his own wrongdoing, and if questioned directly as to whether or not he has done a "bad" thing, he will almost invariably deny it (or at best, if he doesn't deny it, will claim, "Well, *I* couldn't help it").

So Jimmy's mother was expecting too much in wanting him to admit his own wrongdoing, especially right after it had happened. And when she asked him directly if he had knocked over the vase, she was literally pushing him into a lie. Because it was almost a certainty—had she but realized it—that a child of his age would deny his guilt when he was accused directly.

If, for purposes of distributing blame, you find it absolutely necessary to discover whether a 6-year-old did or did not do a certain thing, it is usually easy to find out if you don't accuse him directly. Just say, in Jimmy's case, "Why, how could you reach that high shelf?" He will tell you (not realizing what he is saying), "Oh, I just pushed that chair over and climbed up."

But do not lead him into a lie by asking directly if he did the bad thing. It takes more than 6-year-old maturity before the average child can own up to his misdemeanors, even when he is caught red-handed.

Nor is the average 7-year-old particularly good about taking the blame. In fact, if any wrong has been committed, he is most likely to attempt, at least, to put the blame on somebody. "He did it," or, "It was his fault," are Seven's characteristic alibis in his efforts to shift blame to other shoulders than his own.

Other alibis take the form of self-justification, "I was just going to do it," or, "That was what I meant."

Eight and Nine are, characteristically, getting to be considerably more responsible for their own acts. They may still, on frequent occasion, deny their own guilt. But at least they don't try to blame things on anybody else. At least not all the time.

In fact, at times, children of these ages seem almost too ready to take the blame. "I *always* do it wrong." They promise for the future: "I'll *never* do it again." Or even, "I did it and I'm sorry." They may feel guilty at wrongdoing, and some have been known to apologize spontaneously. But they still are quick with excuses: "He was bothering me!"

Things do improve gradually through the years, but it must be admitted that even by ten years of age most children have not come very far in the ability to take blame. About the most hopeful generalization which can be made is that, *"Some* take blame *part of the time if* the thing is not too bad." The majority frankly admit that they push the blame off onto brothers and sisters if they can possibly manage to do so. Alibiing, also, is very strong even as late as ten. In short, very few even at this age take the blame if they can conveniently get out of doing so.

CHEATING

Evening at Grandmother's. The three children—Jane and Jill, 8-year-old twins, and 6-year-old Bill—are playing a simple three-handed card game. Mother, Grandmother and Father are conversing contentedly in the background, their attention focused more fully on the charming picture of the children at play than on their own conversation.

Till suddenly, Slap! One of the twins reaches over and slaps poor Bill on the face. Bill starts to cry and slaps her back.

"He cheated, Mummy. He always cheats when he's losing," explained the twin to her mother, trying to make herself heard above Bill's sobs.

And so another family evening, and the start of what had looked like a promising visit, was ruined. The adults tended to take sides, but everybody was mad at somebody.

Mother scolded the twins for slapping Bill, "who is just a baby and you ought to be nicer to him."

Father took the stand that it was wrong for Bill to cheat, and that, whereas his sister should not have slapped him, he was actually more at fault than she. That is, slapping was not, in Father's opinion, as bad as cheating.

Grandmother did not express an opinion, but she was extremely downcast to have things going so badly.

All three children were sent to bed, having been thoroughly scolded, but their misdemeanor hung like a cloud over the rest of the evening.

Unfortunately, the average competitive, egocentric 6-year-old has not yet acquired or developed either the ability to lose at competitive games or a full, practical realization of the wrongness of cheating. Put him in a competitive situation and more often than not, if he is losing, he will cheat to win. The response is almost automatic. He needs to be flexible in a game, to change the rules in midstream, if necessary. But he must win, or he crumbles all to pieces or strikes out with ferocity.

Play with one understanding adult, preferably a grandparent, who will both jockey him into place and at the same time let him win, will give his ego the substance which he so badly needs. He'll learn to lose in time, but by slow stages.

Cheating is actually a matter of great interest to the 6-year-old, but most children at that age have come only far enough to be concerned about the cheating of others. They are quick to complain about their playmates, "Lila's cheating!" but they themselves, alas, are equally quick to cheat if they need to do so in order to win.

Things improve by slow degrees in the years which follow. By eight or nine the average child, if not pitted against opponents too greatly skilled, can usually play games without cheating. Eventually, even by nine years of age, he may begin to learn that "the game's the thing" (though he loses this insight in a few years and then later regains it again).

Cheating of another sort, in lessons or examinations in school, is usually not, in ordinary cases, a severe problem in the first ten years—due largely to lack of skill on the part of the cheater before the pre-teen years.

STEALING

"Thou shalt not steal!" A maxim pretty well accepted by law-abiding adults in our culture. However, we have no special reason to believe that the young child is born with any innate tendency one way or the other. In the earliest years he simply grabs whatever he can lay his hands on.

Even in the first two or three years we manage to teach him not to touch certain dangerous or valuable objects. But he is not ready to learn the real distinction between mine and thine and to respect that distinction until much later. And as in many fields of behavior, many children learn to do things the right way by doing them the wrong way first.

Probably the most difficulty with taking things which do not belong to him comes between five and eight years of age. At this time the child is much attracted by bright, pretty or interesting-looking belongings of his mother, by things he wants like pencils and erasers or by money—for itself or mostly for what it can buy. He is not mature enough to withstand his temptation to take these things, even if he has been told time and again that he must withstand it.

So he "steals" something which doesn't belong to him. (His property sense at this time is so limited that he is equally likely to give away something valuable of his own.) There is something almost wistful and charming in what he steals and the way he steals it. At five he may prefer pennies to half dollars. They have meaning to him. At six he responds to the beauty of some trinket and he takes it before your very eyes even though he denies it when accused. At seven his passion for pencils and erasers is so strong that he wants more and more and more—any within hand's reach. And by eight the loose money in the kitchen drawer is indeed a temptation, for he is beginning to know about money, its value and what things it can buy. When the theft is discovered, he is punished and admonished. He probably excuses himself that he "didn't mean to" and he certainly promises that he will "never do it again."

Another day—another theft.

Parents are usually most discouraged and often extremely upset about such happenings. They may feel that they have a juvenile delinquent in the making on their hands. He not only steals but he lies about it when questioned.

The chances are, in most cases, that this early period of stealing will be relatively brief. You can help the child get over this behavior by taking pains to lock up (or otherwise make unavailable) money and other valuables. Tell the child that you are locking them up to *help him remember* that he is not going to take them.

Simply turning a key in a lock is going to do more to prevent pilfering or at least to hold it in check than all the talk and all the punishing in the world.

If the child takes things from his parents' desk or bureau, try giving him one unlocked drawer of his own where he can keep things. Make it interesting and occasionally add that spice that comes with the unexpected—a surprise in his drawer.

If his taking things spreads to friends' houses, you will need to warn the other mothers so that they can keep an eye on him and/ or keep their own valuables locked up. If, in spite of this, you find that he does bring money or property home from the neighbors', he should be expected or helped to return it. (This may be very hard for him, and you may have to return it for him. The fact that he feels his misdemeanor so strongly means that new inner forces are relating to his outer acts and a repetition in the future is less likely.)

Minor pilferings at school are so common in the early grades, especially in the second grade, that some teachers take time at the close of each session for a "pocket emptying." It is surprising to note how many pencils, erasers and such have strayed into pockets other than those of their owners.

At school, such a pocket emptying may be just a routine affair. When things have been taken at home, or at the neighbors', or at a store, of course you will express firm disapproval. But more effective than scolding or punishment is prevention.

When stealing continues beyond seven or eight years of age, several possible reasons may be considered.

1. This particular child may be very immature so far as the ability to understand and abide by general moral teachings is concerned. (Many of our delinquent children fall into this group.) In this case they will have to be treated as though they were younger —in the ways we have just described.

2. It may be that his income, from earnings or allowance, is so far below his actual expenditures that he feels the need of supplementing it illicitly.

3. The stealing may be an indication that there is something seriously wrong with or seriously lacking in the child's life. Some psychiatrists believe that a child steals things to make up for love or other satisfactions which he feels are lacking. You might at least consider this possibility. If you suspect that this is the answer, you may want to find a child specialist to help you solve any stealing problem which may come up.

However, in keeping with the principle of never seek a complicated explanation when a simple one will do, don't seek "deep" reasons and complicated therapy unless you're sure that something simple will not suffice. Good example, proper admonition, prevention and reasonable punishment (making the older child pay back money taken out of his allowance) will take care of the majority of cases of light-fingeredness.

Most important is for parents not to be too deeply shocked, hurt, surprised and despairing when stealing occurs. The remarkable thing is not that some children steal, but that the great majority of children, in spite of temptations and opportunities, can be taught to abide by our culture's rules about private property. It is important for parents to realize that some children need more time than others or more direct assistance to learn the importance of these rules and to be able to abide by them.

MINDING WHEN SPOKEN TO

Minding when spoken to may not be exactly "moral," and not minding may not be exactly "immoral." But certainly one of the important attributes of a "good" child in most people's estimation is that he minds quickly when he is spoken to.

We can't, within the limits of this book, tell you how to make your children mind. Each family situation differs, not only in what the parents expect, but in how skillful they are in getting their children to live up to their expectations and in the readiness and ability of the children to mind when spoken to.

Simple general rules for getting your child to mind are: (1) Be sure that what you demand is not beyond his ability; (2) be sure that you have his attention before you speak; (3) try not to demand too much—don't be always ordering him around.

As we say, getting the child to mind is really up to you. Also, deciding how exactly and how immediately he is to carry out your orders is for you to determine. However, it may help a little to know some of the age changes in readiness and ability to mind which we have found in children of different age levels. Because the ability to mind, like other abilities, changes and grows with increasing age.

18 months: The child of this age does not, as a rule, obey direct commands. In fact he is likely to do exactly the opposite of what you request.

2½ years: The child may obey some simple commands, but in general is imperious and domineering. Techniques and indirect approaches usually work better with him than direct commands.

3 years: At this age most children are much more responsive to directions. Many like to please and to conform, within the limits of their abilities. They are attentive to spoken directions. They respond best to specific rather than general directions and are susceptible to both praise and blame.

4 years: Four is less anxious to please and conform. He likes to do things his own way and enjoys defying the adult. He is out of bounds and resistant in many directions, and is less sensitive to praise and blame than at three.

5 years: Conforming Five needs, invites and accepts supervision and direction. He even asks for directions, and thrives on praise for his conformity.

6 years: Six usually responds slowly or even negatively to commands, though if you can ignore his initial, "No, I won't!" he often later carries out the command spontaneously, as though it were his own idea. He needs a little time and a little leeway. If he says, "No," try, "See if you can do it before I count to ten," or, "I guess you're going to need three chances on that one." If you can give in a little and not demand instantaneous conformity and obedience, things will go more smoothly. However, many Sixes are negative, rude, resistant, saucy and argumentative in the face of direct commands.

7 years: Seven is not as belligerently un-co-operative as is Six, but he often does not respond promptly, does not hear directions and may forget what you have told him. He may start to obey and then get into a detour along the way. Best results are obtained by warning him in advance, reminding him when the time comes and checking to see that he does not get off the track along the way.

8 years: Eight is a little better. He usually delays somewhat in carrying out a request and may argue and find excuses, but he finally obeys with, "If you insist." He prefers to work for an immediate (cash) reward than simply for the sake of helping. Many Eights want, not full directions, which they consider babyish, but just a hint or cue. Thus they prefer the word "dinner" to, "Wash your hands and get ready for dinner." Or if full instructions are given, they may insist that these be worded "just right."

9 years: Considerable improvement here. Many can now interrupt their own activity (so difficult at seven) in response to a request or demand from the adult. However, securing the child's attention in the first place may depend on his interest and willingness to carry out the request. He may wish to postpone the task till later and then may become so busy that he forgets. Even now he needs to be given detailed instructions to begin with, and then reminded. But there is much less arguing back than earlier. If the child does not like the directions, he may look sullen, cross, truculent; but if no issue is made, he will usually obey eventually. Many now prefer a fair appraisal of their work to praise or pay.

10 years: Though there may be some resistance, delay and objection, in general Tens are reasonably good about carrying out commands and reasonably docile about obeying. Most at this age do accept the idea that the parents' word is law.

RIGHT AND WRONG

In thinking about the young child as he does right or wrong, from our point of view, it is important to remember that his own standards of right and wrong are not as well defined as our own. He learns from us, but he learns slowly.

Some children do not seem to try very hard to be good. Others try hard with only partial success, and often ask, "Have I been a good boy today?" on the very days when they have been the worst.

Thus even by six years of age, many children actually cannot always tell good from bad. Most of them have little generalized sense of "goodness" and "badness." Rather, they know that their parents allow and praise certain things, forbid and punish others.

Here are samples of one 6-year-old's lists of "Things to do" and "Things not to do":

Things to do:

1. Keep dresses clean.
2. Keep watches going—winding them.
3. Go to bed at 7:30; get up at 7:30.
4. When people are breaking things, tell them to stop.

Things not to do:

1. Not to say "I am not talking to you."
2. Not to say "Give me the biggest piece of anything."
3. Not to spill crumbs on the floor.
4. Not to set fires.
5. Don't break armchairs.
6. Don't pinch people.

Seven is a little more advanced. He does not have to remember *every single thing* separately. He can generalize a little—that thinking of others is good, that thinking only of yourself is less good.

Thus this same girl's lists at seven contained among other items the following:

Thinking about others:

1. Obeying my mother—picked up the living room.
2. Went to bed willingly—fell asleep quickly.
3. Dressed quickly without dawdling.
4. I don't tip my chair as much as I used to.

Thinking about myself:

1. Eating omelette with my fingers.

2. Saying "Wah."
3. Speaking rudely to my mother: "Yes you will."

And by eight there is already tremendous progress toward generalized concepts of goodness and badness. From this same girl at eight, we have such comments about right and wrong as the following:

1. When some of the people start up a fight, it's not my fault if I want to try and stop the fight even though Miss D. tells us to keep away from fights because the other teachers would think we'd started it. Even if we try to explain to the teachers, they think we did start the fight and were just trying to get away from being punished.
2. In the coat room even though you're not supposed to talk, I can't help it sometimes because other people ask me questions and tempt me to answer them. Do you blame me?
3. I think I ought to have a little more freedom, more freedom about deciding things—like getting up early in the morning. (I used to plan to, then I'd be too tired when I woke up in the morning.)
4. I think I should have rewards for being good, like candy and books I like very much. But I won't always have to be rewarded. Maybe when I'm about 9½ or 10 I don't think I'll have to be rewarded for being good. Then I'll just be good naturally.

Progress, certainly—but Eight still, we must admit, is thinking a good deal more of himself, right or wrong, than he is of others.

Morals at Ten

The child's sense of right and wrong develops slowly. And even when he has matured intellectually to the point where he can, to our satisfaction, tell right from wrong, he is not always emotionally ready to do right and avoid wrong.

"Do it dis way?" asks the 3-year-old, and we believe that he is on his way to conformity. But—"No, I won't. Try and make me!"

says Six. Two is willing but not very ready to do "right." Six may be neither ready nor willing.

In general, however, in spite of ups and downs, things tend to improve with added maturity. And so, in the natural course of things, the child reaches the age of ten, when most children are not only intellectually able to discriminate right from wrong but are emotionally geared to conform to the adult wish that they do right and avoid wrong.

We shall let one of our 10-year-olds speak for herself. (There are always cynics who suspect that children do not tell us the truth—that they make themselves out better than they really are. We do not share this cynicism, but in any event we have the parents' check on the children's statements.)

Yes, I can usually tell right and wrong. It depends on what it is. Unless it was school work. If you were doing some work and it was the wrong question, I might not know. But if somebody was doing something to someone else that was wrong, I would know.

My mother has told me some things; and Sunday School has told me some things; and other things I just know by myself. And the school has told me some things. At school they tell you how to act with other children and things like that. And my mother tells me manners for the table which are right and wrong.

My conscience wouldn't bother me too much if I did wrong; but it would bother me enough to make me say I'm sorry.

Yes [in answer to our question], I certainly try to tell the truth. And I always try to mind mummy except sometimes when I'm looking at television and mummy asks me to go to bed, sometimes I don't hear and sometimes it's too good to miss and I watch it just a little longer.

About swearing, I always try not to. I don't think it's a good thing to do.

I try to be good because I think God wouldn't like it if I was bad.

. . . But even more telling than such comments is the characteristic 10-year-old phrase, "Yes, Mummy lets me (or doesn't let me) do that." The child who is still answering questions by quoting Mummy as an authority is a child who is still conforming—who has not yet reached the teen-age stage of insisting that he be allowed to think things out for himself and to make his own decisions as to right and wrong. (Though even the teen-ager will often need some help in arriving at such decisions.)

DELINQUENCY

Behavior problems serious enough to be termed "delinquent" rarely occur in children in the age range we're discussing in this book. One reason for this is that the very young child has not the ingenuity or strength to carry out very much in the way of serious crime. A more important reason is that we can understand and make allowances for his actions and motives on the grounds that "He's so young," "It's just a stage," "He hasn't learned yet." We excuse his inadequacies in meeting some of society's demands because he is immature.

Finding a 6-year-old who lies or steals, who has moments of nearly ungovernable rage and who thinks the world ought to revolve around him is not much of a surprise to a psychologist, however hard it may be, temporarily, on parents, relatives and the neighborhood. But finding the same behavior in a 14- or 15-year-old can be frightening. (The whole question of *why growth went wrong* is a tremendously complicated one. Yet often it is only when growth does go wrong, or possibly doesn't unfold or move, that we appreciate how complex normal development is.)

In a field where there are more questions than answers (and we aren't even too sure about some of the questions), psychologists of both the professionally trained and the home-grown varieties like to feel that they have *the* answer. And so we could make quite a list, each item of which has been considered *the* cause of delinquency: slums, comic books, progressive education, traditional education, nutrition, divorce, depression, inflation, parental spoiling, parental harshness—and so on and on. Excellent cases for—or against—any of these can be made on the basis of particular children. But no *one* of these can be considered the "exclusive cause."

A good example of misdirected theorizing is the notion that "there are no delinquent children—only delinquent parents." That the parents of delinquent children must shoulder part of the burden of blame can hardly be denied. But to say that delinquency is nearly always the *fault* of the parents is as meaningless as the notion that it is nearly always the *fault* of the child.

The crux of the problem seems to lie in a balance—a balance between the child's basic *individuality* and his *environment*. The first of these, individuality, the basic equipment he brings into the world with him, later is shaped through growth and organized through experience into personality. The many forces we lump together as "environment" include both intimate forces—his family, with its wishes, feelings, methods of discipline—and broader forces—neighborhood and associates, community, customs, laws.

When we consider this relationship between what the individual brings with him into the world and what happens to him after that, we can see at least three broad groups of children who differ in their reactions. Children in the first group seem simply to be made up of basically sturdy stuff. These children are so stable ethically, as in every other respect, that the most extremely adverse circumstances can scarcely distort their behavior. We all know of leaders in almost every field who have risen above the most (theoretically) adverse circumstances. For such children we naturally want to provide the best possible surroundings for development. But their success is essentially of their own making.

There is a second group of children so susceptible to their surroundings that their behavior will indeed be strongly determined by their upbringing. With good upbringing and good surroundings, they become good citizens. Poor upbringing and unwholesome surroundings provide a good chance of their becoming delinquent. For such children, you as parents and you as members of the community will especially need and want to do your very best.

It is from a third group of children, however, that a majority of delinquents seem to come. These children come into the world with one strike—or more—against them from the start. Their inadequacy lies somewhere in their basic individuality. These are not "born criminals." But for one reason or another, the task of growing up to accept and follow the moral laws of our society is hard for them— sometimes just about impossible. Some of these children are retarded in all areas of growth. Their intelligence never develops beyond that of the young child. Some show more specific lacks, developing normally in the area of intelligence, but not developing emotionally— feeling and acting like a 6-year-old when they are in their teens, for example. They may lack inhibition and restraint, or the ability to foresee the end result of their actions. For such children, the environment cannot be just a standard "good environment." It must be better than that; it must be adapted to the very special needs of the particular child—instructing, supervising, making up from the outside for what is lacking in the child.

This group is certainly the one toward whom more effort needs to be directed. If a careful, thorough psychological examination could be made available for every school child, we could then, in the earliest years, spot these potentially deviant children who will likely later, unless prevented, become delinquent. Finding them and dealing with them are, of course, two different things. But finding them is the first step. They must be identified before we can go about protecting society from them and protecting them from their own inadequacies.

Here as elsewhere the best that parents and society can do for our children may not be too good. And here as elsewhere it is not all up to the parents or to society. Even though there is much that they can do, we must always remember that at least part of the answer— sometimes most of it—lies in the organism itself.

Part Three

17

What to Tell About Santa Claus, Deity, Death, Adoption, Divorce

SANTA CLAUS

"THERE really isn't a Santa Claus, is there, Mummy?" Six-year-old Peter regarded his mother searchingly.

Mother hesitated for a moment. She had known that this day would come—but still—questions about Santa, like questions about sex, often pop up when we're not quite prepared for them. She decided to tell the truth.

"No, Peter, there really isn't any Santa Claus."

"That's what I thought," replied Peter comfortably. "He's just a man dressed up, who goes all over the world and comes down the chimney and gives everybody presents."

Thus, as you can see, most children—for Peter is quite typical of others—do not *find out* about Santa Claus all at once. They take from a skeptical environment only as much as they are ready and able to accept.

Two other 6-year-olds, a little further along the road to enlightenment, were overheard by us in the following conversation:

Jetty: "Do you think Santa Claus is real?"

Timothy: "No."

Jetty: "Santa Claus used to be St. Nicholas and then St. Nicholas died, so they just took a man as Santa Claus and put a beard on him."

Perhaps these two anecdotes will help to answer the question: "Should we allow children to believe in Santa Claus?" An inevitable question which we hear every year as Christmastime comes inevitably around.

Most families, we find, don't worry about the problem—in fact, they don't even consider it to be a problem. Their youngest children believe in Santa. The older ones don't. And the transition from belief to disbelief is in most quite painless.

But every year a few parents worry about what will happen when their children *find out* that there is no Santa. They fear that if the child finds out that something he's been allowed to believe really Isn't So, this will undermine his faith in other things that they tell him.

It is our experience that only the extremely fragile child will be harmed by such a "disillusionment." Certainly thousands if not millions of people have believed, and then not believed, and have still been left with a warm spot in their hearts for the whole idea.

Perhaps one of the main reasons why most children are not too much disturbed by the discovery that Santa Claus is not "real" is that, as the preceding anecdotes show, this discovery does not come about all at once. Most children do not believe it the first time that somebody tells them that Santa is not real. They are so far from ready that they probably do not even hear the bad news.

If a child hears that Santa isn't real—when he is very young—he just doesn't "hear" this information because it means nothing to him. Later, when he does "hear" it, it means that he is on the verge of being ready to accept. If he is unhappy and tearful and denies the truth, that too usually means that he is almost ready to accept. Vigorous tearful denial of some enlightenment usually means that a child is on the verge of being ready to understand and believe the new thing.

And even when they do finally hear and can even repeat that there is no Santa Claus, most of them believe only as much as they are ready to believe. This is a comforting thing to know about children—that the human being normally has great powers of self-protection.

AGE DIFFERENCES IN ATTITUDES TOWARD CHRISTMAS

Christmas means very little to the extremely young child—or at least usually means something quite different from what his parents have anticipated. Your 9-month-old baby, instead of being delighted with the large woolly dog which you have provided with such expense and anticipation, may merely howl in fright every time the toy is brought near to him.

Your 2- or 2½-year-old, instead of being the little angel you had expected, just sits by greedily, and every time a present from the tree is offered to anyone else, selfishly inquires, "Anything more for me?" "Anything more for me?"

Here, as in all fields of behavior, if we know what is reasonable to expect and do not expect too much, we are less likely to be disappointed.

Many 2-year-olds whom we have known are not yet ready for Santa Claus. They either are not interested or may even be frightened by him. The tree is the important thing to Two, who gazes at it and its lights starry-eyed. There is also some interest in presents, but not much in the giver.

The 3-year-old has grown up a lot. His interest in Santa may be rather vague and he may be a little hazy as to details, but he is interested. And he is usually pleased and excited by the presents he receives.

Four, as a rule, believes in Santa Claus in every detail. And he is deeply interested in every detail.

But five and six are the real Santa Claus ages, when overwhelming interest and great delight and unshakable belief are expressed. The joy which most children experience in Santa Claus at these ages is surely worth any little disillusionment which may come about later.

The average 5-year-old has an extremely realistic approach to Santa Claus. He definitely thinks of him as a real man living in a real house and having a real wife. He often makes plans to visit him, and likes to write (or at least dictate) letters to him asking for the things he wants.

Six does the same. The first letters he writes, or prints, may be to Santa with lists of the presents he wants to receive. Most 6-year-olds are very firm in their belief about Santa Claus—insistent and emotional. They will often fiercely deny any hint that he is not real.

However, as in many things, this fierce denial may just precede a beginning skepticism. Some 6-year-olds and many Sevens are at least a little bit skeptical and may deny some aspects of the Santa Claus myth, such as that he comes down the chimney.

A few 8-year-olds still believe, but a good many children at eight, and nearly all by nine, are able to substitute a concept of a spirit of Christmas or a spirit of giving for a purely physical Santa. And most make this substitution with only a few pangs and with little real difficulty.

Dr. Gesell has commented on this subject: "Usually a child can assimilate, adore, and in time deny the concept of Santa Claus without suffering any scars of disillusionment."

DEITY

Religion like politics is not a subject on which we should attempt to advise. How much and what kind of religious training or opportunity for religious experience parents give their children is within their joint choice and usually is determined by their own religious background.

However, it is possible for us to tell you a little about the growing capacity of the child for receiving and accepting information about religion. And about the kinds of questions he is likely to ask. In the discussion that follows we are dealing with the factual side of Deity rather than the mystical and reverential side of the subjective experience, even though the latter bursts through spontaneously at certain ages, as at six years, and with certain children.

It has been our finding that under the age of four, most children —except perhaps the very accelerated—give little evidence of what might be termed a religious sense. Some are quite ready to enjoy Sunday school, particularly if it is run along the lines of a good nursery school, as early as three or even two years of age. The truly religious value of such experience is undoubtedly limited. But the social experience can be very valuable.

Not only are many 3-year-olds ready to attend Sunday school, but many of them can be taught to say short prayers. They are often extremely enthusiastic about their nightly praying, though we cannot be certain that their prayers mean much more to most of them than do the nursery rhymes which they also enjoy repeating.

However, at four, the great WHY age, comes a sudden, vigorous and, in some, almost insatiable curiosity about all the many wonders of nature and of life. Not only, "Where did I come from?" but, "Who made you?" "Who made the trees?" "Who made the stars?"

Each parent answers these in his own way. The child wants a simple answer, not a long dissertation. This is a time for large, fluid answers—something any 4-year-old child can grasp hold of. And he seems to be able to grasp hold of the concept of God, the naming of the unknown, as something he wishes to know more about and to penetrate.

How the 4-year-old mind pounces on this concept! His questions almost trip on each other, there are so many. "Who is God?" "What does He look like?" "Is God a gentleman?" "Does he like candy?" "Does he look like Daddy?"

Some adults look somewhat askance at the 4-year-old's very casual acceptance of God almost as a member of the family. But today's parents for the most part recognize this easy acceptance of the idea of Deity as natural for matter-of-fact Four.

Thus, parents are not surprised at the 4-year-old girl who, in the middle of a rainy-day walk with her mother, looked skyward and remarked, "Thank you, God, for making the sidewalk dry in some places. You see I have on my new shoes."

Nor will they take amiss the comment of the 4-year-old boy whose mother questioned him as he sat busily drawing. "What are you drawing?" she asked him.

"A picture of God," he replied.

"But you can't do that, dear," his mother remonstrated. "Nobody knows what God looks like."

"Well, they will as soon as I get this picture done," was the boy's calm reply.

Thus the 4-year-old's concepts and comments may often seem inappropriate to the grownup, but he himself is quite satisfied with his ideas of God.

You are not likely to run into much difficulty with your 4-year-old on this subject of Deity. His why's, it is true, are hard to satisfy fully on this subject as on many others. But most 4-year-olds go as far as they can in their questioning and thinking and then are relatively satisfied to stop without complete information. It is for the adult to answer questions, to guide thinking, but not to give more than the child can absorb.

However, we should mention here a religion different from the usual kind, which tends to prevail with the young child. And that is something which the Swiss psychologist Piaget calls the religion of the parents. Thus, to the average 4-year-old, his parents are all-knowing, all-powerful, eternal. So that actually the 4-year-old may be in small need of a higher power. He leans on his parents who are right there before his eyes. In fact, one little girl neatly verbalized this when she remarked: "I know. God is like Daddy. Only a little bigger."

FIVE-YEAR-OLD AND DEITY

The average 5-year-old child, when it comes to matters of religion, continues Four's marked practical interest in God.

"What does God look like?" "Where does He live?" "When was He born?" "Can He build cars?" "Can you call Him up on the phone?"

Again, as at four, some of these questions may seem inappropriate from the adult point of view. But they represent a probably necessary and natural stage in the child's development.

For some 5-year-olds, as for their younger brothers and sisters, conceptions of God and Santa Claus are not too clearly distinguished. Thus one 5-year-old came home from Sunday school and reported to her family: "You know God? Well he has two names: God and Jesus. You can call him either. I prefer 'God.' Some people don't believe on God. Some children don't believe on Santa Claus. The ones that don't, don't get any Christmas presents. I believe on Santa Claus."

Many are interested in the idea of God's omnipotence, but tend to be rather critical in the case of what they consider to be his mistakes.

Thus one 5-year-old commented to his mother: "God made a mistake when he made mosquitoes. Give me one good reason why he should have made a mosquito."

Another believed that if he himself fell down, it was because God pushed him. Still another, after repeating his bedtime "Now I lay me," turned to his mother and inquired seriously, "Who is it that kills us in the night? Jesus?"

Such comments as these emphasize the fact that though many a 5-year-old enjoys Sunday school and even part of the church service, likes saying his nightly prayers and expresses a lively questioning interest in God—his true comprehension of religious matters is often very restricted and extremely factual.

DEITY AT SIX

The 6-year-old loves to think about religious matters. He loves to pray. He loves to hear stories about God "our Father." He especially loves to hear about "our little Lord Jesus."

He is apt to take all of this very personally and it is extremely meaningful to him. He often loses his factual, detailed reality interest in religious matters and in Deity and enters the land of awe and wonder. The emotion that he feels is unmistakably strong, as shown in his facial expression. But this does not mean he will not become a skeptic at the age of seven.

An extremely religious family is likely to overrate this temporary intense interest. They are likely to make the mistake of believing the child will continue to be as devout and interested as he is at six.

Conversely, a nonreligious family, or one whose concepts of the Deity are more abstract, should not be taken aback when 6-year-old son or daughter comes home from school or Sunday school and discusses in such warm and glowing detail things he has picked up about "God our Father" or "The Little Lord Jesus."

Most 6-year-olds are enthusiastic about Sunday school, even though they do not always behave when there. Many, too, are even more interested in the church service, though here again they by no means can always be counted on to behave, especially for more than half an hour. They behave best and respond most to a colorful ritualistic service with music and pageantry. The singing entrance of the choir, the chanting, the focal point of the altar—all these help them to enter into group worship and to feel awe and wonder spontaneously.

According to Piaget, the Swiss psychologist whom we quoted before, the child of six is himself beginning to discover the limits of human capacity. He transfers to God, of whom he has been told right along, the qualities which he gradually learns to deny man. The feelings which he has up till this time directed to his parents, he now transfers to God—with whom his education has provided him.

And with his typical tendency to go to opposite extremes in anything, Six is apt to show as much interest in the Devil and Hell as in God and Heaven. Thus one little boy told his mother: "If you're good you'll have much fun with God. But if you're bad the Devils put you on the fire and that harms you."

DEITY AT SEVEN

Skeptical Seven! It isn't just that school has educated the child of seven to the point where he no longer takes things so much for granted. Rather, we think, it is that added maturity causes the child to be increasingly questioning and wary. He asks more questions than he did earlier. He requires more proof.

Thus the same boy or girl who at six years of age came home from Sunday school bursting with lively accounts of God and Jesus is not quite so certain at seven. Ask him what he thinks about God and he is apt to reply: "I have never seen him!"

His approach to matters of religion, likely to be so emotional when he is six, again becomes more intellectual at seven. He questions, rather than glowingly repeats what he has been told or has picked up at school or Sunday school. But his questions are quite different from the ones he asked when he was a mere five. He no longer inquires, inappropriately, whether God has a telephone or eats candy.

Now he asks such appropriate questions as: "How did God get up into Heaven?" "How can He see everything and be everywhere all at one time?" Or, "Why don't people come back from Heaven? Is it so wonderful that they don't want to?"

The increasing questioning and especially the increasing skepticism toward matters of religion should not, in our opinion, be a matter for concern by devout parents who wish to have their children grow up to accept the more orthodox doctrines. Actually, the questioning and skepticism of the 7-year-old may express a much more mature and realistic interest in matters of religion than does his earlier, all too easy and complete acceptance of exactly what he may have been told.

His skepticism is not simply rebellion or the expression of an irreligious attitude. Rather it means that these matters concern him but that he is now attaining the maturity of wanting to find out for himself.

He is a bit of a scientist in his own right. When he is read Bible stories that tell about ladders going up to heaven, his modern mind begins to operate and he asks, "What if an airplane came along and knocked them down?"

DEITY AT EIGHT TO TEN YEARS

Eight, in religion as in other matters, tends to show more positive, expansive enthusiasm—less skepticism. Though eight is not, in most children, a particularly devout age, many Eights accept without much question the religious teachings of those about them.

And, typically expansive, they often show much interest in Heaven and in what will happen to them after they die. Some have already reached a stage of believing that the soul but not the body goes to Heaven. But others persist in the notion that the body too goes, after death, to Heaven or Hell, depending on your behavior while alive.

In many children, along with a waning interest in religion, comes a diminished interest in Sunday-school attendance. When and if this diminished interest in Sunday school comes in, many parents have discovered that it works out best if parental emphasis on Sunday school can be diminished for a while. If for a season parents can allow only bimonthly or even monthly attendance, many children will reach their teens with renewed Sunday-school interest. If weekly attendance is insisted upon when the child's own interest is virtually absent or when he may even be resistant—sometimes more harm is done than good.

Some children, of course, wouldn't miss Sunday school for anything. They just naturally enjoy it. Others, spurred on by attendance contests or by extra good teaching, can be held through this period of sometimes flagging interest. Singing in the children's choir will hold many a 9-year-old.

And, as at all ages and in most things, parental example can often have more effect than parental admonition. By eight or nine years of age the average child is bright enough to notice the discrepancy if he himself is sent off to Sunday school while parents stay at home.

By ten years of age, interest in religious matters increases a bit. Of the 10-year-olds we studied, exactly half told us that they did believe in God. But the other half admitted that they either did not believe, never had believed, questioned God's existence or were less interested than formerly.

DEATH

Sooner or later almost every child is faced with some situation which makes it necessary for his parents to talk with him about the question of dying. A member of the immediate family or a close friend dies. Or the death of a pet or even the finding of a dead bird may bring up the question.

How to tell a child about death? As in the case of questions about Deity, or with questions about sex, specifically what you tell the child will be up to you. It will depend on his age, on the intensity and extent of his interest, on the kind of questions he asks.

Always you should answer any question clearly, directly and as truthfully as you can. But not in too great or burdensome detail. If he wants to know more, he will ask further questions.

We can perhaps help you a little by suggesting the general kind and amount of interest and knowledge about the subject of death which we have found characteristic at different ages.

In general, even by four years of age, the child's notions of death are extremely limited. As a rule, no particular emotion is expressed, though the child may verbalize some rudimentary notion that death is connected with sorrow or sadness. (There are of course exceptions. Some children are much disturbed by the death of relatives or of pets even earlier than this.)

By five, in many, the concept becomes more detailed, accurate and factual. Many recognize that death is the "end." Many recognize the immobility of the dead. They may like to avoid dead things —as birds and animals.

Most preschoolers are not ready for anything but the most limited explanation of death. The child even as late as five may have a fairly good, simple understanding, but his attitude is, as a rule, matter of fact and unemotional. For instance, if told that a man fell dead, he may ask, "Did he fall on his back or on his face?"

Most, at five, have a concept of themselves as always living. Only other people die. At five, we get the mere beginning of concern that Mother will one day die. This concern becomes much more marked at six.

Five may utilize the facts he has about death falsely. For instance, one little boy, told about how Abraham Lincoln had been shot, asked at the time of his grandfather's death, "Who shot Grandpa?" Another boy, whose grandfathers both had died but both of whose grandmothers were still alive, inquired, "Do daddies always die first?"

Some, at five and a half, believe in the reversibility of death— you're dead for a while and then you come to life. By six years of age, a new emotional awareness and much clearer concepts are coming in. But before we tell you about six, we'd like to quote to you the letter of a mother who reports her actual experience in telling her 5-year-old about the death of a baby brother.

My son died at five months of age, when my daughter was five years old. There are no other children. We found *truth* to be our most valuable asset. We allowed our little girl to participate in the truth with her eyes, ears and body. The truth to her did not contain the elements of sorrow and grief that it did to us. She danced and sang and played her way through the tragic days of his death, service and burial.

At the minute after the baby's little lungs no longer took in any air she was allowed to see him. Her daddy held her in his arms. She requested to return to "touch" him. She was allowed to and felt his little hand did not squeeze hers in response. Our decision to give her this opportunity was a difficult one for us to make but the next day we were satisfied with our choice because she volunteered: "Daddy, I know Billy's dead because I *saw* him." This was the foundation for the days which followed in which relatives and friends talked, cried and grieved —all or part of which was seen and participated in by her.

We explained death in the simplest terms we knew. She attended the service and was thrilled with the beauty of the flowers. She immediately and since has referred to the cemetery as "fairyland," and has requested to "go out where Billy is." The cemetery has no tombstones permitted and truly looks like a beautiful park.

Helping her to understand and accept the truth has had great benefit for me, her mother. Each time I had to search for simple language with which to explain to her, I found renewed strength in facing the Reality and Finality of what had happened. Her participation helped in another way also. She resented my too prolonged talking of the past —had I done enough for him, all I could? I had, and her reaction helped me to accept that I had, and turn my thoughts to the constructive future.

Each death within a family is different, and the problems are therefore different and also the solution. At no time is it ever easy. As I look back, however, I am grateful that our original decision was to allow her to participate. Each succeeding step we took was in part prompted by her 5-year-old type of reactions. We didn't know till we saw with our eyes just what her reaction would be. With Truth as our guiding goal, we helped her and she helped us.

This little girl obviously shows very superior qualities in accepting the situation as remarkably well as she did. Also she accepts with the realism of the 5-year-old. But the mother's basic principle of relying on the truth at all times was perhaps the fundamental reason that the child was able to accept so well.

Each family of course has to work out the details of its own solutions. The child's questions, the child's age, the circumstances which arise, are different in each case, as this mother notes. This full participation in the situation would not be a good solution in some families. And this same child at six years might respond quite differently and with more anxiety. Also, how much or how little you say will depend on circumstances. But, at any age, things work out best if you stick to the truth and do not try too hard to hide things from the child. If adults are grieving and hiding things at the same time, a child can sense the complexity and falseness of the situation. It is probably much better for the child to face things as they are.

DEATH AT SIX

Five thus can be calm and matter of fact about many things, the idea of death included. Six is violent and emotional about death, as about so many other things. In fact, one of his favorite threats when he is angered may be, "I'll kill you!"

This threat, we regret to report, may be uttered to his mother as well as to friends and brothers and sisters. Yet, at the same time, one of his chief worries may be that his mother may die and leave him.

Thus one 6-year-old inquired directly, "You, my mommie, are you going to die?" Another reported, in slightly garbled fashion: "I don't bite mothers. And if I kick anybody, I say, 'I didn't mean it.' I had a real mother. She died."

Many 6-year-olds, though they still do not realize that they themselves will one day die, are beginning to get the idea that death is often connected with old age and that the older people often die first. One girl thus remarked to her mother, "You will be an old, old lady. And then you will die. And I will have babies."

The notion that death is reversible is very strong at six. Thus one little boy commented, "A boy came back after he died. He was in the funeral with his mother."

Another remarked, "When a man comes and says magic, he can get up again after he is dead. They put him in a grave. He stays in the grave till Saturday—then he can come out."

Still another little boy said to his friend in play, "Always have you been bad. Never have you been good. Now I will make you dead. Never will I make you alive again."

Many 6-year-olds are so emotional about the idea of death that they are not only disturbed by the actuality of it but even by pictures of dead people which they may see in illustrated magazines. Thus, though their ability to understand the notion is considerably increased over what it was at five, many at six are not emotionally able to adjust to the idea of death. So they should be spared contact with the idea, as well as with the actuality, as much as possible.

However, ideas of death and of being killed may spontaneously come into their conversations. Thus one of our 6-year-olds was heard to pray, "Dear Jesus God! Please let me go through a red light without getting killed!" While another 6-year-old remarked to his friend, "I wish you had never been alive. And then other times I don't feel like that at all. Are you like that with your mother?"

DEATH AT SEVEN TO NINE YEARS

Things change again at seven. The average 7-year-old already has a reasonably clear notion of death. But he still is apt to avoid looking directly at this notion by focusing his attention on the coffin, the graveyard, the burial service. In fact, his interest in those details may appear to be rather morbid.

Seven is also much interested in the various possible causes of death: disease, overeating, violence, old age. He now begins to suspect that he himself may one day die. Some strongly deny this. Others view the possibility quite calmly, like the little girl who remarked: "If Granny dies I shall cry, but not for long. I shall be unhappy for you [mother], because you have no Mother. I shall be extra nice and be your Mother . . . I might die next year when I'm eight. I might die before my birthday. Or I might die before Christmas and get no presents. I might die next month—or next week—or this next minute. But I don't feel like it. I want to wait and die when you and Daddy die—it would be nice to die all together."

Seven's plaint, "I wish I were dead," is quite typical of many of his remarks, and should not, as a rule, be taken too seriously, even though it tells us how he feels.

The 8-year-old, less morbid and more expansive than Seven, has usually progressed from an interest in graves and funerals to interest in what happens after death. He may make some such comment as, "After you die, you get buried. You don't feel it. If you're good, you go to Heaven. God takes you out of the box and brings you to Heaven. God makes you alive. If you're bad you go to Hell and the Devil burns you up."

The average 8-year-old, though he understands the subject of death better than he did at seven, is as a rule not too concerned with it and not too much interested in discussing it. By this age many can accept, without too much emotion, the idea that everyone, including themselves, will eventually die.

By nine and ten, most are ready to face the notion of death quite squarely. They no longer concentrate on the funeral or on what happens after. Many now can make reference to the logical or biological essentials: "Not living," or, "When you die you have no pulse and no temperature and you can't breathe." Most Nines and Tens are ready for as full an explanation as you may wish or be able to give.

Though each age has a certain capacity to question and to understand the facts about death, each individual's response is a personal matter. His response is often dependent upon the attitude and emotional factors of his parents and family, which are his guideposts until he can be more surely guided by his own attitude and emotions.

ADOPTION

BLACK AND GRAY MARKET

You're hoping to adopt a baby! Will you get it through the "black" market? The "gray" market? Or will you get it through a recognized and reputable adoption or social agency?

Changes in adoption practice in the last few years have been many. Most of them—but not all—have been in what we consider a desirable direction.

The main change is that adoptions more and more are being carried on in broad daylight, under the supervision of agencies which are staffed and equipped to see that everyone involved in the adoption transaction gets a fair deal.

This shift from black and gray market to properly authorized agencies is described interestingly in a book by Pilpel and Zavin called *Your Marriage and the Law* (Rinehart & Company), which some of you may like to read.

AGENCY ADOPTIONS

Adoption placements which are arranged through properly qualified social agencies have many advantages over those arranged by other methods. Through them the prospective mother is helped to make plans for her immediate present and for her own and her baby's future.

Through them the baby who is to be adopted can be assured of a proper physical examination to determine that he is physically suitable for adoption. Equally important, he can be assured of a thorough developmental or psychological examination to determine that he is of normal mentality and of presumably normal personality make-up.

Such a baby can also be assured that the agency has checked on the desirability and suitability of the adopting parents—not only that they seem to be financially and emotionally ready to provide for a child, but also, if he seems to be a baby of potentially superior ability, that they will be able to give him the education and other advantages which he needs.

For the adopting family, the agency provides a baby who has had such necessary examinations. It also, as a rule, gives some assurance that the child's heredity, so far as it can be determined from what is known of the parents, is not too adverse.

More than this, during the probation period which most states require before an adoption can be made final, the agency, through its workers, provides somebody whom the adopting parents can lean upon, question and consult. In the agency worker they have someone who stands behind them, to whom they can turn if things should go wrong, as they occasionally do, and if the placement doesn't seem to be working out.

However, all is not rosy in today's picture of social-agency-supervised adoptions.

Undesirable Practice in Agency Supervised Adoptions

There is at present a grave error into which some of today's agencies are falling in relation to adoption practice. We call attention to it not to attack the agencies for making this error, but rather to emphasize both for the agencies and for adopting parents how they can easily avoid it.

One of the greatest advances that we know of in adoption practice in the last twenty years has been the policy of giving careful developmental or psychological examinations to every single adoption candidate. Such examinations indicate whether an infant or child is of "normal" mentality and therefore a good adoption candidate, or if he is so subnormal that he is not a fit candidate. They further can to some extent discriminate within the normal group children among those of average, above-average and below-average endowment—thus giving a good clue as to what kind of home each child would best fit.

Working with many local agencies, we ourselves have given hundreds of such examinations and have thus, as time and experience have shown, helped out in seeing that the "right" child gets into the "right" family and that too seriously retarded children are not placed out for adoption. In such an examination even more important than the actual level of development is the degree of integration of the organism, the total force of the personality. The examiner must ask: Is the child emotionally disturbed? Does he possess motivational forces that will produce further growth? These and many other questions and areas of investigation should become a part of any adoption appraisal. Maybe someday we will be able to appraise more fully than we can now and thus avoid the tragedy of misplacement of a child in a home which does not suit him and which he does not suit.

The ideal would be that *every* child up for adoption would have such an examination, as surely as he has a physical examination.

The error which we speak of is the current policy of a few agencies which are, unfortunately, doing away with the psychological examination of candidates for adoption on the grounds that such examinations are unnecessary.

They claim that these are unnecessary because the adopting mother's treatment of the baby, and not the baby's own inherent abilities and disabilities, will determine how he will turn out.

Such an attitude is truly a backward step and is definitely to be decried. To any parent contemplating adoption, we say strongly: Insist on a thorough developmental examination, by a well-qualified person, of any baby you are thinking about adopting.

HEREDITY VS. ENVIRONMENT

It is vital to have such an examination because it can help you to recognize and appreciate just what are the potentialities of the child you are adopting. It can give you an approximate idea of his intellectual level and educability—it can give you valuable clues as to his individuality.

It is most important that you know these things. You as an adopting parent will of course want to give your child the very best opportunities you can provide. You will want to give him every advantage of a good home, love, companionship, understanding. But regardless of what you give him, you are still restricted by what he is basically. In his body, when he is born, he carries the potentialities of what he can become. You can see to it that he has a chance to develop these potentials. But you do not determine the potentials.

Thus it is most important to know ahead of time—is this the kind of child with whom you as a family can be happy and satisfied? Is this a child who can be expected to fit into your home? A thorough developmental examination can go a long way toward helping you answer this question. However it is important to remember that adoption, like natural parenthood, is still a calculated risk.

ADOPTING BABY AND THEN HAVING YOUR OWN

A seeming coincidence which occurs frequently enough to be worth mentioning is this. Parents, discouraged at their long-continued failure to have a family of their own, finally decide to have a family by adoption.

So they adopt a baby. And lo and behold! Before the adoption has even waited out its legal year's waiting period, before it can finally be consummated, along comes a baby of their own.

We shall not here discuss the possible reasons for this happening. We merely comment on it as an extremely interesting sidelight on the whole matter of adoption.

Some of you may be thinking that you would like to adopt a child, but may be putting it off, as some do, for fear you would not love an adopted child as much as you would one of your own. For you, there can be reassurance in the experience of these adopting families which we have just described. Almost unanimously they tell us, and we believe them, that they feel equal affection for their adopted and their own children. This we believe to be the usual and happy experience of adopting parents the world over if their adopted child has within him the potentials of normal development.

HOW TO TELL ABOUT ADOPTION

The mother of an adopted child asked if she could consult us about a problem she had. "I'm worried to death," she told us. "We love our Linda so, and she seems to love us. How am I ever going to tell her the terrible truth? That she is adopted and that we are not her real parents.

"I've wondered if we could possibly keep it from her. But I suppose she'd be bound to find out and then she would hate us."

Linda's mother has a problem, all right, but it is not quite the one she thinks she has.

Telling Linda that she is adopted need not be an insurmountably difficult task. But before her mother can do it effectively, she first of all is going to need to change her own attitude toward adoption.

She must realize that the fact that any child is adopted is not a "terrible" but actually a wonderful and exciting truth.

An adopted child is not one who has come into a family simply in the natural course of events. An adopted child is a chosen child— desired, selected and doubly cherished for this reason. Valentina Wasson's book *The Chosen Baby* (J. B. Lippincott Company) brings this out nicely, and may help you with just what to say to your own adopted child.

Adoption is a marvelous social function. A childless family which wanted and needed a child—a child who needed a family—are brought together.

Your adopted child is different from his playmates, not in a shameful or disgraceful way, but in an exciting and wonderful way. If you realize and believe this, you will be able to impart to your adopted child not only the fact that he is adopted, but your own attitude of joyful confidence in the situation. You can make him glad that he is adopted.

As in giving sex information, your *attitude* is more important than the specific things you say. Remember that you have to impart an exciting and wonderful fact, not a shameful secret.

In this matter of telling the child that he is adopted, as in most other important areas of parent-child behavior, your own common sense and your knowledge of your child's own personality will be your best guides on how to handle the situation. However, here as elsewhere, the specialist can help you specifically. In this instance, with an excellent two-volume book entitled *The Adopted Family* by Rondell and Michaels (Crown). This set consists of one volume of general advice for parents, one volume to be read directly to the child. We believe that you will find it helpful.

However, in the long run the telling is still up to you. Here are a few suggestions.

Within reason, the sooner your child knows that he is adopted, the better. As with sex information, if you yourself do not give it to him in the way you want to—some neighbor, friend, or enemy, will almost certainly give it to him or let it slip out, not realizing the shock such sudden knowledge can produce.

"The sooner the better?" you reply. "Just how soon is that?"

The exact age will vary from child to child. (As with other kinds of information, remember that you do not, on the first occasion, tell the whole story once and for all. A child is usually ready to absorb only a small part of any complex fact when he first asks.) A good time to start in is when your adopted child asks, "Mummy, where did I come from?"

This can be your clue to answer, "You grew in *a* mummy's tummy." At this time, or later, this will lead to questions about, "Did I grow in *your* tummy?" Stick to your original story—"In a mummy's tummy, but not in mine."

This will lead to further questions, either at this time or later, as to why he or she didn't stay with his own mummy. Here you explain that there are two ways of doing it. Some children live with the mummy who produced them. Others live with the mummies who chose them. Either is a good way.

It is surprising how easy it is to impart this kind of information when we feel sure within ourselves. But it is most important not to overemphasize it. As with the imparting of sex information, do not go any further than the child leads you. Also, as with sex information, the child may not believe you at first. Then you can tell him that as he grows older he will understand better. Eight seems to be an age when much that was not comprehended before is often easily understood.

At this age it is almost as though a new dimension had been added to the child's understanding. This new dimension may indeed lead him to penetrate his origin too deeply and many of his questions cannot be answered or must be by-passed. Society has placed the burden of the unknown upon the adopted child and this ordinarily cuts him off from his origins.

So that the inner resolution of the problem is ultimately left to the child as he grows older. One 9-year-old adopted child was already tackling the problem when she said to her adoptive mother, "If you ever should see my mother or my father, say 'hello' for me."

EPITHETS FROM CHILDREN, ATTACKS ON MOTHER

"I hate you, Mummy. I wish you were dead. You aren't my real mother anyway. You're only my adopted mother."

Six-year-old Patty clenches her fists, stamps her foot and, through her tears, shouts these defiant words at her mother, who is hustling her off to bed at the end of a typically tumultuous 6-year-old day.

Once Patty is stormily in bed, her mother talks things over tearfully with Patty's daddy. "I knew it," she complains. "I knew that the day would come when she would throw it up to us that she was adopted."

Fortunately Patty's father was a calm man and also, fortunately, he had a good memory. He could remember back to the time when their own son, now in his teens, had been six or seven years old. "Don't you recall Nat when he was that age?" he asked his wife. "He used to say he was going to get a different mother. And I even remember one spell he had when *he* thought he was adopted.

"I don't think you should take it too seriously, dear," he concluded. "I don't think it's just because Patty is adopted that she talks like this. I suspect that it's just the way children around this age talk when they get mad."

Patty's father is right. Complaints about parents, expressions of wishes for other, better parents and even claims that he knows he is only adopted occur in a great many 6- and 7-year-olds. (Children of this age don't complain just about their parents. School may come in for the same kind of criticism. They want to go back to their old school, or to find a new one.) Complaints about his family do not occur just because the child is adopted, and they are not a special hazard which only adopting parents and not others have to face.

And it is exactly the same with taunts from other children which adopting parents fear for their adopted children. Sooner or later some neighborhood child will shout, "You're only an old adopted child!" How can you help your child to face this?

First, by building up in him the proud confidence that he is a chosen, wanted child—not just accepted because he arrived, but purposely chosen.

And second, by helping him to realize that in every neighborhood there are some children who will pick on any way in which another child is different as a basis for calling names. If you are fatter, thinner, taller, shorter, if you are of a different color or different race or different religion (or even different political party), there are always some children who will call you names about it. Being adopted is not more of a danger in this respect than having freckles or big ears.

Help the child to feel self-confidence in the face of all name-calling. Being adopted is no more of a hazard than being anything else. Having too much money may be to the adolescent just as dangerous. "Thinks he's smart just because his old man has all that dough."

DIVORCE

"How do you go about telling a young child that there is going to be a divorce in the family?"

This is a more common question than many readers might like to think. According to recent statistics, about one in three marriages in our country ends in divorce. In a large percentage of these marriages there are children—and these children, of course, have to be told.

Some of the best advice which we have ever read on this topic is given by J. Louise Despert, M.D., in her recently published book *Children of Divorce* (Doubleday & Co.).

Here, as in other tricky areas, she tells us it is not so much *what* you say as *how* you say it which is important. Certainly it is important to tell the truth. (Though sometimes you do not have to tell *all* the truth all at once.)

But more important than telling the exact factual truth is telling it in a reasonably calm and accepting manner. If your child feels that this is something that you yourself have accepted and adjusted to, there is a good chance that he may be able to accept and adjust to it too.

If, on the other hand, you give the necessary information in a tearful or otherwise emotionally upset manner, he will inevitably be even more disturbed than he otherwise would be.

Most important of all, Dr. Despert feels, is to avoid laying blame on the parent who has left. Emotionally satisfying as it might be to you at the moment, it is important to avoid the natural temptation to picture the absent parent as wicked and erring and to try to get the child onto your "side" in the matter.

Further, it is important not to hold out false hopes to the child. Until things are really decided for sure, it might be best to postpone a definitive talk with your child. But once the prospect of divorce has become a certainty, it is better to present it as such and not to hold out false hopes to the child that perhaps, after all, Daddy (or Mummy) will come back after a while.

When should you have this talk?

The exact day or moment of the day will of course be determined by many small factors special to your particular case. But, in general, the sooner the better probably—once you are certain that divorce is inevitable.

Most parents do not hide things from their children as well as they may think they are doing. If your marriage has been unhappy enough to end in divorce, it is quite certain that even a very young child will be aware that things have not been right. He may then be much relieved, rather than being made more unhappy, to know for sure just what is going to happen. (Or he may become a new factor to help you in making the right decision. We have known of teenagers who have fought like tigers to keep their families together and who have awakened the parents to a realization of what they were doing and caused them to reverse their course.)

Dr. Despert, in preparing her book, reviewed more than a thousand cases of disturbed children who have come to her in recent years.

She found, surprisingly enough, that there were far fewer children of divorce in her group of disturbed children than are found in the general population. But she did find that there was trouble between all, or nearly all, of the parents of the disturbed children who were brought to her for help.

This means, Dr. Despert believes, that it is by no means the legal divorce which causes the children of divorced parents to become unhappy, confused and sometimes even delinquent. Rather it is the unhappiness of the parents which exists before the divorce even takes place. The fact that the parents are unhappy together is the thing that primarily disturbed the children in the family, not the fact that they finally agree to separate.

She calls this unhappiness and incompatibility between parents, which makes the home such a disturbing place for the children of the family, "emotional divorce." And it is emotional divorce, not the actual legal divorce, which she considers the basically harmful factor as far as children are concerned.

"Divorce," she states plainly, "is not automatically destructive to children. The marriage which divorce brings to an end may have been more so."

Whether or not you agree entirely with Dr. Despert, we believe that you will find her book to be both instructive and interesting. Not only for its specific comments about divorce, but for its revealing lights on personality factors in adults, as these make for success or failure in marriage.

As to just what you tell a child about divorce—as with questions of sex or death—just what you say will be different in every case. Roughly it can be something to the effect that when people marry, they hope that they will be happy together and live together always. But that sometimes it doesn't work out that way. And that when it doesn't, and when they cannot live happily together, that they often feel it is better to live apart.

Be sure to explain exactly what all this means in relation to the child—because that of course is what interests him most. Most important, explain that he will still see his daddy (or mummy) and that Daddy (or Mummy) will still love him.

It is important to let the child talk over this problem as much (within reason) as he wants to. But do not let him get the "upper hand" in his questioning. That is, don't let him badger you or make you feel in the wrong. If he starts criticizing or complaining or says he wishes things were some other way or that you ought to have done something different, you will need to be firm. Explain that grownups have to decide things like this for themselves.

DIVORCED MOTHER SHOULDN'T TRY TOO HARD TO MAKE IT UP TO HER CHILDREN

Bringing up children in a "normal" family home is often hard enough, as many of you will testify. Bringing up children in what is commonly described as a "broken" home is, of course, doubly difficult.

It is difficult for many reasons. First, of course, because in such a situation one person, usually the mother, is trying to do the work of two. She alone has to make all the decisions in relation to the child. She alone has to carry them out with no bolstering, "We'll see what Daddy thinks." She alone has to play the role of parent, friend, playmate, with no one to take turns or to take the children off her hands while she enjoys an occasional breathing spell.

All of these functions many divorced mothers perform ably and well.

But there is one situation where we have known many women, in their very effort to do the right thing, to make what seems to us a grave mistake.

This is when they become worried or anxious or oversolicitous of their children in an effort to "make it up to them" because they do not have a father.

Not having a father is a serious lack, but there are a great many handicaps equally severe—serious mental or physical difficulties, being members of a minority group in an excessively intolerant community, living in an "unbroken" home where quarreling and hateful discord is the order of the day.

Nearly all children have to learn to face some adverse circumstances, to accept them, and to go on from there.

If, as a divorced mother, you allow yourself to feel too sorry for your poor son or daughter who is having to grow up without a father's close companionship, your oversolicitude may well do him more harm than the absence of his father.

Even greater is the harm done if the child learns that he can play on your sympathies with regard to this matter. You punish him. He accepts the punishment, but a little later complains sadly, "I wish I had a father like all the other kids." You feel so sympathetic, and perhaps a little guilty that you have caused him to be in such an underprivileged situation, that you either take back the punishment or shower him with some luxury or privilege just to make up to him. We believe that in so doing you are taking your first downward step.

He is deprived, but so in a way are you. Let both of you "make it up" to each other by developing as good a relationship between you as you can. Think more about each other and less about a situation that can't be changed.

VISITING

"My husband and I are divorced," a mother explained to us recently, "and our boy Jim is living with me. His father has the right of seeing him every month. But Jim doesn't like these visits, and every time after he has seen his father he is moody and grouchy and unhappy for several days. Do you suppose these visits are doing him any lasting harm which will show up when he is older? Do you think I should stop them?"

This mother's question brings up several interesting points, each of which is deserving of detailed discussion. We shall here, for brevity's sake, lump them all together.

First, a practical answer to her question—if the father has the legal right to see his son and insists upon exercising it, of course there is little the mother can do beyond taking as calm and matter-of-fact an attitude toward the visits as possible, and then seeing to it that the other aspects of her son's life are as satisfactory and gratifying as possible. From the basis of a healthy, happy home background a sturdy child can absorb and rise above occasional disturbing situations. This is a new adjustment for him to make, which will take time.

This mother needs to be sure that her son's attitude does not arise from and does not reflect her own. A mother may feel that she is being very fair and friendly in what she says to her children about the father who is no longer a member of the family—in fact, she may pride herself on her fairness and objectivity. But, regardless of what she says, if she still feels any traces of natural bitterness and rancor, her children will usually sense this and will react accordingly.

She should also be sure that her child is not playing on her sympathy, and overdramatizing his unhappiness about seeing his father.

However, at certain ages and in certain types of children there commonly come periods when they become extremely antagonistic toward the father who has gone away, regardless of how expertly the mother is dealing with the situation. At such times, many fathers are willing (as a temporary experiment) to lengthen the time between visits and not see the children quite as often.

And lastly, if you are doing the very best you can by your child, do not worry too much that present hurts will "show up later" as having done him lasting harm. If basically sturdy to start with, the average child is extremely resistant to permanent damage. The majority of adults, even nowadays, do not turn up on the analyst's couch because of damaging childhood experiences. A good majority of the population still goes through life reasonably well adjusted despite what may have happened in childhood.

Though difficult, these visits between children and their fathers are the basis for a new relationship which usually pays off in the long run as the child grows older.

Except under the most atypical circumstances it seems desirable, in the case of divorce, for the child or children involved to have an opportunity to visit with and be acquainted with the absent, or non-custodial, parent.

We personally do not approve of split custody. We feel definitely that the child should have his or her *home* with one parent or the other; and that the times with the other parent should be in the nature of visits. It is hard for most children to have two homes.

We also feel that visits should not be too frequent. We think that weekly visits are too much in most cases. Every three or at most every two weeks is usually often enough. However, any visiting arrangement should be flexible and subject to change with circumstances. Arrangements often work out better when the divorced parents do not live in the same city, though this cannot always be avoided.

Perhaps the most important thing is that both parents speak—when they do speak—of the other parent in friendly terms, not disparagingly. It must be expected also that sometimes, until things get well adjusted, visits with the absent parents may cause some upset to the child.

18

What to Do About Discipline

THEORIES OF DISCIPLINE

How to make him mind? Many parents feel that if they had an answer to this one simple question, many of their worst problems would be solved.

In the old days of authoritarian discipline, things were probably easier for parents. Parents were firm, and most children were in awe of parental authority. Strict discipline was maintained in most homes.

Then came a brief era of "permissiveness" when parents spared the rod for fear of repressing their children and harming their psyches. Children brought up permissively were often allowed to do practically anything they wanted to. Parental authority was applied lightly, infrequently and inconsistently. The results were often disastrous.

This era has given way in many households today to what we call *informed permissiveness.* In using informed permissiveness, parents try to understand what they can reasonably expect of their children, keeping in mind always their basic personalities and their ages. They then try to keep their demands within reason. Being sure that they are reasonable, they are firm in their insistence that the child live up to these demands. Thus the child is expected to conform and to obey —but his parents try to see to it that their expectations are not beyond his abilities—as they often were in the old days when authoritarian discipline prevailed.

Understanding your own child's personality and keeping in mind the strong points and weaknesses of the different age levels will help you in following a policy of informed permissiveness with your own children, should you choose to do so.

LEVELS OF DISCIPLINE

There are thus three main current theories of discipline—the strict authoritative which says "No" to almost everything; the permissive, which says "Yes" to almost anything; and what some people call the informed permissive, which says "Yes" or "No," depending on the child's stage of development and what can reasonably be expected and not expected of him. Of these, we believe that "informed permissiveness" is the most effective, though perhaps the most difficult to follow. We should, however, prefer to call the method of discipline which we recommend "developmental discipline." The word permissive implies that the child is getting away with something whether it is his right or not—whether he is ready or not. But when discipline is considered from a developmental point of view, it is growth that is the guide. When the child is not ready, he will be protected from experiences he can't manage. If he insists, he may have to be brought sharply into line or be given substitute experiences that will satisfy him enough to hold him off. And when he is ready, the experience itself becomes his discipline.

But regardless of your general theory, there is a second consideration in this matter of discipline, and that is the level at which you discipline the child.

There are, we believe, desirable ways of disciplining children and there are less desirable ways. We should not expect any parent, nor should parents expect themselves, always to work at the highest or most desirable level. Mothers are frequently overworked. Fathers are often overtired (and vice versa). And the "best" way is not always the easy way.

The easiest way of disciplining, for many, and possibly the least desirable, is the emotional level. You slap, shout and threaten. Some mothers even go so far as to cry or to complain, "You don't love Mummy or you wouldn't act this way."

No mother need blame herself if she descends to this level on occasion. But if these are her customary methods, the chances are that she will not have a well-disciplined child.

The second level is the rational or reasoning level, which involves mostly talking. You explain to the child why bad behavior gets bad results. You urge him to behave better. You tell him how bad his behavior makes you feel. You "isolate" him and tell him that he is too tired to play with the other children. In short, you reason with him. With some children this method works well. With some, it is just so many words wasted.

The third level is, we believe, the most effective, but probably the most difficult because it requires the most knowledge. It is simply to adapt your techniques of discipline to the child's abilities, interests and weaknesses at whatever stage of development he has reached. We call this using *developmental techniques*. This implies understanding the mechanics of behavior at every age level so thoroughly that you know how to motivate or encourage your child toward the kind of behavior you desire. That is, if you understand how a child's organism works, you will understand how best to move him in the direction you choose.

DEVELOPMENTAL TECHNIQUES

Using developmental techniques can be an exciting adventure, particularly when it works. It involves, however, considerable knowledge of the growing organism and what it is like at different ages. An adequate discussion of developmental techniques would require an entire volume in itself. We shall here simply give you examples of such techniques, which may be effective through the preschool years.

We suggest that you may wish to amplify this information by reading the full description of the age levels up to ten in our earlier publication A. Gesell and F. Ilg, *The Child from Five to Ten* (Harper & Brothers). You may also find helpful clues as to specific techniques to be used in the preschool years in A. Gesell and F. Ilg, *Infant and Child in the Culture of Today* (Harper & Brothers) in the section on "Nursery School Techniques."

The section on "Minding" in Chapter 16 page 288 of this present volume discusses age changes in the ability to mind when spoken to and ways of getting the child to mind. Cutts and Moseley's *Better Home Discipline* (Appleton-Century-Crofts) gives practical suggestions on a wide variety of disciplinary problems.

These specific techniques which we give here for motivating pre-school children are merely suggestive. This is by no means a comprehensive list, but merely suggests the *kinds* of things you might find helpful in the early years.

18 months: Keep in mind that the child of this age walks down a one-way street. His favorite word is "No" and his favorite direction "away from." You must expect these reactions and will need to use tricks and techniques to move him in a more positive direction.

Avoid direct commands such as, "Come here!" Instead, lure the child by offering food or a favorite toy, or by playing with some interesting object just out of his reach. Or pick him up and carry him.

Wherever possible, simplify the physical environment to prevent overstimulation and to reduce the number of possible danger areas. So far as you can, keep things he isn't supposed to touch out of reach.

If you use language with him, keep it very simple.

Consult him as little as possible. Streamline routines to avoid opportunities for him to say "No."

2 years: Two is much more positive and docile than he was at 18 months. He will be much more ready to obey. He can modulate his behavior. Help him by keeping situations simple and especially by keeping language simple and direct.

Two is likely to dawdle. Break into this by talk of the next activity; by telling him to "say good-by"; or by leading him by means of an enticing toy.

Warn in advance of a proposed transition: "Pretty soon we'll wash our hands and then have lunch."

Do not expect him to share out of generosity. He may share if you say, "Johnny *needs* that wagon."

2½ years: Two-and-a-half is characteristically an age of opposite extremes. Remember this and try as much as possible to avoid giving the child choices. However, you can sometimes use choices effectively when the choice does not matter: "Do you want the red one or the blue one?"

It is hard for the child of this age to share. Help him to find "something else for Billy to use," but do not expect him to share out of generosity. Two-and-a-half is frequently both aggressive and selfish.

Environmental handling is most important. Shut and if necessary put high bolts on doors. Remove things not to be touched. This is more effective than trying to govern with words.

Except when compliance is essential, give face-saving commands: "How about ——?" or, "Let's ——."

Use words and phrases which are meaningful to the child: "needs," "has to have," "it's time to," "you forgot."

Avoid questions which can be answered by "No," as, "Can you hang up your coat?" Instead ask, "Where does your coat go?"

Don't be afraid to use humor (if it works). If he says angrily, "No, no, no," you say laughingly, "Yes, yes, yes."

3 years: Since this is a "me too" age, you can often motivate children positively by pointing out some other child who is doing the thing "right."

Give suggestions positively. Thus say, "We stand on the floor," rather than, "We don't stand on the table."

Children of this age will do a good deal if motivated by promise of a "surprise."

They respond very well to use of stimulating language. Adjectives such as "new," "different," "big," "strong." Nouns—"surprise," "secret." Verbs—"You could help," "You might try." Adverbs— "How about?" "Maybe."

Many can now listen to reason. "Let's pick up the toys so that we'll have more room for building, after dinner."

Some respond well to imaginative suggestions as, "Can the lumberman pick up those big logs [blocks]?"

The indirect approach often works well. For instance, get a child to take off his outer clothing by your guessing what color his socks are—of course guessing all the wrong colors first.

4 years: Respect the fact that the 4-year-old quite naturally and characteristically behaves in an out-of-bounds manner. Realizing this you can perhaps let it go, part of the time, when he is a little rude, noisy, boastful or rebellious.

At other times, employ his own loved exaggeration in giving directions.

This is an age of tricks and adventure and new ways of doing things. Utilize this. Say, "Let's *skip* out to the dining room."

Use their awaking interest in numbers to motivate them; "Can you get your suit off before I count to ten?" Or, "When the big hand gets to three (or whatever), you may get up."

Giving commands in a whisper is surprisingly effective.

Many at this age are still much interested in imaginary companions. This interest can be used in getting them to comply.

HOUSEHOLD ENGINEERING

The use of developmental techniques, while in most instances extremely effective, does admittedly require a considerable knowledge and understanding of behavior at the different levels of maturity.

A different method of improving the child's behavior is one which requires little more than good common sense and a certain flexibility and willingness to try things which may be a little outside of your usual routine.

This method has been called (though the name of it actually doesn't matter too much) "household engineering."

Household engineering as we use the term means trying to arrange your household with regard to both the spacing and timing of necessary events in such a way that much of the disruptive behavior which bothers you simply does not take place. Thus you set up your daily schedule, or you arrange your household physically, so that the worst danger points simply do not occur.

The possibilities are of course endless. It is probable that you yourself actually employ household engineering much of the time. Here are just a few somewhat random suggestions of the kinds of things we mean. There is nothing specially "scientific" about these suggestions. They are merely intended as examples. You yourself, knowing your family and your own household, can undoubtedly think up many others.

For instance, suppose that two brothers or sisters cannot be together for any length of time without fighting. You may, if you wish, try to deal with this problem by warning, scolding, punishing. Simpler and more effective is to separate them physically. If you don't have the space to do this, you can often work wonders by rearranging their schedules. Hours of naps can be shifted. Sometimes it even pays to have children eat separately. Some schools, in the early years, give a choice of morning or afternoon attendance. This may help. Or the baby-sitter can take one for a walk while the other uses the playroom. Or you may find that quarreling doesn't usually begin until after half an hour of play—so you can let them enjoy this much together and no more. Sometimes a playroom can be sectioned off. Some children need real gates or partitions. Others will respect an imaginary line across the middle of the room.

Or take another example. Suppose that your 4-year-old always behaves badly when company comes. Instead of bribing, threatening, cajoling or punishing, try to arrange it so that child and company do not see too much of each other. Arrange that he will be out of the house or pleasantly occupied in some other part of the house when visitors are present. Or include your guests in your planning. Allow one at a time to spend some time with your child in his room. Thus a social occasion can be salvaged by each guest being willing to give up just a slice of his social time for the sake of a child. This isn't asking too much.

Or consider the following parental complaints and our suggestions for solving the problems which they present:

"My 2-year-old gets into everything! Nothing in the house is safe from him!" A common complaint. What to do? Either fence in the 2-year-old or fence in your possessions. Specific warning and admonition will work in some special situations. The average child of two can be taught not to touch some special and important things—ash trays, Daddy's desk. But if he is the kind who is "into everything," this requires too much watchfulness from the adult. Locks and gates are easier for everyone. Be sure that there is a place for him and his toys in each room of the house. Then he can relate himself to his things. Each room brings change and surprises. He hasn't been forgotten. He is living in a child world in the midst of all of these adult things.

"My 2½-year-old keeps going in and waking Daddy, who has to sleep during the daytime. She disturbs him so much that he cannot get his sleep and therefore is in no shape for his job, which is on a night shift. What do you advise?"

Easy! If Daddy is not firm enough to prevent this behavior unaided, a high lock on Daddy's bedroom door should do the trick. Some 2½-year-olds can be stopped by verbal means alone. But if this is not the case, one firm lock is better than a thousand "No's." The time will come, and soon, with most any 2½-year-old, when a "No" may be sufficient. But till it does, the easy way is often the most effective way for all concerned.

"My 3-year-old has never slept through the night," complains one mother. "She is always up and down—waking, crying, demanding to be taken into our bed. Now with a new baby coming, I'm so worried about what will happen. I'm afraid that they will just wake each other and will never get any sleep."

A well-founded worry! Common sense suggests to us that a wakeful 3-year-old is hard enough in any event without having her share a room with a new baby. And vice versa! If the household is big enough to provide even standing room for a bassinet anywhere but in the 3-year-old's room, we would definitely recommend separation of the two children, at least during the nighttime.

Rearranging your whole family's life just to avoid some difficult area, rather than just "making the child mind," may sound dangerously like giving in to the child. Some fathers, especially, may feel this. But we don't think of it that way. In our experience, trying to adapt the situation to everyone concerned rather than simply trying to fit the child into our notions of how children *ought* to act can help untangle a lot of snarls. A factory manager doesn't simply tell his workers that they *ought* to produce more. Instead he tries to arrange things so that higher production is possible. Similarly, a little creative thinking about some of the most ordinary household routines can often result in improved behavior on the part of the child.

THE DESTRUCTIVE CHILD

Unfortunately, regardless of how well you understand the different ages and how constructively you plan your household arrangements and routines, there are some children who just seem to get into trouble anyway. These are the children generally described as *destructive*.

If your child is unusually destructive, the best discipline may involve finding out *why*. Nina Ridenour, in her excellent pamphlet *When Your Child Is Destructive* (New York State Society for Mental Health, 105 East 22nd St.), states that there nearly always is a reason for destructive behavior.

It may, for instance, be caused by jealousy of a sibling. If so, be sure that the child realizes fully that he is loved, wanted, important. It may be caused by the fact that he is frustrated, either by your restrictions or by his own failings or inabilities. Then try if you can to be less restrictive and to help him work or play more successfully.

If his destructiveness seems largely to be accidental, here are some things you do to try to reduce it:

1. Check over your whole house to see what things you can move or put away so that the child won't get mixed up with them.

2. Lock all doors with high, complicated locks.

3. Give him a large, fenced-in back yard where he can run and climb, play with messy things (mud, water, clay), and also hammer and saw, *under supervision*.

4. Try to stop situations which are likely to end up in accidents— such as bouncing a ball in the living room—*before* the accident occurs. Don't just trust to luck that this time no accident will occur.

5. Realize that carelessness with material things is natural in the majority of children. Many of them will outgrow this in time.

6. Have as many different adults as possible take turns in taking care of him. Mother alone will be absolutely exhausted with full

care of such children. Men can actually control them better than can women.

7. Above all, try to avoid taking him to public places, especially to stores, where his destructive behavior will particularly cause trouble.

8. And lastly, start out by expecting a good deal of wear and tear, at least in all parts of the house which are used by the child.

If, however, his destructiveness seems intentional, Dr. Ridenour suggests that you try things like the following:

1. If your child crumples his father's newspaper or is careless with your books, give him a paper of his own which he may crumple.

2. If he tears up his own books, give him durable cloth books until he is old enough to manage the other kind.

3. If he gets into your bureau drawers, try locking them and also giving him some drawers or a cupboard of his own where he can keep his own things.

4. If he draws on the walls, give him a wall in his own room, covered with beaver board, plain paper, or something of the sort that he can mark on.

5. If he pounds on your best furniture, try giving him other things to pound. A Bingo Bed if he is very young, or, if you have a place for such things, a hammer and boards.

6. If he gets at your scissors and uses them destructively, give him blunt scissors of his own and paper or cloth which he can cut.

7. If he gets into your pocketbook on every possible occasion, give him (or her) a pocketbook of his own to carry around. He may prefer a discarded one of yours to a new one of his own.

8. If he loves messes, give him messy things like clay and sand or finger paints to play with under adult supervision.

9. One of the best remedies for the child who is constantly doing destructive damage is to provide him with materials which you are willing to have him take apart.

Behind all of these suggestions you will see that there lies one main theme: Give the child permissible outlets for his destructive energy until he has matured to the point where added maturity permits him to handle materials constructively, not destructively.

GENERAL SUGGESTIONS

In conclusion, here are a few brief general suggestions about discipline. You may or may not agree with them. Discipline is an extremely individual and personal matter. Each parent knows best what "works" for him and for his child. No outsider can make up your mind for you as to just how you will discipline your children. But the following are suggestions which many have found helpful.

STICK BY WHAT YOU HAVE SAID

In most cases, those parents are most successful who are able to maintain a firm and consistent policy of discipline, and who can be counted on to stick to what they have said. If on occasional second thought you do change your mind, it does no harm to tell the child of your changed verdict and your reason for changing. But in general, life is much simpler for the child if he knows that you can be counted on to do as you say.

MOTHER AND FATHER BACK EACH OTHER UP

Though there are of course many exceptions, it is quite customary for mother and father to have somewhat different ideas about discipline. Fathers as a rule are stricter—mothers are more likely to feel that the child is "just going through a stage and you might as well give in for a while." It is important for the child to feel the consistency of each parent's discipline. Then he comes to know how to expect each one to act. We recall one 4-year-old boy who had never until that moment been spanked by his father. The child rose up in irate wrath, not because of the spanking, but because "Nobody but my mommy can spank me."

Whatever your differences may be, it is extremely important to discuss them in private and to present a united front before the children. And to back up each other's directions. Discipline almost inevitably fails if one parent fails to support, or worse still, criticizes, the other parent's handling in front of the child.

SHOULD YOU DEMAND COMPLETE OBEDIENCE?

This, of course, is a matter which only you can decide. Our own opinion, as you will realize by now, is that if you are sure that your demands are reasonable for a child of the age and temperament of your own, you are justified in firmly insisting that they be carried out. But we also believe that to expect utter, complete and instantaneous obedience no matter what you command is not only unreasonable but impractical. (There is a certain group of unpredictable children who need the extremes of handling of both a tight and a loose rein. These are the children who demand a consistently inconsistent method of control which is both necessary and best for them, even though it is very exhausting for the parents.)

TO SPANK OR NOT TO SPANK

There has been a very marked trend away from spanking in recent years and this is indeed healthy. This trend however is deplored by some who like to hold a heavy hand or rule by force. These advocates still warn about the danger of relaxation of the rule of "spare the rod and spoil the child." But theirs is one of external control without consideration of the inner growth forces. If they took time to look at their method, they would soon realize that it did little good, or if seemingly successful, it more often than not will backfire at a later time.

Parents who believe in a growth process and who recognize their unique place in helping the growth process unfold might profit by the analysis of a spanking episode. Why and how did they reach the point where they had to spank? Could this have been avoided? As each situation is analyzed, it becomes clear that parent and child somehow got off the road. They seemed to have missed or paid no attention to the signposts along the way, and finally they come to a dead end. It is here that forces come face to face with each other and an explosion or a spanking becomes inevitable just to reverse the process and get back on the road again. A spanking may temporarily clear the air, but it is in danger of repetition.

Therefore it is for us, the adults, to think back over each situation to see where we missed the warning signs and how we could have acted differently. Sometimes just waiting along the roadside for a time, doing something together quietly, would have been enough to have given new strength of direction and greater clearness of perception. With these to fortify, one is far less apt to get off the road.

If thus a spanking must occur, it is the parent who is licked, who has failed more often than the child. The parent has in some way failed to support the growth process in the child. He may slowly learn that there are certain ages (as two and a half and five and a half) when he is in greater danger of conflict with the child. He also learns to know the bitter failure of the dead-end of spanking at these ages and that he the parent, often comes out of this fray worse than the child.

Needing to spank suggests failure and that you have somehow missed your way. It is for you to know the direction more fully, to read the sign posts more clearly. And if you do have to spank, recognize fully what you have done. This is the time when preventive methods are in order.

DISCIPLINE TO FIT YOUR TEMPERAMENT AND THAT OF YOUR CHILD

Above all, to be effective, the type of discipline you use is going to need to fit not only your own temperament, but that of your child.

If you are basically a "kiss and slap" type of mother, though you may part of the time be able to restrain yourself and use reasoning or developmental techniques, your handling of the child will always, inevitably, be more emotional than that of the mother whose approach to child-rearing problems is more intellectual.

If you are very quick-tempered, you will at times shout before you think. If you are more even-tempered, you may find it easy to have a quiet discussion with your child. If you are calm and easy-going, you may be able to overlook a good deal without any resentment.

Be assured that there are some advantages and disadvantages to every approach. But most of all know that you must respond within the limits of your own individuality. Working from the true base of your own self, you, the parent, can move in growth just as much as the child can, though the forces of growth are more assured and rapid in the child. Nature has given you, the parent, a second chance, as it were, to develop further through your child. It is unfortunate that some parents let this opportunity go by. It is true that a parent needs to believe in responding within the limits of his individuality. But may he also know that through his own growth his own potentialities may increase.

And the same consideration of limits needs to be given to discovering "what works" with your child. Some children can respond to a lengthy explanation of just why you are making certain demands. Others need the stronger force of verbal expressions of disapproval, isolation, deprivation of privileges. And a relatively small group (we hope) do not respond until they have pushed their parents further and further off the main road until the parent gives up or ends up in the dead end of a spanking. The task of the parent increases within the realms of these three different types of responses. To avoid the third response of physical punishment, the parent often needs to exert heroic efforts and deep understanding. And he needs the support of an environment that can provide multiple supervised outlets and constant change along with good, strong and respected controls.

It is for you the parent to discover what works best with your child. You may find that he responds pretty much the same from age to age or that he shifts his type of response and becomes harder or easier to handle at different ages. But always you can feel secure that if you respect and support the laws of growth, the controls will be steadily given over to the child and your part will be less and less demanding of you. The discipline at first imposed by the parent will eventually be imposed by the growing child on himself. This is the very purpose of discipline—that the child may eventually come into greater self-control.

Postscript

How then, would we summarize briefly the advice which, in our opinion, the child specialist can most helpfully give to the parent?

First of all, it would be that you must have confidence in your own judgment. For all the advice and help you may get from outside, in the final analysis *you* are the one who has to carry out the techniques, put the theories into practice, give the loving care. You are the one who has to deal with your children, day in and day out. Therefore you have to do the things which work with them and which feel comfortable to you. Remember that each child, as well as each family situation, is unique, and that no general rule works for everybody.

Remember, too, that though there is a great deal which you can do to help your child live up to his best potentials, it is not all up to you. And when things go wrong, it is by no means necessarily your fault.

Your child will behave as he does largely because of the kind of person he is. Many things about him—his physical size, his general level of intelligence, even many of his basic personality characteristics—are not within your power to determine. The answer, for better or worse, lies within his organism. Your responsibility is to guide and to understand him—not to try to change him.

It is here that the child specialist can be of assistance to you. His chief role is perhaps to provide you with information which can help you in understanding what it is reasonable to expect—of different kinds of children and of children of different ages. He can also suggest, in a general way through books and other writings, what to do when things seem to be going a little wrong.

When they are going *very* wrong, he can, through public and private clinics, agencies and child-development institutions, give you the same kind of help which you seek from your pediatrician when physical disease threatens or takes over. You should seek him out as freely.

References

1. Ames, L. B., and Learned, J., "Imaginary Companions and Related Phenomena." *The Journal of Genetic Psychology,* 69: 147–67 (1946).

2. Beck, L. F., *Human Growth.* New York, Harcourt, Brace & Co., 1949.

3. Bruch, H., *Don't Be Afraid of Your Child.* New York, Farrar, Straus & Young, 1952.

4. Bullock, A., *Parents' Magazine Book for Expectant Mothers.* New York, McGraw-Hill Book Co., 1954.

5. Coleman, L. D., *Freedom from Fear.* New York, Hawthorne Books, 1954.

6. Cutts, N., and Moseley, N., *Better Home Discipline.* New York, Appleton-Century-Crofts, 1953.

7. ———, *The Only Child.* New York, G. P. Putnam's Sons, 1954.

8. De Schweinitz, K., *Growing Up,* 3d ed. New York, The Macmillan Co., 1953.

9. Despert, J. L., *Children of Divorce.* New York, Doubleday & Co., 1953.

10. Dudley, N., *Linda Goes to the Hospital.* New York, Coward-McCann, 1953.

11. Frankel, L., and Frankel, G., *What To Do With Your Preschooler.* New York, Sterling Publishing Co., 1953.

12. Gesell, A., *Studies in Child Development.* New York, Harper & Brothers, 1948.

13. ———, *Infant Development: The Embryology of Early Human Behavior.* New York: Harper & Brothers, 1952.

14. ———, *et al., The First Five Years of Life.* New York, Harper & Brothers, 1940.

15. Gesell, A., and Ilg, F. L., *Infant and Child in the Culture of Today.* New York, Harper & Brothers, 1943.

16. ———, in collaboration with Louise B. Ames and Glenna E. Bullis, *The Child from Five to Ten.* New York, Harper & Brothers, 1946.

17. Gesell, A., Ilg, F. L., and Ames, L. B., *The Years from Ten to Sixteen*. New York, Harper & Brothers (in press).

18. Grayson, A. B., *Do You Know Your Daughter?* New York, Appleton-Century-Crofts, 1944.

19. Jacob, W., *New Hope for the Retarded Child*. Public Affairs Pamphlet No. 210, 1954, 28 pp. (22 East 38th Street, New York 16, New York).

20. Kanner, L., *In Defense of Mothers*. Springfield, Ill., Charles C. Thomas, 1950.

21. Lawton, S., *The Sexual Conduct of the Teen-Ager*. New York, Greenberg, Publisher, 1951.

22. Levine, M., *A Baby Is Born*. New York, Simon & Schuster, 1949.

23. ———, and Seligmann, J. H., *The Wonder of Life*. New York, Simon & Schuster, 1940.

24. Little, G., *Design for Motherhood*. New York, The Ronald Press, 1953.

25. Menninger, W. C., *et al.*, *How To Be a Successful Teen-Ager*. New York, Sterling Publishing Co., 1954.

26. Neisser, E., *Brothers and Sisters*. New York, Harper & Brothers, 1951.

27. Paullin, E., *No More Tonsils*. New York, Island Press Co-operative, 470 W. 24 St., 1947.

28. Pemberton, L., *The Stork Didn't Bring You*. New York, Hermitage House, 1948.

29. Pilpel, H., and Zavin, T., *Your Marriage and the Law*. New York, Rinehart & Co., 1952.

30. Podolsky, E., *The Jealous Child*. New York, Philosophical Library, 1954.

31. Redlich, F., and Bingham, J., *The Inside Story—Psychiatry and Everyday Life*. New York, Alfred A. Knopf, 1953.

32. Richardson, F. H., *How To Get Along with Children*. Atlanta, Ga., Tupper & Love, 1954.

33. Ridenour, N., *When Your Child Is Destructive*. New York State Society for Mental Health, 105 E. 22 St., 1947.

34. Rondell, F., and Michaels, R., *The Adopted Family*. New York, Crown Publications, 1951.

35. *Scholastic Magazine,* Teen Age Book Club. 351 Fourth Avenue, New York, N. Y.

36. Sever, J. D., *Johnny Goes to the Hospital*. Public Relations Department of the Children's Medical Center, 300 Longwood Avenue, Boston 15, Mass., 1953.

37. Sheldon, W., *The Varieties of Temperament*. New York, Harper & Brothers, 1942.

38. Spock, B., *Pocketbook of Baby and Child Care*. New York, Pocket Books, 1946.

39. Strain, F. B., *Being Born*. New York, Appleton-Century-Crofts, 1954.

40. Ullmann, F., *Getting Along with Brothers and Sisters*. Science Research Associates, S. Wabash Avenue, Chicago, Ill., 1950.

41. Wasson, V., *The Chosen Baby*. Philadelphia, J. B. Lippincott Co., 1939.

Index

Index